Sources Of American Spirituality

Eastern Spirituality In America

SELECTED WRITINGS

Edited by Robert S. Ellwood

PAULIST PRESS
New York ♦ Mahwah

Acknowledgments: The publisher gratefully acknowledges the use of the following materials: *Introduction to Christopher Isherwood and Swami Prabhavananda*, by Aldous Huxley, in THE SONG OF GOD: BHAGAVAD-GITA, copyright 1944, 1972, pp. 11–22 of Mentor edition. Reprinted with permission of Vedanta Society of Southern California. "The Salt of the Earth," by Swami Prabhavananda, in THE SERMON OF THE MOUNT ACCORDING TO VEDANTA, copyright 1963, pp. 36–58 of Mentor edition. Reprinted with permission of Vedanta Society of Southern California. From THE SCIENCE OF RELIGION by Paramahansa Yogananda (Los Angeles, 1982), used with permission of Self-Realization Fellowship. KRSNA CONSCIOUSNESS: THE TOPMOST YOGA SYSTEM, by A.C. Bhaktivedanta Swami, copyright 1970, pp. 24–44 (Chapters 3–5). Reprinted with permission of the Bhaktivedanta Book Trust. NAMU DAI BOSA: A TRANSMISSION OF ZEN BUDDHISM TO AMERICA, by Nyogen Senzaki, Soen Nakagawa Roshi, and Eido Tai Shimano Roshi. Published by The Zen Studies Society. "Ignorance and Enlightenment" and "Spiritual Enlightenment," in ZEN FOR AMERICANS, copyright 1906 as SERMONS OF A BUDDHIST ABBOTT, pp. 126–45, by Soyen Shaku. Reprinted with permission of Open Court Publishing Co. BEAT ZEN, SQUARE ZEN, AND ZEN, by Alan W. Watts, Copyright 1959 by Alan W. Watts. San Francisco: City Light Books. Reprinted by kind permission of Mary Jane Watts. From THE TIBETAN BOOK OF THE DEAD, by W.Y. Evans-Wentz, pp. 10–18 and 28–35. Copyright 1960 by W.Y. Evans-Wentz. Reprinted by permission of Oxford University Press, Inc.

Library of Congress Cataloging-in-Publication Data

Eastern spirituality in America.

   (Sources of American spirituality)
   Bibliography: p.
   Includes index.
   1. Hinduism—Doctrines. 2. Buddhism—
Doctrines. 3. Taoism—Doctrines. 4. Theosophy.
5. United States—Religion—19th century.
6. United States—Religion—20th century.
I. Ellwood, Robert S., 1933-   . II. Series.
BL1055.E27 1987   294   86-30391
ISBN 0-8091-0388-5

Published by Paulist Press
997 Macarthur Boulevard
Mahwah, N.J. 07430

Printed and bound in the United States of America

CONTENTS

PREFACE   1

GENERAL INTRODUCTION   4

I. INTRODUCTION   5

II. HINDUISM   45
Neo-Vedanta:
1. Swami Vivekananda: Address at the
   World's Parliament of Religions   51
2. Swami Prabhavanada: The Salt of the Earth   61
3. Aldous Huxley: Introduction to
   The Song of God: Bhagavad-Gita   79
4. Paramahansa Yogananda: The Science of Religion   87
Bhakti:
1. Swami Bhaktivedanta: Krishna Consciousness   98

III. BUDDHISM   114
Zen:
1. Soyen Shaku:
   a. Address at the World's Parliament of Religions   121
   b. Two Sermons   125
2. Nyogen Senzaki: Selected Short Sermons   136
3. Alan Watts: Beat Zen, Square Zen, and Zen   162
Tibetan Buddhism:
1. W.Y. Evans-Wentz: The Tibetan
   Book of the Dead   181

IV. TAOISM   195
    1. Thomas Merton: The Way of Chuang Tzu   199

V. THEOSOPHY   215
    1. H.P. Blavatsky: Isis Unveiled   219

BIBLIOGRAPHY OF GENERAL WORKS
ON EASTERN SPIRITUALITY IN AMERICA   235

INDEX   237

PREFACE

The religions of the East have exercised an influence, direct and indirect, on American culture and the American soul. My endeavor in this volume will be to present representative texts exploring the sources and nature of this influence. These texts should give the reader some impression of how Hinduism, Buddhism, Taoism, and Theosophy—a portmanteau conveying East to West and West to East—appear in the traveling guises that have made them options within general American spiritual culture.

It is hoped that the reading selections following will provide an overview of Eastern spirituality as it has historically been presented to Americans. At the same time, it has been necessary to define rather strictly what can be covered in a single volume. Certain principles have had a role in governing the selection of material:

1. Islam and Islamic-derived movements, such as Baha'i, Subud, and various Sufi groups, have been excluded. It can be argued that, as a monotheistic religion rooted in the same Semitic culture-area as Judaism and Christianity, Islam should be considered a Western rather than an Eastern religion. In any case, to have included spokesmen for these groups would have been to attempt more than could be done well in a volume of this scope.

2. Writers have been selected who have addressed a "mainstream" occidental-American audience as well as, or instead of, ethnic Asian-American religionists. They are thus persons who have had some impact on American spiritual culture as a whole.

3. At the same time, early Transcendentalist and other writers, such as Emerson and Thoreau, whose general Eastern sympathies

1

did much to prepare the ground for American Eastern spirituality but who are easily accessible elsewhere, are not included. I have preferred to devote more space to persons closely connected with the concrete, institutional forms American Eastern spirituality took beginning with the Theosophical Society and the World's Parliament of Religions of 1893, and developed in the subsequent course of Eastern spiritual thought in America. (Not all writers in the volume, however, were adherents of any particular Eastern group. One, Thomas Merton, was a Roman Catholic monk, and another, Alan Watts, never formally identified himself with any Eastern religion. Both, however, had a part in the East-West dialogue of this century that cannot be overlooked in a volume of this sort, and help suggest the diversity of persons who have participated in introducing the spiritual East to the West.)

4. To illumine that diversity, I have tried to strike a rough balance between writers of Eastern and Western background, to include lay as well as clerical authors, and to bring in some ''name'' writers such as Merton and Aldous Huxley, who not only said what they had to say very well, but were well enough known to have had a broad influence.

Our topic is Eastern spirituality in America, but the question of who—or what—is American in this context is somewhat tricky. In the nature of the case, important figures in a great transcultural movement, such as the introduction of Eastern spirituality into a Western society, are likely to be international peripatetics, with no abiding cities Eastern or Western. This has been the way it was. The seminal events for the institutional Americanization of Eastern spirituality were the founding of the Theosophical Society in New York in 1875 and the celebrated World's Parliament of Religions in Chicago in 1893. Thus it has seemed important to include American writings of Blavatsky, and the parliament addresses of Vivekananda and Soyen Shaku, plus other American sermons of the latter, even though these three were not resident in America more than a few years. Two of the other writers, Huxley and Watts, were expatriate Britishers, and all except one were in fact born outside the United States. Ironically, the sole American-born writer, W. Y. Evans-Wentz, authored the only selection not penned in the United States. His famous *Tibetan Book of the Dead* was done while that scholar was in the field in India and Tibet, and while he was academically affiliated with Jesus College, Oxford; I have included material from it because he was American born and raised, and later spent many years of retirement in San Diego, and because of the book's immense influence in the American Eastern scene.

Thus, while all of the writers in this volume were in important ways international, transcultural figures—and in this lay their significance—it has also been possible to arrive at a commonsense understanding of what sort of writings are appropriate for inclusion in a volume that is part of an American spirituality series. All the authors spent some time in America, and (with the one exception noted) all selections were actually written there. All have had a demonstrable impact on American spirituality, the majority being major interpreters of important Eastern spiritual movements drawing largely occidentals.

One requirement of the Paulist Press series The Sources of American Spirituality has been that writers represented must be deceased. Some Eastern movements in America now fairly important, mainly those deriving from the 1960s' milieu, from Transcendental Meditation to Nichiren Shoshu, have had to be excluded here because the authors of their most important writings were still alive at the time of composing this volume. One exception is Swami Bhaktivedanta of the International Society for Krishna Consciousness; he died in 1977, and I have put him in because he is one of the best spiritual thinkers of the 1960s set and represents a unique type of Eastern religion in America, bhakti devotionalism.

The limitation of these selections to personalities more past than present has helped define the book's perspective. I have wanted to document the background in American life of this kind of spirituality—in the words of the series title, its sources—showing that it is more than a recent phenomenon, but one that has taken various forms as American society itself has changed.

Brief bibliographies are placed at the end of the introduction to each chapter or major section. Only works about the religion in question in America, and about the particular writers selected, have been cited; general books about Hinduism, Buddhism, or Taoism, and lists of other works by the writers, mostly very prolific, have been omitted as beyond the scope of this book. Our focus has instead been on the ideas and rhetoric of their message to occidental America.

Robert Ellwood
University of Southern California

GENERAL INTRODUCTION

O my brave soul!
O farther farther sail!
O daring joy, but safe! are they not all the seas of God?
O farther, farther farther sail!
—Walt Whitman, "Passage to India"

The Sources of American Spirituality series attempts to portray the fullness of the American spiritual odyssey. Thus far the series has presented the writings of Walter Rauschenbusch, William Ellery Channing, Elizabeth Seton, and Charles Hodge, and has traced the development of Catholic devotion to the Holy Spirit in the nineteenth century. This present volume illustrates the intention to move beyond well-studied, "main line" traditions to those less known, though often equally important, sources of influence that have helped shape the soul of the American people.

The tendency to limit discussion of American religion to its European and Near Eastern derivatives is common, despite over a century of participation in the religions of the East that has had a palpable effect on the culture of our nation. Certainly the Beat Generation of the 1950s and the social transformations of the 1960s owed a great deal to the influence of Eastern religions, perhaps more than the casual observer, or even the not so casual participant, was aware. But before those recent phenomena, the influence of Eastern religions was felt. Countless high schoolers encountered a clue of its influence a century and a half ago in Emerson's poem "Brahma," or in Thoreau's journal of his ascetical hermitage at Walden Pond, or in Whitman's lyrical "Passage to India." It was front page news in 1893 when the World's Fair in Chicago included a global Parliament of Religions that featured speeches by the Hindu monk Swami Vivekananda and the Zen master Soyen Skaku. That event was the impetus for the creation of many programs for the comparative study of religion at colleges and universities. In the margins of our cultural experience the influence of the east has also been seen. The occult Theosophical movement of Helena Blavatsky, the Swedenborgian musings of Andrew Jackson Davis, the mysterious rappings of the Fox sisters—all were tinged with a trace of the East.

All this and more is skillfully illustrated in the introduction, notes, and text selections of this volume. The study of such a diverse phenomenon presents many challenges to the student. Professor Ellwood has used his considerable gifts as a scholar and a stylist to create a pleasing work that avoids the deadly traps of banality on the one hand, and pedantry on the other. It is my hope that this book will offer our readers the opportunity for a journey to the East as it has been reflected in our own culture.

John Farina

I

INTRODUCTION

HISTORICAL OVERVIEW OF
EASTERN RELIGION IN AMERICA

The mainstream of American religion has long possessed two overseas focuses, two "centers out there," in Victor Turner's expression.[1] Both lie across the narrower ocean to wash American shores, the Atlantic. One is the Europe of American religion's predominate institutional and ethnic roots, the Europe of Rome and Wittenberg and Geneva. The other, beyond Europe, is a tiny Holy Land at the eastern end of the Mediterranean.

But Americans have also long been aware of another spiritual pole in the world, one often much more vaguely defined as "the East." It is broadly comprised of India, China, Japan, and their environs, vast lands lying across the Pacific from America as does Europe across the Atlantic. While the major sources of America's spiritual heritage may have been brought over the smaller sea, the country has faced toward Asia as well in matters of the spirit, just as it has in commerce, diplomacy, and war.

Indeed, the spiritual East is a presence that has long haunted America, in the form of its great faiths like Hinduism and Taoism, and its great sages from the Buddha to Mahatma Gandhi. Eastern religion has been praised, denounced, and misunderstood, but it has

---

1. Victor Turner, "The Center Out There: Pilgrim's Goal," *History of Religions* 12, no. 3 (February 1973); 191–230.

not been wholly ignored. For some Americans it has been the faith associated with their own ethnic heritage. For others it has had the appeal of a radical and exotic alternative. Either way, by now American Eastern religion shows every sign of being deeply and permanently interwoven into the spiritual life of an increasingly pluralistic society.

The stream of Eastern spirituality in America contains three distinct currents. First, as a general intellectual and cultural influence, it has been a real presence since the eighteenth century, a presence that expressed itself most pervasively through nineteenth-century Transcendentalism but did not take institutionalized form until late in that century. Intellectual Orientalism continues, of course, to exercise influence independent of concrete groups and leaders; a recent example is the spate of books pointing to congruence between a Vedanta-Buddhist-Taoist world view and that emerging from modern physics.[2]

Second, Eastern spirituality has articulated itself through organizations that look toward Eastern religious traditions but have been patronized largely by Americans of occidental descent. Groups like the Vedanta Societies, the Self-Realization Fellowship, Zen centers, and a host of more recent institutions have drawn a diversity of occidental seekers who have found in them a response to a personal spiritual quest.

Third, Eastern spirituality has taken the form of religious institutions primarily meeting the needs of Americans of Asian ethnic background. These range from Chinese-American Buddhist temples to the more recent wave of Hindu temple building sponsored by Indian-Americans; they include outposts of Asian "new religions" from Japanese Tenrikyo to Vietnamese Cao Dai.

In the discourse and selections presented in this volume, we shall emphasize the second current of Eastern spirituality by stressing the writings of persons who addressed a general American audience but who, in some but not all cases, were associated with an Eastern group serving primarily occidental Americans. Many were,

---

2. See, for example, Fritjof Capra, *The Tao of Physics* (Boulder, Colo.: Shambhala, 1975); and Gary Zukav, *The Dancing Wu Li Masters* (New York: Morrow, 1979).

however, persons who also had a strong impact on intellectual life as a whole. (The rationale for the selections is presented in the Preface.) Let us now look at the three currents in more detail.

The general Eastern intellectual influence came first. Indeed, the impact of the East on the spiritual and social movements that helped shape America is one of those issues that can be traced back indefinitely. Exchange between India and the Hellenistic and Roman worlds was brisk; while specifics have proved hard to document, Jain, Buddhist, and Vedanta ideas could well have affected Neoplatonism and Gnosticism, as they certainly did Manichaeism. The seminal importance of these movements for subsequent Western, including Christian, thought goes without saying.

Later, the rise of Islam and enmity between it and Christendom separated Europe from India and East Asia, save for a brief period—the age of Marco Polo—when the all-conquering Mongols kept trade routes open. But it was not until the Age of Exploration that the spiritual East was rediscovered.

Interestingly, an early important influence was not from Hinduism or Buddhism, but from the great Chinese spiritual/political philosophy, Confucianism. As retailed in the West by writers such as the eminent Jesuit missionary Matteo Ricci (1552–1610), the doctrine of the ancient Chinese sage looked like a foundation for a rational humanistic society based on simple Deism. It much appealed to Enlightenment thinkers of the stamp of Leibnitz or Voltaire, weary of Europe's despotisms and sanguinary religious wars. As one element in the Age of Reason mentality, the idealized Confucian state is a factor in the background of the American Declaration of Independence and the Constitution.

The Confucian Enlightenment's influence in America is reflected in several positive citations of the Chinese philosopher in the work of Benjamin Franklin, who called for closer study of China in the preface to the first volume of the American Philosophical Society's *Transactions* (1771).[3] At the same time, other accounts by trav-

---

3. Carl T. Jackson, *The Oriental Religions and American Thought: Nineteenth-Century Explorations* (Westport, Conn.: Greenwood Press, 1981), pp. 14–15. See also Harlee Creel, *Confucius: The Man and the Myth* (New York: John Day, 1949), Chap. 15, "Confucianism and Western Democracy," pp. 254–78.

elers and missionaries to Asia were appearing that enlarged on the exotic and grotesque features of those lands of "idolatry." America was long to live with a split image of the East of almost schizoid proportions, simultaneously idealizing and demonizing it beyond the human range. Both sides are represented in the brief account of Eastern religion in Hannah Adams' pioneer comparativist work, *A View of Religion.*[4] Attempting to be fair but suffering from inadequate sources, she mentions, for example, bizarre yogic practices, but also appreciates Hindu tolerance and architecture.

If Chinese intellectual influences predominated on America's Eastern front in the eighteenth century, the nineteenth was the century of India. Indian spirituality, as understood in that century, appealed to the great turnings that marked the era: toward idealism in philosophy, and toward romanticism in letters. India's popularity was abetted by the entrenchment of the British raj, which enhanced both its fascination and its accessibility, whether through books or travel, to the English-speaking world. The roots of nineteenth-century Indology lay in the great seminal translations from Sanskrit begun in the last decades of the previous century, including those of Franklin's close friend, the brilliant English scholar Sir William Jones. A little later, the translations of the *Upanishads* and other texts by the equally acute Hindu reformer Ram Mohan Roy (1774–1833) made a particular impact because of the Easterner's open sympathy with Unitarian Christianity.[5]

Roy's work seems to have been a major source for the Orientalism of Emerson and Thoreau, and it was through their Transcendentalist distillation that philosophical Hinduism first reached a wide American audience. Emerson prudently refrained from citing the East at length in his public writings, revealing the depth of his interest in it only in his letters and journals. The full extent of Eastern influence on the sage of Concord, and the reliability of his grasp of Oriental thought, remain subjects of scholarly controversy, but unquestionably the Emersonian impetus helped renew the spiritual East in the consciousness of fresh American generations.

---

    4. Hannah Adams, *A View of Religions* 3rd ed. (Boston: Manning & Loring, 1801).

    5. See William Bysshe Stein, ed., *Two Brahman Sources of Emerson and Thoreau* (Gainesville, Fla.: Scholars' Facsimiles & Reprints, 1967).

In particular, he participated in shifting the center of attention from China to India, and from Enlightenment to romantic and idealist styles of reacting to what the East had to offer. Spiritual seekers turning eastward now hoped less to find a rational God and a utopian social order than to share in something like Herman Hesse's paradigmatic *Journey to the East,* a quest for sunrise lands of ultimate origins and supreme mystic wisdom.[6] That vision involved a subtler salvation than the Western evangelist's heaven to gain and hell to shun. Emerson himself well expressed it in the lines of his celebrated and controversial poem "Brahma," based on a passage from the *Upanishads:*

If the red slayer think he slays,
Or if the slain think he is slain,
They know not well the subtle ways
I keep, and pass, and turn again.

The strong gods pine for my abode,
And pine in vain the sacred Seven;
But thou, meek lover of the good!
Find me, and turn thy back on heaven.[7]

Emerson's less cautious Transcendentalist colleague Henry Thoreau, however, evidenced greater specific familiarity with the wisdom of the East. He vividly evoked the romantic "Yankee Hindoo" mood in phrases such as those of a famous passage from *Walden:*

In the morning I bathe my intellect in the stupendous and cosmogonal philosophy of the Bhagvat-Geeta, since whose composition years of the gods have elapsed, and in comparison with which our modern world and its literature seem puny and trivial. . . . The pure Walden water is mingled with the sacred water of the Ganges.[8]

---

6. Herman Hesse, *Journey to the East* (New York: Farrar, Straus & Giroux, 1956).

7. First published in *Atlantic Monthly,* November 1857.

8. Henry David Thoreau, *Walden* (New York: New American Library, 1942), pp. 198–99.

The same romantic sense that the East, particularly India, represents a civilization immeasurably more primordial and spiritually wise than the raucous and seemingly masterful West was later renewed by Walt Whitman in "Passage to India." It was written in 1871 after that ambiguous triumph of Western technology, the opening of the Suez Canal, facilitated travel by spiritual seekers and many others to the lands of ancient wisdom while highlighting the contrast between the West's kind of knowledge and theirs.

> Passage O soul to India!
> Eclaircise the myths Asiatic, the primitive fables.
> Not you alone proud truths of the world,
> Nor you alone ye facts of modern science,
> But myths and fables of old, Asia's, Africa's fables,
> The far-darting beams of the spirit, the unloos'd dreams,
> The deep diving bibles and legends,
> The daring plots of the poets, the elder religions . . .
> Passage to more than India!
> Are thy wings plumed indeed for such far flights?

"Passage to more than India . . ." The words suggest that the quest was finally not for the heat and dust of the land then basking in the heyday of the British Empire, but for something of which that storied country and its people themselves were but symbol, an Eastern sapience now dimly perceived, yet primeval and ultimate beyond all else in this world.

Those who held this vision of the East in nineteenth-century America were, of course, a small minority. For most, the nations of Asia were exotic and colorful, perhaps, fit goals for Yankee traders of the more adventurous sort, but all the same barbaric and heathen lands with which spiritual commerce ought to flow the other way in the form of Christian missionaries. Indeed, the combined imperialist, commercial, and religious invasions of the East in that century seemed overwhelming, a river in full flood compared to a trickle in the other direction, liable to drown those timeworn civilizations before they could fully impart their gifts to the world. But movement in human history is rarely in one lane only, and as the nineteenth century advanced, a spiritual undertow from East to West gathered force.

The undertow owed its power in large part to its ability to relate to three existing Western mindsets. First, the already-mentioned romanticism, with its elevation of exalted feeling and purpose over reason and its comfortable coexistence with philosophical idealism, easily induced a warm pantheistic glow for which Eastern religions provided ready language. Their glamor was enhanced by another romantic theme, love of the distant and the past. For many romantics the Walter Scott cult of chivalry and medieval gothic sufficed, but in others the yearning for the far frontiers of the spirit could take them inwardly—or physically by steamship or caravan—to the unimaginably old and far places to which Thoreau and Whitman had alluded, to immensely ancient temples reflecting in lotus ponds or banked by Himalayan snows. In sum, romanticism helped open the road for the East's westward progress by implanting the ideal of a spiritual quest for wisdom from far away and long ago, which would be apprehended more by mystical experience than by reason, and which would probably culminate in a sovereign sense of cosmic Oneness—in an Emersonian Oversoul. The first great alliance of romanticism and the spiritual East in America was Transcendentalism, though it was simultaneously forged by such Germans as Schlegel and Schopenhauer; the romanticist/orientalist mood is well reflected in the rhetoric of such later movements as Theosophy and Vedanta.

The second aperture for the East was the Western occult tradition, which enjoyed something of a propitious revival in the nineteenth century. This tradition's Neoplatonic roots likewise gave it a vision of the One mediated through the many, together with the picture of an adventurous spiritual quest through which the treasure of the One is finally gained. This "alternative" Western spiritual heritage, with Hellenistic roots and branches running through medieval kabbalism and magic, which flowered in Renaissance alchemy, astrology, and esotericism, reached American shores as early as 1694, when a "Rosicrucian" society to study such matters was established in Pennsylvania.[9]

Nineteenth-century Western occultism was in no small part simply a survival of the Renaissance world view as it flourished before it was eclipsed by the victory of Copernican-Newtonian science. Finely articulated for readers of English in much Elizabethan literature, that world view was based on medieval concepts abetted by the new discovery of classical sources, by the new Renaissance spirit of intellectual expansiveness, and by the new science, which seemed initially to march well with it.

The Renaissance and Elizabethan world view's three basic pillars were Ptolemaic astronomy, the "Great Chain of Being" concept of a hierarchy of increasingly superior intelligences linking heaven and earth, and the notion of "correspondences." The last refers to the idea that relationships and lines of force conjoin various elements of the universe, with man a microcosm at the center. "As above, so below." Planets and zodiacal signs, gemstones, herbs, and organs of the human body have connections capable of both philosophical and magical application. Belief in astrology, ceremonial magic, and the classical medicine based on humors and bodily "airs" comfortably consorted with this world view. So did the darker belief in witchcraft, although it also had sources in scriptural affirmations of Satan and his power; some, like the Puritans, hounded witches while rejecting horoscopes as unbiblical.

Under the impetus of the new science and the spirit of the Age of Reason, this world view steadily decayed through the seventeenth and eighteenth centuries. But as it decayed it fragmented, so that a person might hold to certain of its tenets while denying others. Benjamin Franklin, for example, ridiculed astrology but eloquently defended the higher concept of the Great Chain of Being with its implication that evil is a matter of perspective. Others, while acknowledging the Copernican universe and the positive achievements of the new science, retained a hold on astrology or the magic of stones. It was possible to deprecate naive occultism while recogniz-

9. See Herbert Leventhal, *In the Shadow of the Enlightenment: Occultism and Renaissance Science in Eighteenth Century America* (New York: New York University Press, 1976).

ing the old spiritual hierarchies and the Neoplatonic ennoblement of mystical or theurgic experience, as did the Englishman Francis Barrett in *The Magus* of 1801.[10] But epigoni of the old like him were at the same time in the vanguard of something else, an "underground" Western occultist tradition distinct from the intellectual establishment of the day. Yet the older world view was not without outward power. Much of its lore and symbolism went into Freemasonry, a yeasty force in the eighteenth and nineteenth centuries, when colorful wizards like Cagliostro and Saint-Germain represented the underside of the Enlightenment.

In the early nineteenth century, two movements flourished in America that brought about a revitalization of the tradition and helped prepare it for the Eastern influx. These were Swedenborgianism and Mesmerism. Emmanuel Swedenborg (1688–1772), after a brilliant career in Sweden as a scientist, turned to religion and a long series of visionary experiences.[11] He confided that he had seen Christ, met God personally, been a witness of the Last Judgment beginning in 1757 on a spiritual plane, and conversed with spirits of the departed in the many mansions of heaven and hell. He wrote voluminously on the sacred wisdom he had gleaned from these encounters. Central to Swedenborg's thought is a version of the idea of correspondences, stressing that earthly forms are but counterparts of entities in the realm of spirit, and an educative vision of life after death, in which souls are not so much rewarded or punished as sent to school to enable them to advance to higher planes.

Swedenborgian ideas were circulated in America through books and by the Swedenborgian "New Church." They spread vigorously on the upper frontier, carried by such apostles of the new faith as John Chapman ("Johnny Appleseed"). Marguerite Block, in her history of American Swedenborgianism, speaks of a "Swedenborgian wave" in the 1840s that washed through intellectual America and watered the early shoots of Transcendentalism.[12] After the ex-

---

10. Francis Barrett, *The Magus, or Celestial Intelligencer* (London: Lackington, Allen & Co., 1801; facsimile reprint ed., Secaucus, N.J.: Citadel, 1975).

11. See George Trobridge, *Swedenborg: Life and Teachings* (New York: Swedenborg Foundation, 1968).

12. Marguerite Block, *The New Church in the New World* (New York: Henry Holt, 1932), pp. 158–59.

ample of the Stockholm sage himself in his traffic with the Other
Side, it needed but a spark for such tinder to become Spiritualism,
which in turn prepared a path for such vehicles of Eastern influence
as Theosophy and its progeny.

The flint and steel for that spark were offered by Mesmerism,
which enjoyed a complementary vogue in America in the 1830s and
1840s. Franz Mesmer (1734–1815), the Austrian father of modern
hypnotism, discovered through various techniques the therapeutic
effect of suggestion given to patients in trance or semi-trance
states.[13] He interpreted the effect through a doctrine of "animal magnetism," a cosmic force communicated to the sufferer by his pro-
cedures. This force, he held, could also awaken latent powers of
psychism and spiritual wisdom, enabling one to tap a universal spiritual source. Mesmer's findings helped to produce, on the one hand,
medical hypnosis and psychoanalysis. On the other hand they were
a potent rationale and dynamic for nineteenth-century occultism, a
role reflected in the remark of H. P. Blavatsky, the Theosophist, that
Mesmerism is the most important branch of magic and, indeed, the
true base of what is called magic or miraculous.

The immediate American upshot in the effervescent 1840s was
the combination of Mesmerist trance with Swedenborgian world
view to beget Spiritualism, with its communication with the departed
through trance-mediumship. In 1847 Andrew Jackson Davis, a student of Swedenborg and a practitioner of Mesmerism who became
the leading philosopher of Spiritualism, published his *Principles of
Nature, Her Divine Revelation and a Voice to Mankind.*[14] Delivered
out of a trance to scribes, this monumental work of nearly eight
hundred pages fused a Swedenborgian view of spiritual planes to a
deistic interpretation of the earth's creation and history, Fourierist
utopianism, and an exuberently optimistic vision of the future.

During the next year, the vision sprang to life as the Fox sisters
of Hydesville, New York, reported the mysterious tappings that set

---

13. See Vincent Buranelli, *The Wizard from Vienna* (New York: Coward,
McCann and Geoghegan, 1975); and Robert C. Fuller, *Mesmerism and the American Cure of Souls* (Philadelphia: University of Pennsylvania Press, 1982).

14. Andrew Jackson Davis, *Principles of Nature, Her Divine Revelation and
a Voice to Mankind* (New York: S. S. Lyon and W. Fishbough, 1847).

religious Spiritualism on its erratic course. A national craze in the early 1850s, it soon settled down to a relatively modest institutional life, but had a marked if sometimes indirect effect on spiritual experimentation to come. As Whitney Cross commented, for many Spiritualism was a step on the road to some more liberal or ''modern'' form of religion; its critique of the conventional churches and its speculative mood ''must have tended to obliterate any remnants of literal-mindedness and orthodoxy embedded in its converts.''[15] Not seldom this liberation was to ease openness to the East, as among Theosophists, even though Spiritualism itself displayed small orientalist concern.

The third strand of nineteenth-century thought and life with which the East meshed was the scientific. At first glance this correlation may seem at odds with the other two, romanticism and occultism, but a moment's reflection may tell us that in historical context all three fit together. Nineteenth-century occultism had romantic affinities, but it, and above all Spiritualism, claimed also to be the most ''scientific'' of faiths. It claimed to be based on empirical evidence rather than authority, comported well—like science—with freedom and democracy, and in the eyes of writers like Davis looked toward a bright future of endless human progress in this world and beyond.

Similarly, much ink was spilled by Western apologists for Eastern religion, and increasingly by Eastern pundits with a Western education and audience in mind, to assert the unique compatibility of those ancient faiths with the modern scientific outlook. Among those in this book, writers such as Swami Vivekananda of Vedanta or Soyen Shaku of Buddhism stressed the empirical, rational, nontheistic, and nonfideistic character of such concepts as karma and universal oneness. At the same time, they ignored or allegorized the more miraculous and mythical aspects of their traditions. But while Western aficionados of Eastern spirituality may have been reassured by this rhetoric, despite the dry and abstract air it often gave the religion of the Hindus and Buddhists, it is doubtful if many were really

---

15. Whitney R. Cross, *The Burned Over District: The Social and Intellectual History of Enthusiastic Religion in Western New York* (New York: Harper and Row, 1965), p. 348.

converted by it; it probably helped rationalize an appeal that was at heart more romantic or mystical. Nonetheless, the use of the word *science* as a touchstone by advocates of Eastern religion remains: The book by Paramahansa Yogananda from which we shall quote is entitled *The Science of Religion,* and in the excerpted passage from his *Krishna Consciousness* Swami Bhaktivedanta compares the "science of Krishna" with "material science."[16]

THEOSOPHY

Whether the appeal was romantic, occult, or scientific in background, the East in America gradually moved from a diffuse influence to one that, without losing its general cultural impact, also took institutional form as the nineteenth century advanced. The first important institutional development was the founding of the Theosophical Society in New York in 1875. While initially Theosophy was not primarily Eastern-oriented, and has always aimed at promoting not "Easternism" alone but the "Ancient Wisdom" it perceives lying behind all religion East and West, its complex career has made it an important conveyor of oriental ideas to America.

The principal founders of the Theosophical Society were a remarkable pair. Helena P. Blavatsky (1833–1893) was an occultist and world traveler of aristocratic Russian background, celebrated for her girth, enigmatic gaze, sharp tongue, and aura of mystery and psychic power. Her close companion was Henry Steel Olcott (1832–1907), journalist and lawyer of contrasting sturdy middle-class American origin. Drawn by common Spiritualist interests, the two first met in 1874, shortly after Blavatsky's arrival in America, at the home of the dour Eddy brothers in Chittenden, Vermont, where nightly spirit-manifestations were allegedly taking place.

Back in New York, the Russian and the American continued their esotericist friendship and were soon sharing an apartment. Blavatsky began to persuade her willing pupil that "Brahma Vidya" or

---

16. A. E. Bhaktivedanta Swami Prabhupada, *Kṛṣṇa Consciousness: The Topmost Yoga System* (Los Angeles: Iskon Books, 1970).

"Eastern Spiritualism" was far loftier than the Western variety, displaying to him intriguing "phenomena" based on her training in it.

When the Theosophical Society was formed in the fall of 1875, however, it centered chiefly on the study of Western occultism, as that which underlay the civilization that had nourished it. Olcott, in his inaugural address as president of the Theosophical Society, provided incisive insight into basic tensions and visions of the day as he said:

> If I rightly apprehend our work, it is to aid in freeing the public mind of theological superstition and a tame subservience to the arrogance of science. However much or little we may do, I think it would have been hardly possible to hope for anything if the work had been begun in any country which did not afford perfect political and religious liberty. It certainly would have been useless to attempt it except in one where all religions stand alike before the law, and where religious heterodoxy works no abridgment of civil rights.
>
> Our Society is, I may say, without precedent. From the days when the Neoplatonists and the last theurgists of Alexandria were scattered by the murderous hand of Christianity, until now, the study of Theosophy has not been attempted.
>
> To the Protestant and Catholic sectaries we have to show the origin of many of their most sacred idols and most cherished dogmas; to the liberal minds in science, the profound scientific attainments of the ancient magi. Society has reached a point where *something* must be done; it is for us to indicate where that something may be found.[17]

Here in a few words we find a perception of a need and the hour that explains much, not only of Theosophy, but of many other new spiritual movements in the late nineteenth century. On the one hand,

---

17. "Inaugural Address of the President of the Theosophical Society," facsimile centenary edition (Theosophical Society of America, Wheaton, IL, 1975).

thinking people are becoming more and more afraid that conventional theological Christianity is out of date and out of touch; on the other hand, taken by itself the science that has done so much to discredit traditional faith fails to meet all human needs and reveals its own "arrogance." What is called for is "something" new that is also very old, coming from a day when universal wisdom and the human heart were less at odds, which shows the common ground of all religions while puncturing the pretensions of priesthoods in both church and laboratory. Finally, we note that only in America could this new stage in spiritual understanding fully mature, for only here is there adequate freedom of thought and faith.

Soon the interests of the nascent Theosophical Society began shifting more and more toward India, and beyond it to mysterious Tibet, seen as the greatest surviving reservoirs of the ancient wisdom so much choked off elsewhere by ecclesiastical bigotry and scientific materialism. Blavatsky's first major work, *Isis Unveiled,* published in 1877, while fundamentally based on Western occult thought, declares that the "practical blending of the visible with the invisible world" had found a "refuge" in "the chief lamaseries of Mongolia and Thibet," and that there "the primitive science of *magic*" was "practiced to the utmost limits of intercourse allowed between man and 'spirit.' " She urged the "pretended authorities of the West" to "go to the Brahmans and Lamaists to the far Orient, and respectfully ask them to impart the alphabet of true science."[18]

Not long after, in 1878–1879, the "Theosophical Twins," as Olcott liked to call himself and Blavatsky, put these words in effect by themselves removing from America to India. They were drawn initially by the Hindu Arya Samaj of Swami Sarasvati Dayananda, with whose efforts to restore the primordial faith of India they felt a common bond. But relations with it did not go well, and the pair pursued an independent and initially quite rewarding work of spreading Theosophy among Englishmen and Indians alike in the subcontinent; in 1880 both formally became Buddhists, in Ceylon, and

---

18. Helena P. Blavatsky, *Isis Unveiled,* 2 vols. (New York: J. W. Bouton, 1877; facsimile ed., Wheaton, Ill.: Theosophical Publishing House, 1972), II: 616, *passim.* [Cited Adlai E. Waterman, "Epilogue to the Centenary Edition, The Inaugural Address . . ."]

Olcott went on to work energetically on behalf of Buddhism and Buddhists as well as Theosophy.

As Theosophists believing in the convergence of all religions and in the "ancient wisdom" behind them all, they did not mean to imply by their Buddhist submission an exclusive conversion, but this partial shift of attention in 1880 coincides with a new phase in Western and especially American oriental spirituality, the vogue for Buddhism.

BUDDHISM AND THE WORLD'S
PARLIAMENT OF RELIGIONS

As we have seen, Western interest in the East has shifted from one Eastern venue to another over the generations, in the process often revealing more about the West and its changing aspirations than about the East. The Enlightenment idealized Confucian China; the era of romanticism and Transcendentalism, Vedantic India. Buddhism, less well studied and understood in the early years of the century, seemed to compete poorly with the wisdom of the *Upanishads* and the *Bhagavad-Gita*. Emerson clearly regarded its nirvanic "nothingness" and its lack of even the most impersonal God with distaste, speaking of Buddhism's "icy light"; he clearly preferred the warm affective mysticism he found in the Hindu classics.

But by the 1880s a trend toward Buddhism was under way. A key event was the publication in 1879 of Sir Edwin Arnold's long epic poem on the life of the Buddha, "The Light of Asia."[19] Its romantic depiction of the Enlightened One received an enthusiastic response on both sides of the Atlantic, doing much to implant a sympathetic image of Buddhism in the mind of a generation.[20] In 1883 Phillips Brooks, the popular Bostonian Episcopal clergyman, could write wryly of "these days when a large part of Boston prefers to consider itself Buddhist rather than Christian."[21]

---

19. Edwin Arnold, *The Light of Asia* (London: Trubner & Co., 1879).

20. See Brooks Wright, *Interpreter of Buddhism to the West: Sir Edwin Arnold* (New York: Bookman Associates, 1957).

21. Cited in Jackson, *Oriental Religions and American Thought*, p. 141.

The great event of the nineteenth century's closing years was the World's Parliament of Religions, held in Chicago in 1893 in conjunction with the Columbian Exposition and World's Fair.[22] Organized by Protestants of liberal bent, the parliament was a religious milestone in several respects. Though its sponsorship reflected the cultural domination of American religious life by "mainstream" Protestantism in that era, it also indicated the increasingly progressivist and universalistic outlook of at least one of its wings. Further, and most important for us, the parliament, to which spokesmen of all recognized world religions were invited, represented the first time most Eastern faiths were presented in the West by well-qualified interpreters.

Their speeches, two of which are included in this volume, created a sensation. To hear or read firsthand the words of one immersed from birth in one of those fabled, primordial traditions to which Transcendentalism and Theosophy had, as it were, only pointed with awe from afar, was a momentous experience. To be sure, conservative religionists in America and abroad roundly denounced the parliament. But others, doubtless prepared by more diffuse orientalizing influences from *Walden* to "The Light of Asia", responded more positively. Out of their response there emerged the first Asian religious institutions in America primarily serving occidental seekers, the early Vedanta Societies and Zen centers. The parliament also did much to encourage the development of comparative religion as an academic subject in American colleges and universities. It was followed by a spate of courses and textbooks in that field, which undoubtedly had an indirect impact on the growth of such institutions.

At the same time, it must be noted that the parliament's spokesmen for Asian religions tended to be devotees of their own traditions who were at the same time persons of Western education and modern ideas. They were characteristically reform-minded men eager both

---

22. On the World's Parliament of Religions, see John Henry Barrows, ed., *The World's Parliament of Religions,* 2 vols. (Chicago: Parliament Publishing Co., 1893), which includes all major papers; Jackson, *Oriental Religions and American Thought,* Chap. 13; and Joseph M. Kitagawa, "The 1893 World's Parliament of Religions and Its Legacy," 1983 John Nuveen Lecture, Chicago: The Divinity School and the Baptist Theological Union of the University of Chicago, 1983.

to bring their own religions in line with what they perceived to be the most up-to-date scientific and moral thought, and to present them to Westerners as wholly compatible with that thought. Not seldom the double task gave their apologetics a quality that may strike present-day readers as at once overly truculent and ingratiating. But one must appreciate the difficult and courageous position they were in, under suspicion for giving away too much by traditionalists at home, likely to be considered just another benighted heathen abroad until proven otherwise by the power of their words.

A good example was Swami Vivekananda, the founder of a modern Hindu monastic order, the Ramakrishna Mission, who made a stunning impression on the parliament and the American public. A young man of brilliant intellect, he had received a good education in Western science and philosophy, and considered himself a free-thinker, before suddenly becoming a disciple of the great Hindu saint Ramakrishna, shortly before the latter's death. In his many books and vigorously delivered lectures, Vivekananda interpreted Hinduism in terms of a universalistic and rationalized Vedanta philosophy, treating its gods and myths as allegories. Through the Ramakrishna Mission he promoted educational and social work in India, seeking to raise Hindu standards of both philanthropy and intellectual sophistication. At the same time he and his followers established centers, often called Vedanta Societies, in the West dedicated to promulgating Hindu teachings of a simple Advaita (philosophical nondualist) Vedanta sort; they have had an impact on certain writers and thinkers, among others. Vivekananda contended that while India needed the material knowledge of the West, the West desperately required the spiritual wisdom India had to offer.[23]

The Japanese Zen spokesman at the parliament, Soyen Shaku, was also a remarkable person whose education and life spanned both cultures. He was instrumental in bringing to America his student, the layman D. T. Suzuki, whose long succession of books and lectures did much to create the Western vogue for Zen. Soyen also organized a Buddhist-Christian conference in Japan in 1896, and it was a monastic disciple of his, Sasaki Shigemitsu, who

---

23. A readable source is Christopher Isherwood, *Ramakrishna and His Disciples* (New York: Simon and Schuster, 1965).

eventually established the most influential early Zen work in America, the Buddhist Society of America, later the First Zen Institute of New York, in 1930.

The World's Parliament of Religions, then, was pivotal in the transition of the East in America from the sort of literary influence exercised by Thoreau, Arnold, or even Blavatsky, to its decisive augmentation by institutions. It is to a survey of these groups that we must now turn. First, however, a few general remarks on their history and sociology may be in order.

CHARACTERISTICS OF EASTERN RELIGIOUS
GROUPS IN AMERICA

The fundamental sociological reality of Eastern religious groups appealing to occidental Americans derives from their need to offer an attraction powerful enough to outweigh the normal pull of conventional religion. Against the latter's dependence on family, ethnic, and community ties, and one's psychological needs for integration into those structures, the outsider must present powerful compensation. Quite apart from the issue of relative philosophical merits, then, Eastern religions in America as institutions must offer effective alternative social-psychological worlds.

Those worlds are essentially built around four factors, generally present in some form in all institutionalized Eastern religion in America, though the relative importance of each may vary. The characteristics of Eastern groups will be considered under four headings: charisma, intellectual expression, intensity of experience, and worship and sociology.

Charisma

First is charismatic leadership. Though the religion may be old in its homeland, in the American context it will possess features of a new, emergent religious movement. Prominent among them, as we know from the work of Max Weber, is a fairly fluid structure centered on the authority of a powerful central leader rather than on highly defined institutionalization.[24] American Eastern groups have typically been focused on one person, living or deceased, like Ramakrishna or Vivekananda of Vedanta, Paramahansa Yogananda of Self-Realization, or Bhaktivedanta of Krishna Consciousness. He will be presented as in the great Eastern tradition of spiritual masters—gurus, sages, Zen *roshis*—who are the beneficiaries of special training, initiation, and inner experience, and exist as the present incumbents in a long lineage of such persons.

Thus the charismatic leader is one who is (a) the founder or living teacher of the group, (b) recipient of a special call or initiation upon which the group is based, (c) uniquely qualified to teach or impart a special technique for spiritual experience, such as a method of meditation, chanting, or devotion, (d) uniquely entitled to call and empower disciples to which this authority may be passed, and (e) the object of a special devotion, in line with the Eastern tendency to blend freely the sacred and the teacher of the sacred, so that the charismatic teacher, or after death his portrait or image and relics, is offered quasi-divine honors. After the passing of the founder and the first generation, the group may undergo the Weberian "routinization of charisma," as have the groups of the above-mentioned personalities, but the cultus of the semi-deified founder is likely only to be enhanced by time.

Intellectual Expression

The second major area of distinctive focus is that of intellectual expression. While Eastern religions have both monistic and theistic strands, it is the former that predominate in American Eastern religion appealing to occidentals. That is to be expected, since the "nondualist" strands of Hinduism, Buddhism, and Taoism offer the most striking contrast to the conventional Judeo-Christian personal, monotheistic God. The needs of those who desire a more theistic faith would presumably be adequately met in most cases by the indigenous religion, and alienation sufficient to motivate the choice of a foreign alternative, with all the socio-psychological

---

24. See Max Weber, *The Sociology of Religion,* trans. Ephraim Fischoff (Boston: Beacon Press, 1963), Chap. 4.

strain that entails, lacking. The major exception is Krishna Consciousness, but it advances devotion to Krishna as a personal God in the context of an intensely Indian cultural milieu and utopian social idealism.

Certain common themes, though expressed in varying language, link most Eastern religion in occidental America. These include pantheistic (or better, nondualist) universalism, a sense of the divine within such as may arise from meditation or mystical experience, and a belief that the ultimate goal of spirituality is a lasting felt union, called enlightenment or God-realization, with that inward and universal divine. More specifically, these religions present a cosmos whose fundamental reality is an infinite, nondualistic, conscious though transpersonal Reality—Brahman, the Tao, the Dharmakaya. The same Reality dwells within, as the Atman or Buddha-nature, and is the true nature of all things. It is not always known, however, for when sense-objects are glimpsed partially or through egocentric eyes they are not seen as the divine taking many forms, but rather delude, being maya or magnets of that attachment which leads to suffering. The cure is found in cleansing the doors of perception and finding the true divine Self through meditation, pure devotion, or other techniques taught by the group. Also common is belief in karma and reincarnation.

Let us pause for a moment to consider together these first two characteristics of Eastern religions in America, the highly charismatic teacher in a long lineage, and the impersonal Absolute, which is, for the most part, the ultimate teaching. For the two go together in a manner of almost paradoxical fascination. The more the Transcendent is put beyond all name and form, past even the ghost of personhood, the more it seems its earthly incarnations exude a pungent vitality that intoxicates disciples, pure distilled water turned to rich wine on contact with human flesh and blood.

Christopher Isherwood, in his compelling though highly personal account of his relationship with Swami Prabhavananda of the Vedanta Society of Southern California, *My Guru and His Disciple,* found that he could describe what he was looking for as "this thing." Words like God and soul had been ruined by bad experiences with Western churchly religion, and what appealed to him about Vedanta was that in it he did not have to use that language. So, when he started meditating, he said that "I was just to sit quiet for ten or fifteen minutes twice a day, morning and evening, and keep reminding myself of 'this thing'—what it was and why one should want to make contact with it. That was all." Prabhavananda, however, under whose guidance he came to meditate, was far more than a "thing," though the "thing" was in him. His eyes, for example, "were soft, dark, and moist, with yellowish whites," and "whenever I describe their effect upon me, the reader must remember that I am really describing how Prabhavananda—or 'this thing'—was using them on that particular occasion."[25]

Helena Blavatsky was certainly among the most tangy personalities in the annals of the human race. Her companion, Henry Steel Olcott, who must have known her better than anyone else, speaks of her as "an enfeebled female body, 'in which . . . a vital cyclone is raging much of the time'—to quote the words of a Master."[26] In his *Old Diary Leaves,* he never tires of describing her infinite variety: her temper, her razor-sharp tongue, her childish tricks and capriciousness, yet also her generosity and remarkable wisdom, above all the states when she seemed in contact with beings and mysteries as far beyond the normal human ken as the Himalayan heights that sheltered her Masters are above the plain. Olcott can only insist that

> just because I did know her so much better than most others, she was a greater mystery to me than to them. It was easy for those who only saw her speaking oracles, writing profound aphorisms, or give clue after clue to the hidden wisdom in the ancient Scriptures, to regard her as an Earth-visiting *angelos* and to worship at her feet; she was no mystery to them. But to me, her most intimate colleague, who had to deal with the vulgar details of her common daily life, and see her in all her aspects, she was from the first and continued to the end an insoluble riddle. How much of her waking life was that of a responsible personality, how

25. Christopher Isherwood, *My Guru and His Disciple* (New York: Penguin Books, 1981; first published 1980), p. 40.

26. Henry Steel Olcott, *Old Diary Leaves, First Series* (Adyar, Madras, India: Theosophical Publishing House, 1895, 1941), p. 50.

much that of a body worked by an overshadowing entity?
I do not know.[27]

Yet this enigma shrouded in rather too ample and solid flesh
herself taught that the strange Masters and demigods whose ram-
buctious instrument she was were only midpoint between Earth and
the ultimate. In her most mature work, *The Secret Doctrine,* she
writes of ''an Omnipresent, Eternal, Boundless and Immutable
PRINCIPLE, on which all speculation is impossible, since it transcends the power of human conception and can only be dwarfed by
any human expression or similitude. It is beyond the range and reach
of thought—in the words of the *Māndūkya Upanishad,* 'unthinkable
and unspeakable.' '' It is the ''Rootless Root'' of ''all that was, is,
or ever shall be''; of it Consciousness and Matter are but ''two symbols.'' Further, ''the Eternity of the Universe *in toto*'' is a ''boundless plane,'' ''the playground of numberless Universes incessantly
manifesting and disappearing,'' called the ''Manifesting Stars'' and
the ''Sparks of Eternity''—in this awesome hyperspace the Pilgrim,
her name for the individualized consciousness moving from life-
form to life-form over the duration of universes, is but a transient,
for ''the Eternity of the Pilgrim is like a wink of the Eye of Self-
Existence.''[28]

Then there is Alan Watts, that sometime student and teacher of
Zen who liked going his own way, who described in his autobiography *In My Own Way* his understudying the Zen *roshi* Sokei-an of
the First Zen Institute of New York. (Sokei-an, or Shigetsu Sasaki,
was a student of Soyen Shaku, excerpted like Watts himself later in
this volume.) Watts portrays Sokei-an vividly, with his ''head
shaped like a short watermelon,'' his bohemian poet past, his ribald
stories, his skill as a woodcarver. Watts decided he wanted to ''study
with Sokei-an without his knowing it.'' He therefore observed the
Zen master in his personal and everyday life, which said more than
his formal discourse. He noted that ''he never fidgeted, but moved

27. Henry Steel Olcott, *Old Diary Leaves, Second Series* (Adyar, Madras,
India: Theosophical Publishing House, 1900, 1954), p. viii.

28. Helena P. Blavatsky, *The Secret Doctrine,* vol. 1 (Adyar, Madras, India:
Theosophical Publishing House, 1971), p. 82.

slowly and easily, with relaxed but complete attention to whatever was going on.'' At the same time, there was no ''purpose'' in what he did, for he liked to disconcert ''serious'' students of his wisdom by proclaiming that ''Zen is to realize that life is simply nonsense, without meaning other than itself or future purpose beyond itself. The trick is to dig the nonsense, for—as Tibetans say—you can tell the true yogi by his laugh.''[29] This meaningless meaning was appreciated by the same Alan Watts, who wrote, not only *The Way of Zen*, but also a book called *This Is It*, in which he gave his own labelless label to what Isherwood termed ''this thing.'' He concludes an account of a revelatory experience by saying, ''I saw that everything, just as it is now, is IT.''[30]

Intensity of Experience

In the third characteristic of Eastern religious groups in America, after charismatic leadership and distinctive doctrine, the group depends on an intensity of experience generated by its characteristic practices as well as its intellectual outlook. Here the Eastern faith may well contrast with the rather cool, socially oriented worship of much conventional religion. While it may have its comparatively restrained lectures and services of public worship, it may also go much further than mainstream Western churches in offering highly specific methods of yoga, meditation, chanting, or ritual involving the whole self, mind and body, which for many practitioners produce deeply felt spiritual experience and tangible results.

Typically, the Eastern religious group catering to occidentals centers its teaching and practice on one relatively simple and sure technique, such as Transcendental Meditation or the six-syllable chant of Nichiren Shoshu. Even when, as in Vedanta or Zen, the intellectual component is wide and deep, actual practice for most followers is fairly uncomplex meditation aided by a little ritual and chanting. The proffered practices are, of course, only a few out of

---

29. Alan Watts, *In My Own Way* (New York: Random House, Vintage Books, 1973), pp. 165–66.

30. Alan Watts, *This Is It* (New York: Pantheon Books, 1958, 1960), p. 30; *The Way of Zen* (New York: Pantheon Books, 1957).

many in the immense storehouse of such resources held by the religions of the East. But their advocates sincerely believe them to be supreme, and they are ones that for many give definite and immediate results, in the form of peace of mind, alteration of consciousness, a sense of power, or answered prayer. In one way or another the practices yield felt results strong enough to counter the family, ethnic, or community matrix of more conventional religion.

Worship and Sociology in Eastern Religious Groups

The fourth factor is the sociological aspect of the Eastern religion's expression. The community nature of Eastern religious groups is inseparable from the overall experience they engender for participants, particularly over against conventional religion. Some long-established groups, such as the Vedanta Societies and the Self-Realization Fellowship, offer a standard Sunday-morning-service style of participation. But they generally also present other classes and activities more closely related to practice, including the opportunity for personal spiritual guidance from a qualified teacher, and have an inner highly committed or monastic core. A broad spectrum of participatory styles is available, from the almost total communalism of some Krishna or Zen centers to the groups offering only occasional lectures or classes that do not conflict with Sunday-morning religion, or even those that are little more than mailing lists for publications and tapes.

In any case, a salient characteristic of Eastern groups, as of other alternative religions, is that they afford a diversity of styles of participation. Frequently, they enable a person to have one type of relationship to conventional religion and another to the Eastern. Not a few regular Sunday churchgoers also take yoga or meditation classes in an Eastern venue on some other day with little sense of inner inconsistency, or attend an occasional Theosophical lecture. On the other hand, Eastern groups may offer opportunities to those who wish them for a higher level of shared spiritual activity or communalism than is easily available in conventional religion, particularly for lay adherents.

The various Zen centers around the country are good examples. Generally, these centers offer intensive spiritual experience together with flexibility in ways for members to relate to the group. American

Zennists, including priests, may be male or female, married or celibate, earn their living on or off the premises, and be in residence for longer or shorter periods of time. Yet the point of being connected with a Zen center is to be able to engage in sustained Zen practice. Participants typically do zazen, or Zen meditation, for at least a half hour morning and evening, engage in Zen study if that is their bent, and schedule regular interviews with the *roshi,* or Zen master.

One vivid illustration, though one more monastic in style than most because of its isolated location, is the already-legendary Zen Mountain Center at Tassajara Hot Springs in the California mountains east of Carmel. The journalist Rasa Gustaitis described a visit to it in the sixties in her book *Turning On.* The center was indeed a sociological "new family" centered around a distinctive practice, zazen. The community rose before the sun to gather in the zendo, or meditation hall. "Dark shapes move toward the zendo. Outside its door, sandals and shoes are lined up in neat rows. People bow as they enter, facing the long room lit by kerosene lamps attached to the walls."[31] Gustaitis found the pain in her legs sometimes excruciating as she sat unmoving in the proper posture, and much of her time outside the zendo was spent in such communal tasks as washing dishes. Meals were ritual occasions, with food first offered on an altar, begun and ended with chants, and much bowing and kneeling as the simple fare was served. Yet she found that as she lived the Zen life a bubbly inward joy kept trickling down, despite the cold, the pain, the hours, the work, and the stylized regimen, and that this joy was abetted not only by the compensation of the natural hot springs baths for which Tassajara Hot Springs was named. It was rather that living and doing Zen somehow brought "beauty and meaning to the smallest moment." The *roshi* there once said in a lecture that Buddhism is actually "nothing but living your own life, little by little."[32]

But clearly that "living" is made meaningful not because the *roshi* or anyone else *says* it is meaningful, but because ritual and an attitude of care and attention suggested by it inform the smallest details of everyday life. Community support for this attitude, expressed

31. Rasa Gustaitis, *Turning On* (New York: New American Library, 1970; first published 1969), p. 155.
32. Ibid., p. 166.

in ritual, reinforces this secure and happy outlook of meaningfulness until it is reified as joy running deep within each participant. For in the last analysis religions teach more by what is done, or sanctioned in practice by the religious community, than by what is said. Practices can focus and then dispense those states of mind the religion values as expeditiously as the words of doctrine or the example of the charismatic leader, for significant doing injects value right into the thick of life and shows it to be, at least ideally, held communally. This is particularly true when, as is the case with most Eastern religions in America, praxis centers on one simple, sure activity like zazen. Zazen is really meditation only insofar as it is total clarity and awareness of mind, and that Zen awareness should not end when the practitioner arises.

The Hare Krishna movement, represented in this volume by the writings of Swami Bhaktivedanta, also focuses on a simple central practice, the Hare Krishna mantra or chant. Adherents recite it constantly on a rosary, and it is the basis of *samkirtan,* the lively group dancing and chanting done several times daily in temples, and often on the streets. It is significant that this practice has a powerful evangelistic appeal, more it would seem than the movement's theology or publicity. J. Stillson Judah, in his study of the movement, found that 38.18 percent of members interviewed reported first encountering it in street *samkirtan*—more than in any other single circumstance—and since these were persons who later joined, the effect was apparently positive.[33] Indeed, the impact was sometimes overwhelming. One devotee reported the first Krishna service he attended as follows:

> Because of certain feelings, I did not join in—at first. However, I saw the devotees chanting, and those magic words, magic words, "Hare Krishna, Hare Krishna, Krishna Krishna, Hare Hare/ Hare Rama, Hare Rama, Rama Rama, Hare Hare!" So I finally gave in and joined them, repeating over and over again. It certainly felt good afterwards.

---

33. J. Stillson Judah, *Hare Krishna and the Counterculture* (New York: John Wiley, 1974), p. 162.

Two days later I went to *kirtana* at the devotee's private house. This time it hit me! I was lost in bliss, divine bliss! . . . I was overwhelmed! Now Krishna Consciousness really had a hold on me, and I can't believe it's all happened so fast![34]

The same theme of the power of the chant is reiterated in the promotion of the movement itself. Gregory Johnson describes a multicolored poster from the sixties that read:

Stay high forever. No more coming down. Practice Krishna Consciousness. Expand your consciousness by practicing the Transcendental Sound Vibration. Hare Krishna. . . . The chanting will cleanse the dust from the mirror of the mind and free you from all material contamination. . . . Try it and be blissful all the time.[35]

Johnson added, "In attracting adherents, its chanting ceremonies seemed to be much more significant than its doctrines. On many occasions I observed visitors who had been fully absorbed in chanting and dancing leave the temple quietly when the post-mantra doctrinal discussions began."[36] This was reinforced by one devotee who said, "Kirtan is the most exciting and sublime experience I have ever had. Every day I feel it again."[37] Certainly some adherents have been drawn to Krishna Consciousness by its teachings, its art, its color, its Indian cuisine and cultural aura, its utopian social vision, and its close-knit communalism. But for many it seems to be in the practice that it all comes together, that one intensely and personally touches the core reality from which the rest flows.

Since their appeal is not based on family, ethnic, or community identity in most cases, Eastern groups for occidentals understandably

---

34. From unpublished paper by Gregory Johnson; cited in Judah, *Hare Krishna,* p. 169.

35. Gregory Johnson, "The Hare Krishna in San Francisco," in *The New Religious Consciousness,* ed. Charles Y. Glock and Robert N. Bellah (Berkeley: University of California Press, 1976), p. 36.

36. Ibid., p. 37.

37. Ibid., p. 38.

tend to draw people as individuals, often appealing to isolated people whose needs are not met by churches revolving around those identities. A higher percentage of members or attenders are likely to be single, widowed, divorced, or young people who have not yet settled down, than is true of the membership of mainline churches and synagogues. Within Eastern groups, moreover, greater specificity as to social characteristics may obtain than in family-based churches, some comprised largely of older women, others of young people. However, generalizations in this respect are unwise, and the trend seems to be toward leveling as Eastern groups themselves mature and become more family-based.

PERIODS IN THE HISTORY
OF EASTERN RELIGION IN AMERICA

The history of institutionalized Eastern religion in America for occidentals falls into three fairly distinct periods. The first was a period of largely verbal and intellectual emphasis, the second an era of the charismatic teacher, the third a time when Easternization as a total life-style and a spiritual way clearly discontinuous with conventional religion was in demand.

The first period, the era before World War I, was dominated by the Theosophical and Vedanta Societies, though the pioneer Zen work of Soyen Shaku's disciples was also present. The Theosophical and Vedanta preeminence meant the preponderance of a highly verbal and intellectual style, based, for most people, on reading books and hearing lectures. The idea-content was Eastern in large part, though under heavy syncretistic or modernizing tendencies. But the practical or worship and sociological forms of expression of these groups were reassuringly familiar to Americans drawn eastward by books and thoughts of the Transcendentalist sort. One might have heard lectures in the Chautauqua style, or in the case of Vedanta witnessed a simple service with a rather cerebral sermon reminiscent of liberal Protestantism.

In both cases, symbols of continuity with American culture and religiosity in the style of worship and institution shared center stage with ideas from far away. Even in the presentation, the rationality and compatibility of Eastern ideas with the most advanced Western thought was suggested by both rhetoric and lecture-hall setting. To be sure, both Theosophy and Vedanta, though different, made much of masters with extraordinary powers, and of subtle planes and forces little known to science. But those claims were not presented as logic-shattering enigmas, as they might have been by a Zen master, but as realities ultimately amenable to reason though far beyond the cutting edge of today's science. Admittedly, too, a pungent aroma of miracle and mystery surrounded the original avatars of those movements, Blavatsky and Ramakrishna. However, they were figures always exotic to the American scene, and were deceased by early in the American history of their movements, the archetypal magus quickly becoming sacred legend.

But if the spirit of the pre–World War I Eastern group was one of intellectualized verbal expression in a format continuous with the liberal Protestant, the next period, that between the wars, saw the return of the magus in force. The twenties and thirties were the era of the Krishnamurti enthusiasm in Theosophy, of Yogananda of Self-Realization, of a slowly growing interest in living masters in India from Mohandas Gandhi to Aurobindo and Ramana Maharishi, of the gradual growth of American Zen under living Japanese *roshis* like Sasaki, of the First Zen Institute, and Senzaki Nyogen, excerpted in this book. Such movements centering on living personalities inevitably were more fluid and informal than the older ones during this period. It is worth noting, however, that their second generation produced some redoubtable apostles too, such as Katherine Tingley, Annie Besant, and C. W. Leadbeater in Theosophy, or Swami Prabhavananda, of the Vedanta Society of Southern California.

The postwar era, and especially the 1960s—which were seminal for so much new Eastern religious activity, saw a fresh spirit emerge. Aided by the easing of U. S. immigration laws, a new set of Asian teachers arrived in America, from Swami Bhaktivedanta of Krishna Consciousness to Jiyu Kennett, the English woman Zennist who, after studying in Japan, founded the Mount Shasta Abbey in California. In the yeasty sixties' spiritual environment, the long-standing enthusiasm for the living teacher and special technique persisted.

But postwar America also displayed a new cosmopolitanism more willing than before to cast the old aside entire, and eager to experiment not only with new ideas, but also with new foods, hair-styles, and life-styles to go with them. The yearning now seemed virtually to be for symbols of discontinuity with conventional American religion. Seekers and finders were eager to surround themselves with full-fledged Eastern culture in groups that met and acted in ways pointedly different from those of standard churches.

One was not satisfied with the ideas and isolated spiritual techniques of the East. Zen, yoga, Krishna, Tibetan and other groups adopted the dress, diet, and art of their distant holy lands, often to the extent of a separatist communalism. The range of this searching for discontinuity was, of course, uneven. By the 1970s and 1980s some backtracking was evident as groups born of the spiritual exuberance of the 1960s sought better integration with general American society for the long haul.

But the basic character of this generation of Eastern groups remains. They exhibit a desire not just for a new idea or practice, but for an entire new religious way of being in the world, including a different way of relating to one's religious authority and group. They wish to symbolize this disjuncture in important life-style and cultural ways. Instead of a service of sermon and sacrament, *satsang,* a discourse with questions and answers, might be conducted by a spiritual teacher. He would be seated rather than standing behind a pulpit, and the hour would be evening or late afternoon instead of Sunday morning. In place of traditional Sunday best, everyone would wear loose, open-necked clothes with an Eastern flair of a sort more suitable to yoga or lotus-posture meditation. Incense would float in the air, and perhaps also the chant of mantras or sutras in an ancient tongue few could follow but whose very sounds charged the room with energy. And so it would go.

THE SPECTRUM OF EASTERN RELIGIOUS GROUPS

Our introductory remarks must now move to an overview of the specific groups that have made up the Eastern spiritual presence in America, and of whose teachers the selections in this book are representative. We will look at them in terms of the three periods, with attention to doctrine, worship, and sociology. It must be emphasized that not all the groups named here are represented by selections in this book. They are discussed in order to afford the reader a glimpse of the full spectrum of Eastern religion in America, but space and the criteria of selection, outlined in the Preface, do not permit reading material from all.

1. *Theosophical Groups.* The modern Theosophical movement is not strictly religious by its own definition, since its basic groups have seen themselves as teaching organizations presenting an "ancient wisdom" underlying religion as well as having congruities with scientific and philosophical thought, but as not inculcating any creed or specific religious practice. However, derivative groups, from "I Am" to the Liberal Catholic Church, are religious by any normal definition. Further, modern Theosophy should not be thought of as essentially Eastern either, since its standard literature from H. P. Blavatsky's *Isis Unveiled* and *The Secret Doctrine*,[38] makes very extensive use of Western sources such as Neoplatonism and the Kabbala as well as Vedas and Puranas—which in fact often seem less well digested than the former and subjected to Gnostic or Neoplatonist presuppositions.

Nonetheless, as we have seen, the Theosophical movement has had a major role in introducing Eastern ideas to America, and the journey of Blavatsky and Olcott to India was a paradigm of countless later pilgrimages by American seekers. Ideas such as karma and reincarnation received their earliest and probably most effective popularization in America through Theosophical initiative.

The largest Theosophical Society has its international headquarters at Adyar, in Madras, India. The largest of "Adyar" Theosophy's some forty-five national branches is that in India itself; the American branch, headquartered in Wheaton, Illinois, is next in size and influence. These features have tended to keep East-West dialogue and Eastern-based teaching prominent in this wing of the movement. The two other groups, the United Lodge of Theosophists and the Theosophical Society continuing the work of the former Point Loma community, together with the numerous devolutions of

---

38. H. P. Blavatsky's *Isis Unveiled* (New York: J. W. Bouton; 1877), *The Secret Doctrine* (London: Theosophical Pub. Co., 1888).

Theosophy, have tended to be more Western in emphasis without rejecting Theosophy's universality.[39]

2. *Hindu-Derived Groups.*   A large number of groups with Hindu background have been established in America. Typically, those appealing chiefly to occidentals have been based on the work of a single guru, whose teaching is broadly Advaita Vedanta, stressing the divine within, and who offers a particular initiation and spiritual method for realizing it. Here are the few of the largest, most representative, and most solidly established of such groups.

• *The Ramakrishna Mission and Vedanta Societies.*   The oldest groups in the Hindu category are societies formed under the influence of Swami Vivekananda and his spectacular performance at the World's Parliament of Religions. Commonly called Vedanta Societies, they are autonomous groups, each under the spiritual guidance of a monk of the Ramakrishna Mission headquartered in Calcutta, India. The first was founded in New York in December 1895; others soon followed in such major cities as Boston, Chicago, San Francisco, and Los Angeles. The most prominent has come to be the Vedanta Society of Southern California, with several centers, including a monastery and a convent. Long under the leadership of the distinguished teacher and translator of Sanskrit classics Swami Prabhavananda (1893–1976), it became the spiritual home of such well-known intellectuals as Aldous Huxley and Christopher Isherwood.

• *The Self-Realization Fellowship.*   The second important movement of Hindu background in America began to take shape in 1920, when Paramahansa Yogananda (1893–1952) arrived in this country, although the group was not formally founded until 1935. Mystic, yoga teacher, and author of the popular *Autobiography of a Yogi*,[40] Yogananda, with his appealing personality and effective yogic methods for attaining spiritual awareness, drew bands of fol-

---

39. See Bruce F. Campbell, *Ancient Wisdom Revived: A History of the Theosophical Movement* (Berkeley and Los Angeles: University of California Press, 1980).

40. Paramahansa Yogananda, *Autobiography of a Yogi* (Los Angeles: Self-Realization Fellowship, 1946).

lowers across the country. Headquartered in Los Angeles, the Self-Realization Fellowship offers both services centered on the ideal of the unity of religions and classes in kriya yoga, the technique taught as basic by the founder.

- *Yoga groups.* A large number of yoga classes and groups, under the tutelage of both Indians and occidentals, can be found throughout America. Most are centered on hatha-yoga, the yoga of postures and breathing exercises, and many clients participate in them more for physical than religious reasons. The spiritual meaning of yoga as a path to inner realization is seldom entirely missing, however. Among the movements in which spiritual as well as physical yoga are emphasized are those created by disciples of the famous Indian yoga teacher Sivananda (1887–1963). In America these include the Sivananda Yoga Vedanta Centers of Swami Vishnu Devananda and the Integral Yoga Institute of Swami Satchidananda.

- *Transcendental Meditation.* In 1959 the Maharishi Mahesh Yogi first brought Transcendental Meditation, or TM, to the Western world. Since then the movement, centering around teaching a simple method of meditation and initiating people into it, has had a colorful and controversial history. In the flamboyant sixties its temporary endorsement by entertainment celebrities catapulted it to fame; in the seventies, in somewhat more sober guise as a "scientific" technique, it experienced dramatic growth and then decline. But TM has done much to raise Western consciousness of Eastern spirituality.

- *The Divine Light Mission.* This movement has also had a meteoric rise and fall. Its leader, Maharaj Ji (b. 1957), came to the United States in 1971 as the Perfect Master, an embodiment of God. Widely publicized as the "teenage guru," he enjoyed a brief, largely counterculture vogue. After peaking in 1974, however, the movement has dwindled, rent by defections and estrangement between the guru and his mother after the former's marriage to an American woman.[41]

41. On the Divine Light Mission, see James V. Downton, Jr., *Sacred Journeys: The Conversion of Young Americans to Divine Light Mission* (New York: Columbia University Press, 1979); and David G. Bromley and Anson D. Shupe, Jr., *Strange Gods: The Great American Cult Scare* (Boston: Beacon Press, 1981), pp. 42–46.

- *The Satya Sai Baba Movement.*   The spiritual figure Satya Sai Baba (b. 1926) has exerted great influence in modern India both through his simple Vedic teachings and his charisma, abetted by countless stories of miracles he has performed. Although he has never come to America, a number of Americans have become his disciples, and Sai Baba centers appear to be growing in the 1980s.

- *Rajneesh Movement.*   The teacher known as Rajneesh (b. 1931) advocates a way based on mental calm and full self-expression. His group engendered great controversy in the mid-1980s after its attempt to gain control of a town in Oregon, its legal problems due to alleged immigration law violations, major defections, and Rajneesh's dramatic apparent attempt to flee the country, subsequent arrest, and return to India.

- *The International Society for Krishna Consciousness.*   The "Hare Krishna" movement is virtually unique among Hindu-based groups in the West in enjoining a bhakti-type devotionalism to Krishna as "the Supreme Personality of Godhead" rather than a form of transpersonal nondualism. Its richly hued temples, rites, and dress, together with its closely knit communities, have also brought controversy. In the 1980s the movement showed signs of entering a time of troubles. It was brought to America in 1965 by Swami Bhaktivedanta (1896–1977), a prolific writer and able exponent of the bhakti way of life.

3. *Groups Related to Sikhism.*   The Sikh religion, a monotheistic faith founded by Guru Nanak (1469–1539), is centered in the Punjab, where Hinduism and Islam meet. It has inspired several sectarian movements, most related to the Sikh belief in a succession of living true gurus, or authoritative teachers and leaders of the faith, after Nanak. The great majority of Sikhs believe that the succession ended with the tenth, Gobind Singh (1666–1708), when authority passed to the Sikh scriptures, the Holy Granth. Certain recent sects, often not founded by Sikhs but partly inspired by their ideal of a living succession, have emerged and come West.

- *Radhasoami Satsang.*   Founded by Shiv Dayal (1818–1878), this movement teaches a cosmology of the gnostic sort, explaining the creation as an "overflow" from God as it descended and mingled with *maya* or illusion. Its practices enabling the ascent of the soul back to its source emphasize following *anhad sabda,* divine sounds heard only in consciousness. The movement came to America as early as 1911 and grew considerably during the sixties.

• *Ruhani Satsang.* Radha Soami has experienced several schisms resulting from disputes over succession to the guruship. Several autonomous groups in the United States that share the name Ruhani Satsang are led by followers of Kirpal Singh (1896–1974), who separated from Radha Soami in 1951 after a controversial succession.

• *Eckankar.* Eckankar, "the ancient science of soul travel," was founded in 1965 by the American Paul Twitchell (d. 1971), who claimed to be nine-hundred-seventy-first in a succession of living Eck masters. Eckankar's emphasis on the inner ascent of the soul, spiritual sound, and the importance of a succession of living masters is reminiscent of Radha Soami. Despite controversy, the movement has been successful in America.

• *Sikh Dharma.* In 1968 a Sikh called Yogi Bhajan came to the United States. He founded a group called 3HO (Healthy, Happy, Holy Organization) and taught practices known as kundalini yoga. Soon, however, he led his followers more and more into normative Sikhism under the aegis of the Sikh Dharma. His largely occidental disciples wear distinctive white garb and tend to live communally in ashrams located in major cities.

4. *Buddhist Groups.* Organized Buddhism for occidentals in America began with the work of Soyen Shaku and his students after the 1893 World's Parliament of Religions. Subsequently other forms of Buddhism besides his Zen have had an appeal for Westerners, although other Buddhist traditions, such as Shingon and Pure Land, have maintained an almost exclusively Asian-American following in this country. Some of the groups with important occidental adherence are listed here:

• *Zen Centers.* As we have seen, the First Zen Institute (originally the Buddhist Society) was established in New York in 1930 by Sokei-an Sasaki Roshi. Another Japanese monk, Nyogen Senzaki (1876–1958), had come to America in 1905, the same year as

Sokei-an, but did not begin preaching Buddhism until twenty years later. He established zendos in San Francisco and Los Angeles in 1928 and 1929 respectively. His major influence, however, has been through his American students, who have been responsible for Zen centers from New York to Hawaii.

The postwar years were the season of great growth for American Zen. Inspired by the books and lectures of D. T. Suzuki and his cadets such as Alan Watts, and by Americans who had experienced the Zen-enriched culture of Japan firsthand during the Occupation, Zen enjoyed a vogue in the 1950s. It was associated with, but not limited to, the "Beat" movement in art, letters, and lifestyle. That interest eventuated in the establishment of major Zen centers in Los Angeles (1956), San Francisco (1959), Rochester, New York (1966), and elsewhere. By the early 1970s the first *roshis* (Zen masters) of occidental descent, including Richard Baker of San Francisco and later Santa Fe, Phillip Kapleau of Rochester, and Robert Aitken of Honolulu, had received dharma transmission and headed important centers, a significant step in occidental Buddhism's coming of age.

- *Nichiren Shoshu.*   Nichiren Buddhism, founded by the prophet Nichiren (1222–1282), with its emphasis on the Lotus Sutra (the sacred chant that aligns one with its power for benefit in this life as well as the next) as sole scripture and the idea of a new dispensation, has been a potent source of new religious movements in modern Japan. Greatest of all has been Soka Gakkai, the dynamic lay Nichiren movement that grew phenomenally in postwar Japan, coming to America in 1963. In 1967 it became Nichiren Shoshu of America (NSA), later Nichiren Shoshu Academy. Stressing practical as well as spiritual benefits of chanting and a joyful, active life-style, NSA has flourished in the American setting. Other Nichiren groups, Rissho Kosei Kai and Reiyukai, have also found a place here although they have been less successful in attracting occidentals than has NSA.
- *Tibetan Buddhism.*   Enigmatic Tibet, that isolated realm at the "roof of the world" with its colorful culture and profound Buddhist faith in the mysterious Vajrayana or Tantric tradition, has long fascinated the rest of the world. That was never more the case than in sixties' counterculture circles, when *The Tibetan Book of*

the Dead[42] and Tibetan religious art, with its mandalas and fiercefaced deities, were the rage. At the same time, Tibetan lamas, refugees from the Communist Chinese takeover of their homeland, were arriving in the West. Soon the interest and the spiritual masters found each other, and several centers for Tibetan Buddhism were established. Tarthang Tulku founded the Nyingmapa Center in Berkeley, California, in 1969, and in 1970 the more eclectic Chogyam Trungpa began a center in Vermont, later transferring his main effort to Boulder, Colorado, where his works include a Buddhist studies center, the Naropa Institute. Several other Tibetan Buddhist activities also appeared in the 1970s.

• *Theravada Buddhism.* The 1970s also brought a certain growth of interest in Theravada, the quieter southern school of Buddhism found in Sri Lanka, Thailand, Burma, Cambodia, and Laos. In 1976 Jack Kornfield and Joseph Goldstein, both of whom had studied Theravada deeply in southeast Asia, established the Insight Meditation Center in Barre, Massachusetts, to teach vipassana meditation, the meditation of analysis leading to nirvanic realization. Several other Theravada centers have also appeared.

5. *Taoism.* This great mystical and aesthetic tradition of China has had a real impact on American Eastern spiritual consciousness at least since the sixties, though one more diffuse than that of the foregoing groups. The *Tao te ching,* the classic of Lao Tzu (6th century B.C.E.?), has been widely read and the relevance of its deep naturalism to the anxiety and ecological crises of our era noted. The East Asian exercises and martial arts, from Tai chi chuan to Aikido, profoundly shaped by Taoism, have grown rapidly in popularity. Taoism's cultural influence can also be gauged by the immensely successful *Star Wars* movies, for the "Force" central to them is clearly derived from the martial arts and appears to be none other than the *ch'i* or *ki* utilized by them and rooted in Taoist spirituality. Taoist centers have appeared in America and seem to be growing in number in the 1980s but—unless one counts the innumerable martial

---

42. *The Tibetan Book of the Dead* (London: Oxford University Press, 1927).

arts schools—are only the proverbial tip of the iceberg of Taoism's overseas influence.

6. *Ethnic Asian Religion.*   Although our principal focus in this book is on Eastern religion for occidentals, a brief account of ethnic Asian religion is necessary for balance and because interaction between the two strands, ethnic and occidental, has had a role in the American evolution of both. By the time of the 1980 census, somewhat over two million people in the United States were Asian-Americans from traditionally Buddhist countries, including an older immigration represented by some 800,000 Chinese and 700,000 Japanese, and a newer immigration of Koreans, Vietnamese, and others. In addition there were some 300,000 Indians of Hindu or Sikh background. Only a minority of the Asian-American population is active in traditional religions, but their numbers have been sufficient to maintain a visible presence of Buddhist, Hindu, Sikh, and other Asian temples in the larger cities and the major magnets of Asian immigration, the West Coast and Hawaii.

The first wave of Asian immigration consisted of Chinese who came to California in Gold Rush days, numbering 60,000 by 1860. A Chinese temple appeared in San Francisco in 1853, and there were eight in the area by 1875. They were the syncretistic temples characteristic of Chinese popular religion, with Buddhist, Taoist, and Confucian features; several examples of these early centers of Asian worship survive.

Although they traveled earlier to Hawaii (not yet a U.S. possession), Japanese immigrants did not arrive on the mainland in large numbers until the end of the nineteenth century. Far more than Chinese, Japanese religion in America took an organized denominational form. The Buddhist Church of America was founded in San Francisco in 1899; its Jodo Shinshu (Pure Land or Amidist) form of Buddhism has been predominant among Japanese-Americans. But other forms of Buddhism, including Zen, Shingon, Nichiren, and Jodo, have also established churches, as have several of the "new religions" of Japan such as Tenrikyo, Konkokyo, and World Messianity.

Early immigration from India was almost exclusively Sikhs from the Punjab. A Sikh temple was opened in Stockton, California, in 1912. U.S. immigration laws, however, severely curtailed immigration from India, as from other parts of Asia, between 1917 and the passing of new legislation in 1946 and 1964, which enabled it to increase rapidly. New Sikh temples were built in several places in California and in major cities across the country. By the 1980s over 100,000 Sikhs were in the United States.

Many Hindu Indians have also come to the United States since World War II, nearly 200,000 by the 1980s, though the erection of major Hindu temples began later than in the case of Buddhism and Sikhism. Some persons of Hindu background were content to attend Hindu centers catering mainly to occidentals, such as the Vedanta Societies or the ISKCON Krishna temples. By the 1980s, however, imposing temples representing a diversity of Hindu traditions and supported mostly by ethnic Hindus were appearing from New York to Los Angeles. Small groups of Jains and Parsees can also be found in the United States.

Ethnic and occidental Eastern religious groups have long maintained essentially separate courses despite occasional fraternization. However, spiritually adventurous Westerners have always found their way, in very small numbers, to Asian-American temples, whether as friendly visitors, attenders, members, or spouses of members. But as language and cultural barriers gradually break down over generations and American society continues in its increasingly pluralistic direction, one can expect that distinctions between the two strands will slowly diminish and eventually vanish.

II

HINDUISM

Movements in India to reform and reinterpret Hinduism, stimulated by pervasive contact with the Christian West, gathered force in the nineteenth century. Two powerful if not entirely consistent drives impelled them: to meet through apologetics and reform efforts the often-searing criticisms of Hindu faith and society leveled by missionaries and liberal faultfinders from the West, and to shore up the defenses of Hindu tradition before it was overwhelmed by the same West. Examples were the Brahmo Samaj of Ram Mohan Roy (1772–1833), whose work as we have noted in the introductory chapter influenced the Transcendentalists, and the Arya Samaj of Dayananda (1824–1883), a more conservative movement that attracted the attention of early Theosophists. Broadly speaking, early and mid-century movements like these exalted the monistic and monotheistic strands in the Vedas and the *Bhagavad-Gita* while deploring Hinduism's mythological and polytheistic strata. They promoted high ethical ideals, social reform, and intellectual renewal. But they reached only an elite in India, while winning much sympathy but few real converts in the West.

A second stage, often called Neo-Vedanta, emerged in the closing decades of the nineteenth century. Part of a broader "Hindu renaissance" aligned with the sentiment from which the Indian independence movement was growing, it managed to combine a liberal modern temperament with a broad affirmation of Hindu culture as a whole. Neo-Vedanta was chiefly associated with the saintly Ra-

45

makrishna (1834–1886) and his disciples, especially Swami Vivekananda (1863–1902), though its spirit is reflected in other modern
thinkers, such as the philosopher Sarvepelli Radhakrishnan (1888–
1975).

Neo-Vedanta centers on a belief that Hinduism has an immensely valuable spiritual message for the world, which can be con-
fidently promulgated. The message is based on the traditional
sources of Vedanta, particularly the Advaita or nondualistic Vedanta, which its advocates generally espoused, the *Upanishads* and
the rigorous development of their essential themes of India's preem-
inent philosopher Shankara (c. 8th cent. C.E.). The tradition's radical
nondualism shows all things to be manifestations of Brahman or
God, and religiously underscores the divine within as that Reality
most to be sought, both in oneself and in others.

The Neo-Vedanta reinterpretation stressed further the tradition's implicit theme of universalism, stressing that the divine
within oneself and all things was the true end of all religions. It
further emphasized its implicit validation of such modern ideals as
human equality, democracy, and rational, scientific thought. The
influential disciples of Ramakrishna saw this outlook supremely
exemplified in the life and teachings of this Hindu saint, at once
a saint in the classic mold, ecstatic, indifferent to money and other
worldly things, and engaged in his own way with modern concerns. He had, for example, pursued experientially the spiritual
paths of several religions, finding to his own satisfaction that they
were all roads to the same place.

Neo-Vedanta was put into full intellectual expression, however, by others. None had a more dynamic impact than the brilliant, tireless Vivekananda, who might be called Ramakrishna's
Saint Paul. He expounded his thought in a series of books and addresses, which basically offered rationalized versions of longstand-
ing Hindu themes, from yoga to Advaita. After Ramakrishna's
death, he, with another disciple, Swami Brahmananda, founded the
Ramakrishna Order of Monks, at first comprised only of the master's direct disciples. Soon others joined; it is now both a very influential monastic order in Hindu India and the supplier of swamis
to the world who come West at the invitation of Vedanta societies
(or similar groups) in Europe and America. In 1897 Vivekananda
formed the Ramakrishna Mission as an outreach agency of the Or-

der; it does teaching and social welfare work in India and elsewhere.

The Ramakrishna Order has given America a series of distinguished monks, including Swami Nikhilananda, scholarly head of the Ramakrishna-Vivekananda Center in New York, and Swami Akhilananda, head of the Vedanta Center of Boston and noted for his work in the psychology of religion. None, however, has exceeded in reputation Swami Prabhavananda, for many years head of the Vedanta Society of Southern California. It was his privilege to lead a relatively large center that included among its adherents such well-known writers as Gerald Heard, Aldous Huxley, and Christopher Isherwood. In collaboration with Isherwood and others, he translated a number of Vedanta classics into English for the popular reader, as well as publishing several volumes of addresses and sermons, often giving Vedantic interpretations of Christian texts.

Others besides those in the tradition of the Ramakrishna Order and Mission have presented the universalistic Neo-Vedanta message. Among them was Paramahansa Yogananda of the Self-Realization Fellowship. Like the others he first found his way in America through friendship with liberal Protestants, first coming to the United States to attend a congress of religious liberals in 1920, and deciding to stay. As we have seen, he founded the Self-Realization Fellowship in 1935. Using a technique known as kriya yoga, it seeks the Vedantic goal of realizing the divine within, and finds the same theme in all great religions. Other Vedanta-oriented groups may be found in America, some of which began by separating themselves from the Vedanta Societies or the Self-Realization Fellowship.

Bibliography

Bridges, Hal. *American Mysticism: From William James to Zen.* New York: Harper and Row, 1970.

Ellwood, Robert. *Religious and Spiritual Groups in Modern America.* Englewood Cliffs, N.J.: Prentice-Hall, 1972.

Harper, Marvin Henry, *Gurus, Swamis, and Avataras: Spiritual Masters and Their American Disciples.* Philadelphia: Westminster, 1972.

Isherwood, Christopher. *My Guru and His Disciple.* New York: Farrar, Straus, Giroux, 1980. About Swami Prabhavananda.

————. *Ramakrishna and His Disciples*. New York: Simon and
    Schuster, 1965.
Nikhilananda, Swami. *Vivekananda: A Biography*. New York: Ra-
    makrishna-Vivekananda Center, 1953.
Thomas, Wendell. *Hinduism Invades America*. Boston: Beacon
    Press, 1930.

Hindu Selections

This address, together with Vivekananda's vigorous personality, cre-
ated a powerful impression in the congress and the nation. It may be con-
sidered the charter of Neo-Vedanta Hinduism in the West, for it strikes its
basic themes: the eternal Vedas as more basic than other expressions of Hin-
duism, an unapologetic but spiritualizing interpretation of its myths and
"idols," stress on the quest for the divine within and ultimate liberation, a
tone that aligns the faith with the rationalistic and idealistic movements of
the age, rejecting the language of sin in favor of that of imperfection and
incompleted progress, while striving to add to idealism the riches of Ve-
dantic depth and power.

Hinduism as a Religion*

Three religions now stand in the world which have come down
to us from time prehistoric—Hinduism, Zoroastrianism and Judaism. These all have received tremendous shocks and all of them
prove by their revival their internal strength, but Judaism failed to
absorb Christianity and was driven out of its place of birth by its all-
conquering daughter. Sect after sect has arisen in India and seemed
to shake the religion of the Vedas to its very foundations; but, like
the waters of the seashore in a tremendous earthquake, it has receded
only for a while, only to return in an all-absorbing flood, and when
the tumult of the rush was over these sects had been all sucked in,
absorbed and assimilated in the immense body of another faith.

From the high spiritual flights of philosophy, of which the latest
discoveries of science seem like echoes, from the atheism of the Jains
to the low ideas of idolatry and the multifarious mythologies, each
and all have a place in the Hindu's religion.

Where then, the question arises, where then the common center
to which all these widely diverging radii converge? Where is the

---

*Reprinted from J. W. Hanson, ed., *The World's Congress of Religions at
the World's Columbian Exposition* (Chicago: J. W. Iliff, 1894), pp. 366–76.
Slightly edited.

common basis upon which all these seemingly hopeless contradictions rest? And this is the question which I shall attempt to answer.

The Hindus have received their religion through the revelation of the Vedas. They hold that the Vedas are without beginning and without end. It may sound ludicrous to this audience—how a book can be without beginning or end. But by the Vedas no books are meant. They mean the accumulated treasury of spiritual laws discovered by different persons in different times. Just as the law of gravitation existed before its discovery and would exist if all humanity forgot it, so with the laws that govern the spiritual world; the moral, ethical and spiritual relations between soul and soul and between individual spirits and the father of all spirits were there before their discovery and would remain even if we forgot them.

The discoverers of these laws are called Rishis and we honor them as perfected beings, and I am glad to tell this audience that some of the very best of them were women.

Here it may be said, that the laws as laws may be without end, but they must have had a beginning. The Vedas teach us that creation is without beginning or end. Science has proved to us that the sum total of the cosmic energy is the same throughout all time. Then, if there was a time when nothing existed, where was all this manifested energy? Some say it was in a potential form in God. But then God is sometimes potential and sometimes kinetic, which would make him mutable, and everything mutable is a compound, and everything compound must undergo that change which is called destruction. Therefore God would die. Therefore there never was a time when there was no creation.

Here I stand, and if I shut my eyes and try to conceive my existence, "I," "I," "I," what is the idea before me? The idea of a body. Am I, then, nothing but a combination of matter and material substances? The Vedas declare, "No." I am a spirit living in a body. I am not the body. The body will die, but I will not die. Here am I in this body, and when it will fail, still I will go on living. Also I had a past. The soul was not created from nothing, for creation means a combination, and that means a certain future dissolution. If, then, the soul was created, it must die. Therefore, it was not created. Some are born happy, enjoying perfect health, beautiful body, mental vigor, and with all wants supplied. Others are born miserable. Some are without hands or feet, some idiots, and only drag out a miserable existence. Why, if they are all created, why does a just and merciful God create one happy and the other unhappy? Why is He so partial? Nor would it mend matters in the least to hold that those who are miserable in this life will be perfect in a future life. Why should a man be miserable here in the reign of a just and merciful God?

In the second place, it does not give us any cause, but simply a cruel act of an all-powerful being, and therefore it is unscientific. There must have been causes, then, to make a man miserable or happy before his birth, and those were his past actions. Why may not all the tendencies of the mind and body be answered for by inherited aptitude from parents? Here are the two parallel lines of existence— one that of the mind, the other that of matter.

If matter and its transformation answer for all that we have, there is no necessity of supposing the existence of a soul. But it cannot be proved that thought has been evolved out of matter. We cannot deny that bodies inherit certain tendencies, but those tendencies only mean the physical configuration through which a peculiar mind alone can act in a peculiar way. Those peculiar tendencies in that soul have been caused by past actions. A soul with a certain tendency will take birth in a body which is the fittest instrument of the display of that tendency, by the laws of affinity. And this is in perfect accord with science, for science wants to explain everything by habit, and habit is got through repetitions. So these repetitions are also necessary to explain the natural habits of a new-born soul. They were not got in this present life; therefore, they must have come down from past lives.

But there is another suggestion, taking all these for granted. How is it that I do not remember anything of my past life? This can be easily explained. I am now speaking English. It is not my mother tongue; in fact, not a word of my mother tongue is present in my consciousness; but, let me try to bring such words up, they rush into my consciousness. That shows that consciousness is the name only of the surface of the mental ocean, and within its depths are stored up all our experiences. Try and struggle and they will come up and you will be conscious.

This is the direct and demonstrative evidence. Verification is the perfect proof of a theory, and here is the challenge thrown to the world by Rishis. We have discovered precepts by which the very depths of the ocean of memory can be stirred up; follow them and you will get a complete reminiscence of your past life.

So then the Hindu believes that he is a spirit. Him the sword cannot pierce, him the fire cannot burn, him the water cannot melt, him the air cannot dry. He believes every soul is a circle whose circumference is nowhere, but whose center is located in a body, and death means the change of this center from body to body. Nor is the soul bound by the condition of matter. In its very essence it is free, unbound, holy and pure and perfect. But somehow or other it has got itself bound down by matter, and thinks of itself as matter.

Why should the free, perfect and pure being be under the thraldom of matter? How can the perfect be deluded into the belief that he is imperfect? We have been told that the Hindus shirk the question and say that no such question can be there, and some thinkers want to answer it by the supposing of one or more quasi perfect beings, and use big scientific names to fill up the gap. But naming is not explaining. The question remains the same. How can the perfect become the quasi perfect; how can the pure, the absolute, change even a microscopic particle of its nature? The Hindu is sincere. He does not want to take shelter under sophistry. He is brave enough to face the question in a manly fashion. And his answer is, "I do not know." I do not know how the perfect being, the soul, came to think of itself as imperfect, as joined and conditioned by matter. But the fact is a fact for all that. It is a fact in everybody's consciousness that he thinks of himself as the body. We will not attempt to explain why I am in this body.

Well, then, the human soul is eternal and immortal, perfect and infinite, and death means only a change of center from one body to another. The present is determined by our past actions, and the future will be by the present. The soul will go on evolving up or reverting back from birth to birth and death to death—like a tiny boat in a tempest, raised one moment on the foaming crest of a billow and dashed down into a yawning chasm the next, rolling to and fro at the mercy of good and bad actions—a powerless, helpless wreck in an ever raging, ever rushing, uncompromising current of cause and effect. A little moth placed under the wheel of causation which rolls on, crushing everything in its way and waits not for the widow's tears or the orphan's cry.

The heart sinks at the idea, yet this is the law of nature. Is there no hope? Is there no escape? The cry that went up from the bottom of the heart of despair reached the throne of mercy, and words of hope and consolation came down and inspired a Vedic sage and he stood up before the world and in trumpet voice proclaimed the glad tidings to the world, "Hear, ye children of immortal bliss, even ye that resisted in higher spheres. I have found the ancient one, who is beyond all darkness, all delusion, and knowing Him alone you shall be saved from death again." "Children of immortal bliss," what a sweet, what a hopeful name. Allow me to call you, brethren, by that sweet name, heirs of immortal bliss; yea, the Hindu refuses to call you sinners.

Ye are the children of God. The sharers of immortal bliss, holy and perfect beings. Ye divinities on earth, sinners? It is a sin to call a man so. It is a standing libel on human nature. Come up, live and shake off the delusion that you are sheep—you are souls immortal, spirits free and blest and eternal; ye are not matter, ye are not bodies. Matter is your servant, not you the servant of matter.

Thus it is the Vedas proclaim, not a dreadful combination of unforgiving laws, not an endless prison of cause and effect, but that, at the head of all these laws, in and through every particle of matter and force, stands One "through whose command the wind blows, the fire burns, the clouds rain, and death stalks upon the earth." And what is His nature?

He is everywhere, the pure and formless One, the Almighty and the All-merciful. "Thou art our Father, Thou art our Mother, Thou art our beloved Friend, Thou art the source of all strength. Thou art He that bearest the burdens of the universe; help me to bear the little burden of this life." Thus sang the Rishis of the Veda. And how to worship Him? Through love. "He is to be worshiped as the One beloved, dearer than everything in this and the next life."

This is the doctrine of love preached in the Vedas, and let us see how it is fully developed and preached by Krishna, whom the Hindus believe to have been God incarnate on earth.

He taught that a man ought to live in this world like a lotus leaf, which grows in water, but is never moistened by water; so a man ought to live in this world, his heart for God and his hands for work.

It is good to love God for hope of reward in this or the next world, but it is better to love God for love's sake, and the prayer goes, "Lord, I do not want wealth, nor children, nor learning. If it be Thy will I will go to a hundred hells, but grant me this, that I may love Thee without the hope of reward—unselfishly love for love's sake." One of the disciples of Krishna, the then emperor of India, was driven from his throne by his enemies and had to take shelter in a forest in the Himalayas with his queen, and there one day the queen was asking him how it was that he, the most virtuous of men, should suffer so much misery, and Yudhisthira answered, "Behold, my queen, the Himalayas, how grand and beautiful they are! I love them. They do not give me anything, but my nature is to love the grand, the beautiful; therefore, I love them. Similarly, I love the Lord. He is the source of all beauty, of all sublimity. He is the only object to be loved. My nature is to love Him, and therefore I love. I do not pray for anything. I do not ask for anything. Let Him place me wherever He likes. I must love Him for love's sake. I cannot trade in love."

The Vedas teach that the soul is divine, only held under bondage of matter, and perfection will be reached when the bond shall burst, and the word they use is, therefore, Mukta—freedom—freedom from the bonds of imperfection; freedom from death and misery.

And they teach that this bondage can only fall off through the mercy of God, and this mercy comes to the pure. So purity is the condition of His mercy. How that mercy acts! He reveals Himself to the pure heart, and the pure and stainless man sees God; yea, even in this life, and then, and then only. All the crookedness of the heart is made straight. Then all doubt ceases. Man is no more the freak of a terrible law of causation. So this is the very center, the very vital conception of Hinduism. The Hindu does not want to live upon words and theories; if there are existences beyond the ordinary sensual existence, he wants to come face to face with them. If there is a soul in him which is not matter, if there is an all-merciful universal soul, he will go to Him direct. He must see Him, and that alone can destroy all doubts. So the best proof a Hindu sage gives about the soul, about God, is, "I have seen the soul, I have seen God."

And that is the only condition of perfection. The Hindu religion does not consist in struggles and attempts to believe a certain doctrine or dogma, but in realizing; not in believing, but in being and becoming.

So the whole struggle in their system is a constant struggle to become perfect, to become divine, to reach God and see God, and in this reaching God, seeing God, becoming perfect, even as the Father in heaven is perfect, consists the religion of the Hindus.

And what becomes of man when he becomes perfect? He lives a life of bliss, infinite. He enjoys infinite and perfect bliss, having obtained the only thing in which man ought to have pleasure—God—and enjoys the bliss with God.

So far all the Hindus are agreed. This is the common religion of all the sects of India, but then the question comes—perfection is absolute, and the absolute cannot be two or three. It cannot have any qualities. It cannot be an individual. And so when a soul becomes perfect and absolute, it must become one with the Brahman, and he would only realize the Lord as the perfection, the reality of his own nature and existence—existence absolute; knowledge absolute, and life absolute. We have often and often read about this being called the losing of individuality as in becoming a stock or a stone. "He jests at scars that never felt a wound."

I tell you it is nothing of the kind. If it is happiness to enjoy the consciousness of this small body, it must be more happiness to enjoy the consciousness of two bodies, or three, four, five; and the ultimate of happiness would be reached when it would become a universal consciousness.

Therefore, to gain this infinite, universal individuality, this miserable little individuality must go. Then alone can death cease, when I am one with life. Then alone can misery cease, when I am with happiness itself. Then alone can all errors cease, when I am one with knowledge itself. And this is the necessary scientific conclusion. Science has proved to me that physical individuality is a delusion, that really my body is one little, continuously changing body in an unbroken ocean of matter, and the Advaitam is the necessary conclusion with my other counterpart, mind.

Science is nothing but the finding of unity, and as soon as any science can reach the perfect unity it will stop from further progress, because it will then have reached the goal. Thus, chemistry cannot progress further, when it shall have discovered one element out of which all others could be made. Physics will stop when it shall be able to discover one energy of which all others are but manifestations. The science of religion will become perfect when it discovers Him who is the one life in a universe of death, who is the constant basis of an ever-changing world, who is the only soul of which all souls are but manifestations. Thus, through multiplicity and duality the ultimate unity is reached, and religion can go no further. This is the goal of all—again and again, science after science, again and again.

And all science is bound to come to this conclusion in the long run. Manifestation and not creation is the word of science of today, and the Hindu is only glad that what he has cherished in his bosom for ages is going to be taught in more forcible language and with further light by the latest conclusions of science.

Descend we now from the aspirations of philosophy to the religion of the ignorant. At the very outset, I may tell you that there is no polytheism in India. In every temple, if one stands by and listens, he will find the worshipers apply all the attributes of God, including omnipresence, to these images. It is not polytheism. "The rose called by any other name would smell as sweet." Names are not explanations.

I remember, when a boy, a Christian man was preaching to a crowd in India. Among other sweet things, he was asking the people, if he gave a blow to their idol with his stick, what could it do? One of his hearers sharply answered: "If I abuse your God what can He do?" "You would be punished," said the preacher, "when you die." "So my idol will punish you when you die," said the villager.

The tree is known by its fruits, and when I have been amongst them that are called idolatrous men, the like of whose morality and spirituality and love I have never seen anywhere, I stop and ask myself, "Can sin beget holiness?"

Superstition is the enemy of man, but bigotry is worse. Why does a Christian go to church? Why is the cross holy? Why is the face turned toward the sky in prayer? Why are there so many images in the Catholic church? Why are there so many images in the minds of Protestants when they pray? My brethren, we can no more think about anything without a material image than we can live without breathing. And by the law of association the material image calls the mental idea up and vice versa. Omnipresence, to almost the whole world, means nothing. Has God superficial area? If not, when we repeat the word we think of the extended earth, that is all.

As we find that somehow or other, by the laws of our constitution, we have got to associate our ideas of infinity with the image of a blue sky, or a sea, some cover the idea of holiness with an image of a church, or a mosque, or a cross. The Hindus have associated the ideas of holiness, purity, truth, omnipresence, and all other ideas with different images and forms. But with this difference: Some devote their whole lives to their idol of a church and never rise higher, because with them religion means an intellectual assent to certain doctrines and doing good to their fellows. The whole religion of the Hindu is centered in realization. Man is to become divine, realizing the divine, and, therefore, idol, or temple, or church, or books, are only the supports, the helps, of his spiritual childhood; but on and on man must progress.

He must not stop anywhere. "External worship, material worship," says the Vedas, "is the lowest stage, struggling to rise high; mental prayer is the next stage, but the highest stage is when the Lord has been realized." Mark the same earnest man who was kneeling before the idol tell you, "Him the sun cannot express, nor the moon nor the stars, the lightning cannot express him, nor the fire; through Him they all shine." He does not abuse the image or call it sinful. He recognizes in it a necessary stage of His life. "The child is father of the man." Would it be right for the old man to say that childhood is a sin or youth a sin? Nor is it compulsory in Hinduism.

If a man can realize his divine nature with the help of an image, would it be right to call it a sin? Nor, even when he has passed that stage, should he call it an error? To the Hindu, man is not traveling from error to truth, but from truth to truth, from lower to higher truth. To him all the religions, from the lowest fetishism to the highest absolutism, mean so many attempts of the human soul to grasp and realize the infinite, each determined by the conditions of its birth and association, and each of these mark a stage of progress, and every soul is a young eagle soaring higher and higher, gathering more and more strength till it reaches the glorious sun.

Unity and variety is the plan of nature, and the Hindu has recognized it. Every other religion lays down certain fixed dogmas, and tries to force society to adopt them. They lay down before society one coat which must fit Jack and Job and Henry, all alike. If it does not fit John or Henry he must go without a coat to cover his body. The Hindus have discovered that the absolute can only be realized or thought of or stated through the relative, and the images, cross or crescent, are simply so many centers, so many pegs to hang the spiritual ideas on. It is not that this help is necessary for every one, but for many, and those that do not need it have no right to say that it is wrong.

One thing I must tell you. Idolatry in India does not mean anything horrible. It is not the mother of harlots. On the other hand, it is the attempt of undeveloped minds to grasp high spiritual truths. The Hindus have their faults; but mark this, they are always toward punishing their own bodies and never toward cutting the throats of their neighbors. If the Hindu fanatic burns himself on the pyre, he never lights the fire of inquisition. And even this cannot be laid at the door of religion any more than the burning of witches can be laid at the door of Christianity.

To the Hindu, then, the whole world of religion is only a traveling, a coming up, of different men and women, through various conditions and circumstances, to the same goal. Every religion is only an evolution out of the material man, a God—and the same God is the inspirer of all of them. Why, then, are there so many contradictions? They are only apparent, says the Hindu. The contradictions come from the same truth adapting itself to the different circumstances of different natures.

It is the same light coming through different colors. And these little variations are necessary for that adaptation. But in the heart of everything the same truth reigns. The Lord has declared to the Hindu in His incarnation as Krishna, ''I am in every religion as the thread through a string of pearls. And wherever thou seest extraordinary holiness and extraordinary power raising and purifying humanity, know ye, that I am there.'' And what was the result? Through the whole order of Sanskrit philosophy, I challenge anybody to find any such expression as that the Hindu only would be saved, not others. Says Vyas, ''We find perfect men even beyond the pale of our caste and creed.'' How, then, can the Hindu, whose whole idea centers in God, believe in the Buddhism which is agnostic, or the Jainism which is atheist?

The whole force of Hindu religion is directed to the great central truth in every religion, to evolve a God out of man. They have not seen the Father, but they have seen the Son. And he that hath seen the Son hath seen the Father.

This, brethren, is a short sketch of the ideas of the Hindus. The Hindu might have failed to carry out all his plans. But if there is ever to be a universal religion, it must be one which will hold no location in place or time; which will be infinite, like the God it will preach; whose Son shines upon the followers of Krishna or Christ, saints or sinners, alike; which will not be the Brahman or Buddhist, Christian or Mohammedan, but the sum total of all these, and still have infinite space for development; which in its Catholicity will embrace in its infinite arms and find a place for every human being, from the lowest groveling man, from the brute, to the highest mind towering almost above humanity and making society stand in awe and doubt His human nature.

It will be a religion which will have no place for persecution or intolerance in its polity, which will recognize a divinity in every man or woman, and whose whole scope, whose whole force, will be centered in aiding humanity to realize its divine nature.

Ashoka's council was a council of the Buddhist faith. Akbar's, though more to the purpose, was only a parlor meeting. It was reserved for America to proclaim to all quarters of the globe that the Lord is in every religion.

May He who is the Brahma of the Hindus, the Ahura Mazda of the Zoroastrians, the Buddha of the Buddhists, the Jehovah of the Jews, the Father in heaven of the Christians, give strength to you to carry out your noble idea.

The star arose in the east; it traveled steadily toward the west, sometimes dimmed and sometimes effulgent, till it made a circuit of the world, and now it is again rising on the very horizon of the east, the borders of the Tasifu, a thousand fold more effulgent than it ever was before. Hail, Columbia, motherland of liberty! It has been given to thee, who never dipped hand in neighbor's blood, who never found out that shortest way of becoming rich by robbing one's neighbors—it has been given to thee to march on in the vanguard of civilization with the flag of harmony.

2. SWAMI PRABHAVANANDA: THE SALT OF THE EARTH

This sermon by Swami Prabhavananda, leader of the Vedanta Society of Southern California from 1929 until his death in 1976, well illustrates the flavor of Western Vedanta in the twentieth century. One of a number on Christian texts preached by this eminent monk, it characteristically endeavors to build bridges between the great religions while pressing for an inward or universal meaning for such concepts as Incarnation and Knowl-

edge. At the same time, Swami Prabhavananda takes the occasion to fa-
miliarize hearers (and readers) with such Hindu sources as the *Bhagavad-
Gita* and the sayings of Ramakrishna.

*"The Salt of the Earth"**
[Matthew 5:13–37]

Ye are the salt of the earth: but if the salt have lost his sa-
vour, wherewith shall it be salted? it is thenceforth good
for nothing, but to be cast out, and to be trodden under foot
of men.

In India, when a disciple comes to a teacher, the teacher tries
first of all to give him a firm faith in himself, and a feeling that weakness and cowardice and failure have no part in his true nature. In the
second book of the Bhagavad-Gita, almost the first words which Sri
Krishna, the divine incarnation, says to Arjuna are: "What is this
weakness? It is beneath you. . . . Shake off this cowardice!"

Just as you can see the contents of a cupboard through its glass
doors, a great teacher can see into your heart. But he does not condemn you for your faults and weaknesses. He knows human nature.
Because he realizes that when you feel weak and depressed you cannot achieve anything, cannot grow spiritually, he gives you confidence in yourself.

The teacher sees not merely what you are at present, but also
the capacities you will develop. Many years ago a young swami, who
was about to leave India to preach in America, went to see Swami
Turiyananda. When this great disciple of Sri Ramakrishna praised
the young monk highly, the latter protested: "But sir, I don't have
any of the qualities you are praising!" Then Turiyananda said:
"What do you know about yourself? I see what you are going to
unfold!" We all have the power to unfold the divinity latent within
us, but the teacher gives us confidence in our ability to do it.

---

*From Swami Prabhavananda, *The Sermon on the Mount according to Ve-
danta.* Copyright © 1963 by Vedanta Society of Southern California. Reprinted by
permission.

At the same time we must remember the beatitude: "Blessed are the meek . . ." Meekness and faith in oneself must go together. The faith which Christ instilled in his disciples by calling them "the salt of the earth" was not faith in the lower self, the ego, but faith in the higher Self, faith in God within. With such faith comes self-surrender, freedom from any sense of ego.

Sri Ramakrishna illustrated this truth with an incident from Hindu mythology. He told how Radha, the foremost of the shepherdesses, whom Sri Krishna loved best, became apparently very egotistical. When the other shepherdesses complained to Sri Krishna about her, he suggested that they ask Radha. "Certainly I have an ego," said Radha. "But whose ego is it? It is not mine, for everything I have belongs to Krishna." A person who has surrendered everything to God has no ego in the ordinary sense. He cannot be vain or proud. He has strong faith in the true Self within him, which is one with God.

This saying of Jesus, "Ye are the salt of the earth . . ." reminds me of a saying my master used to quote to us: "You have the grace of God, you have the grace of the *guru* [the spiritual teacher], and you have the grace of God's devotees; but for the lack of one grace you may be cast out." What is that one grace? It is the grace of one's own mind, the will to struggle for perfection. If, in spite of all those graces which would otherwise make us "the salt of the earth," we lack the grace of our own mind, we may be "trodden under foot of men." We must strive hard to surrender ourselves wholeheartedly to God—in order that the divinity within us may become manifest.

> Ye are the light of the world. A city that is set on an hill cannot be hid.
> Neither do men light a candle, and put it under a bushel, but on a candlestick; and it giveth light unto all that are in the house.

A great spiritual teacher gathers pure souls around him and teaches them, not only by word of mouth, but by actual transmission of spirituality. He does not simply give them self-confidence; he actually illumines the hearts of his disciples and makes them the light of the world. For only those who have obtained illumination through union with the light which dwells in the hearts of all can become the light of the world. Only such illumined ones are fit to teach mankind; only they can carry on the message of a divine incarnation. When Sri Ramakrishna met anyone who wished to teach the word of God, he would ask: "Have you the divine commission?" Only he who has seen God can receive his commission, his direct command to teach. Religion degenerates when taught by unillumined men. It is no good relying on a degree at a theological college; books cannot give illumination. One may have studied scriptures, history, philosophy—one may be versed in theology, dogmas, and doctrines, and give wonderful sermons—and yet be a baby when it comes to spiritual life. In order to transform people's lives, one must first light one's own candle.

According to Vedanta, there are two kinds of knowledge. The first, the lower, consists of academic knowledge, such as science and philosophy. Even knowledge of the scriptures is considered lower knowledge. The second, the higher knowledge, is the immediate perception of God. A man who is enlightened by this higher knowledge does not need encyclopedic information in order to expound the scriptures; he teaches from inner experience.

Swami Adbhutananda, one of Sri Ramakrishna's disciples, was such an enlightened man. Among his brother monks he was unique in that he had had no formal education at all. He came to Sri Ramakrishna as a young servant boy who did not even know how to sign his name. Sri Ramakrishna tried to teach him the Bengali alphabet, but Adbhutananda could not manage to read even the first vowel correctly. And yet we who were privileged to meet him in his later life saw the wisdom of this unlettered man. One day, several young monks came across a difficult passage in the Upanishads, the ancient scriptures of the Hindus. They could not understand it, although they referred to a number of commentaries. Finally they asked Adbhutananda for an explanation. As the Swami did not know Sanskrit, the young monks phrased the passage in his vernacular. Adbhutananda thought for a moment; then he said: "I've got it!" Using a simple illustration, he explained the passage to them, and they found wonderful meaning in it.

A man who has seen God does not need academic knowledge in order to teach religion. His heart has been purified and illumined, and his light shines forth and gives comfort to everyone. He does not

have to go out looking for disciples. Sri Ramakrishna used to say that
when the lotus blossoms the bees come from all around, of their own
accord, to gather the honey. "Make that lotus blossom!" he used to
tell his disciples.

When such an illumined soul appears, and spiritual aspirants
gather around him, they cannot help thinking of God and loving him.
In the presence of such a soul they feel that God-realization is easy.
This was my own experience at the feet of Sri Ramakrishna's disciples. It is not hard to understand; there is no mystery about it. When
you go to visit a lawyer, what kind of thoughts come into your mind?
Thoughts about legal matters. With a doctor, you think about sickness and medicine. These thoughts come to you because the person
you are with at the moment is living in that particular atmosphere.
So, also, with a holy man. You may not know anything about him,
but this is the test: When you come into his presence, the thought of
God will come to you—even though the holy man may be talking of
something quite different.

Of course, you have to be a seeker after the truth of God in order
to be susceptible to a spiritual atmosphere. If you are not interested
in God-realization, Christ himself may stand before you to teach
you, and you will not appreciate him or recognize his greatness. You
will turn from him as the many turned from him two thousand years
ago. But if you are a spiritual aspirant and come into the presence of
an illumined soul, you cannot do other than glorify God, because in
his presence you will feel the presence of the Father. This is what
Jesus was speaking of when he said to his disciples:

Let your light so shine before men, that they may see your
good works, and glorify your Father which is in heaven.

And then he said:

Think not that I am come to destroy the law, or the prophets: I am not come to destroy, but to fulfil.
For verily I say unto you, Till heaven and earth pass, one
jot or one tittle shall in no wise pass from the law, till all
be fulfilled.
Whosoever therefore shall break one of these least com-
mandments, and shall teach men so, he shall be called the

least in the kingdom of heaven: but whosoever shall do and
teach them, the same shall be called great in the kingdom
of heaven.

Jesus here speaks of the mission of the divine incarnation,
called the *avatar* by the Hindus and the Son of God by the Christians.

The concept of the avatar evolved from the theory of the Logos
in both Western and Eastern philosophy. In the West, the theory of
the Logos was first developed by the Greeks to bridge the gulf that
separates man from God, the known from the unknown. In its earliest
uses the Logos was identified with one or another of the physical
elements. Plato projected the Logos as the cosmic purpose, the supreme Good, under which all lesser ideas—i.e., eternal archetypes
of things, relations, qualities, and values—are subsumed. Later, the
Stoics denied the validity of Plato's supersensual archetypes. They
perceived the principle of reason to be immanent and active in the
universe. Philo, an Alexandrian Jew and contemporary of Jesus,
combined Stoic reason with Plato's transcendentalism, and added
them to Hebraism. He declared that the Logos was not only immanent in the universe but was transcendent as well, one with God. The
author of the Fourth Gospel then used Philo's Logos theory as the
basis for his interpretation of the life of Christ, but gave it new vision
to serve the theological needs of Christianity. In addition to attrib-
uting a real personality to the Logos, he emphasized, not its creative
aspect but its redemptive function, its communication of spirituality
to men. He stressed, moreover, the conception of the Logos as Word
rather than Reason, interpreting it as an expression of the divine will,
an outpouring of God's goodness, power, light, and love. To quote
St. John: "In the beginning was the Word, and the Word was with
God, and the Word was God. . . . And the Word was made flesh,
and dwelt among us (and we beheld his glory, the glory of the only
begotten of the Father), full of grace and truth." The Logos, the
"only begotten of the Father," was "made flesh" in Jesus Christ.

In the Vedas (most ancient of the world's scriptures) we find
passages which are almost identical with the opening sentence of the
Gospel according to St. John: "In the beginning was the Lord of
Creatures; second to him was the Word." "The Word was verily
Brahman." According to the Hindus, Brahman conditioned by
maya, his creative power (which is the basis of mind and matter), is

first manifested as the eternal undifferentiated Word, out of which the concrete sensible world then evolves. To the Hindus, therefore, the Word is incarnated in all beings, each of whom may directly realize God through the divine power of the Word. But like St. John, Hindus believe that in a special sense the Logos is made flesh in the avatar—the avatar being the descent of God, whereas the ordinary man ascends toward God.

There is this important difference between the Hindu and Christian concepts of divine incarnation: Christians believe in a unique historical event, that God was made flesh once and for all time in Jesus of Nazareth. Hindus, on the other hand, believe that God descends as man many times, in different ages and forms.

In support of the view that Jesus was God's unique representative on earth, Christians often quote his saying: "I am the way, the truth, and the life: no man cometh unto the Father, but by me." But when we study the sayings of other world teachers we find that they made almost identical statements, equally declaring themselves to be incarnations of the Godhead. For example, Sri Krishna says: "I am the goal of the wise man, and I am the way." "I am the end of the path, the witness, the Lord, the sustainer. I am the place of abode, the beginning, the friend and the refuge." "Fools pass blindly by the place of my dwelling here in the human form; and of my majesty they know nothing at all, who am the Lord, their soul." "Fill your heart and mind with me, adore me, make all your acts an offering to me, bow down to me in self-surrender. If you set your heart upon me thus, and take me for your ideal above all others, you will come into my Being."

Similarly, Buddha reveals that he is the way: "You are my children, I am your father; through me you have been released from your sufferings. I myself having reached the other shore, help others to cross the stream; I myself having attained salvation, am a savior of others; being comforted, I comfort others and lead them to the place of refuge." "My thoughts are always in the truth. For lo! my self has become the truth. Whosoever comprehends the truth will see the Blessed One."

What are we to do? Whose words shall we accept—Jesus' or Krishna's or Buddha's? The point is this: If we take the "I" or "me" of these teachers to refer to a mere historical man, we can never understand their statements. We must know that when Jesus, Krishna, and Buddha say "I" or "me," they are not asserting the ego, the lower self, as ordinary embodied souls do. They are asserting their divinity, their identity with the universal Self. They are telling us that the Father, the Godhead, is reached through the grace of the Son, the Incarnation. To the Hindus, the statements of these avatars are not contradictory—they are equally true, evoked by the same divine inspiration. Therefore the Hindu accepts all the great sons of God who are worshiped in different religions.

Of course the validity of the avatars is not proved by their claim to be the way of enlightenment or salvation. First, it is revealed by their unique power to transmit spirituality and transform men's lives by touch, look, or wish. Jesus manifested this power when he breathed on his disciples and said to them, "Receive ye the Holy Ghost." Sri Krishna manifested this power when he gave Arjuna divine sight, so that the disciple might see the universal form of God. Secondly, the validity of the avatars is shown by the revelation of their divinity in transfiguration. Jesus appeared transfigured before Peter, James, and John. Sri Krishna appeared transfigured before Arjuna, as described in the eleventh chapter of the Gita. The life and Gospel of Sri Ramakrishna record instances in which the Master gave the realization of God to his disciples by touch and appeared transfigured to several devotees in the form of their chosen aspect of God.

But, the question may be asked, why should God have descended as man more than once? What purpose was accomplished? An answer may be found in the Hindu theory, borne out by history, that spiritual culture moves in waves, a repeated surging and falling. After a fall in a nation's spiritual life, when truth and righteousness have been neglected and forgotten, an avatar is born to relight the flame of religion in the heart. Sri Krishna says:

> When goodness grows weak,
> When evil increases,
> I make myself a body.
>
> In every age I come back
> To deliver the holy,
> To destroy the sin of the sinner,
> To establish righteousness.

As if to fulfill Sri Krishna's promise, Buddha appeared. At the time of Buddha's birth, spiritual culture in India was at a low ebb; it consisted wholly in the observance of rituals and sacrifices, for people had forgotten the simple fact that religion is primarily a matter of direct experience. Similarly, at the time of Jesus' advent, the externals of the Jewish faith were usurping its inner truth. He came to purify and revivify the religion of the Jews.

From time to time, then, a divine incarnation is needed to reestablish the eternal spirit of religion. By his living example the Incarnation shows mankind how to be perfect even as the Father in heaven is perfect. The avatar thus really becomes the way, the truth, and the life. But it is always the same supreme Spirit which embodies itself in the avatar. God is one without a second. He who came as Sri Krishna, and as Buddha, came again as Christ, and as other avatars; he merely chose a different dress. To suit the particular needs of successive ages, with each coming, God reveals a new and characteristic presentation of the eternal truth of religion.

When an avatar is born on earth, he assumes the human body with certain consequent limitations and sufferings, such as hunger and thirst, illness and death. But his advent differs radically from the birth of ordinary embodied souls. In the words of Jesus: "Ye are from beneath; I am from above." According to the Hindu view, ordinary souls are born in consequence of their *karmas* (the effects of their thoughts and deeds of the past). They are born in a particular environment, with particular aptitudes dictated by the desires and tendencies they have created in a previous life. They are products of evolution; they are tied by the fetters of ignorance and live under the spell of maya, the veiling power of Brahman, which makes the absolute Reality appear as the universe of many names and forms. They are slaves of *prakriti,* of primordial nature.

The birth of a Krishna, a Buddha, or a Jesus, however, is the result of free choice. He has no karmas, no cravings or past tendencies. He does not yield to the domination of maya but puts maya under subjection. He appears in human form solely for the purpose of doing good, out of compassion for mankind. Sri Krishna says:

I am the birthless, the deathless,
Lord of all that breathes.
I seem to be born:

It is only seeming,
Only my maya.
I am still master
Of my prakriti,
The power that makes me.

He who knows the nature
Of my task and my holy birth
Is not reborn
When he leaves this body:
He comes to me.

Compare with these last lines the words of the Bible: "But as many as received him, to them gave he power to become the sons of God, even to them that believe on his name."

To worship a Christ or a Krishna is to worship God. It is not, however, to worship a man as God, not to worship a person. It is to worship God himself, the impersonal-personal Existence, in and through the Incarnation; it is to adore him as one with the eternal Spirit, transcendent as the Father and immanent in all hearts. In this context, St. Paul's testimony about Christ is of special relevance. He says: "For in him dwelleth all the fulness of the Godhead bodily. And ye are complete in him, which is the head of all principality and power." Of equal weight is St. John's statement that the same Word which was "in the beginning" and "was God" was made flesh in Christ. In this passage, the author of the Fourth Gospel reminds us that his master was not a mere historical man, but that he is the eternal Christ, one with God from beginningless time. And this view seems to be validated by Jesus, who said: "Before Abraham was, I am."

A Hindu, then, would find it easy to accept Christ as a divine incarnation and to worship him unreservedly, exactly as he worships Sri Krishna or another avatar of his choice. But he cannot accept Christ as the *only* Son of God. Those who insist on regarding the life and teachings of Jesus as unique are bound to have great difficulty in understanding them. Any avatar can be far better understood in the light of other great lives and teachings. No divine incarnation ever came to refute the religion taught by another, but to fulfill all religions; because the truth of God is an eternal truth. St. Augustine said: "That which is called the Christian religion existed among the ancients, and never did not exist from the beginning of the human race until Christ came in the flesh, at which time the true religion, which already existed, began to be called Christianity." If, in the history of the world, Jesus had been the sole originator of the truth of God, it would be no truth; for truth cannot be originated; it exists. But if Jesus simply unfolded and interpreted that truth, then we may look to others who did so before him, and will do so after him. And, in fact, as we read the teachings of Jesus, we find that he wishes all of us to unfold that truth: "And ye shall know the truth, and the truth shall make you free." He has come, he declares, not to destroy the eternally existing truth, but to fulfill. This he did by restating it, giving it new life by presenting it in a new way.

Again and again men forget that these presentations of the divine incarnations are meant to be unfolded in their own lives. They cling too devotedly to the letter, the outward form, of the avatar's message and lose sight of its undying spirit. These are the scribes and pharisees; the jealous guardians of a tradition which has become obsolete. That is why Christ says:

> For I say unto you, That except your righteousness shall exceed the righteousness of the scribes and Pharisees, ye shall in no case enter into the kingdom of heaven.

The scribes and Pharisees forget the first commandment, to "love the Lord thy God with all thy heart, and with all thy soul, and with all thy mind." They are very ethical, upright men in their way; but they cling to forms and outward observances, and this leads them toward intolerance, narrowness, and dogmatism. The righteousness which exceeds the righteousness of the scribes and pharisees is the very opposite of this. It is an ethic which regards the observance of forms and rituals, not as an end in itself, but as a means to enter into the kingdom of heaven.

God is beyond relative good and evil. He is the absolute good. When we unite ourselves with him in our consciousness, we transcend relative righteousness. This truth has often been misunderstood. It does not mean that we should condone immorality, for ethical life is the very foundation of spirituality. At the beginning of spiritual life we must consciously abstain from harming others, from falsehood, theft, incontinence, and greed; we must observe mental and physical purity, contentment, self-control, and recollectedness of God.

But the urge to live a truly ethical life and to practice spiritual disciplines comes to us only if we try to live the first commandment—if we learn to love God, and struggle to realize him. Without that idea, morality degenerates into the external decorum of the scribes and pharisees. But when the first commandment is observed, then the second commandment follows as a matter of course. When we love God, we must love our neighbor as our self—because our neighbor is our very Self.

Through the practice of self-control, the inner restraint of the passions, we develop spiritually toward union with the absolute good. The man who attains this ultimate state does not have to discriminate consciously between right and wrong, or practice self-mastery. Holiness and purity become his very nature. He transcends relative righteousness and enters the kingdom of heaven.

> Ye have heard that it was said by them of old time, Thou shalt not kill; and whosoever shall kill shall be in danger of the judgment:
> But I say unto you, That whosoever is angry with his brother without a cause shall be in danger of the judgment: and whosoever shall say to his brother, Raca, shall be in danger of the council: but whosoever shall say, Thou fool, shall be in danger of hell fire.

It is not enough to obey the commandment: "Thou shalt not kill." Even the thought of killing, of hatred, is as deadly as the act. We may pretend to ourselves that it does not matter what we think, as long as we act rightly. But when the test comes, we always betray ourselves, for the thought controls the act. When the test comes, if our minds are full of hatred, that hatred will express itself in acts of violence and destruction and murder. Standing up in the pulpit and talking about love will not help us; it will not stop war and cruelty, when there is no love in our hearts. Love will not come to us simply because we say we have it, or try to impress other people with the seeming sweetness of our natures. It comes only when we have controlled our passions inwardly and have subdued our ego. Then divine love grows in us, and with it love of our fellow men. But the love of God has to be won through self-discipline, which we have neglected to practice. We have forgotten the aim of life—to realize and see God. That is our whole difficulty, and that is why when Jesus asks us to love our enemies, we are unable to obey him, even if we wish to do so. We do not know how.

We cannot love God and hate our neighbor. If we really love God, we will find him in everyone; so how can we hate another? If we harm anyone, we harm ourselves; if we help anyone, we help ourselves. All feelings of separateness, exclusiveness, and hatred are not only morally wrong, they are ignorant, because they deny the existence of the omnipresent Godhead.

> Therefore if thou bring thy gift to the altar, and there re-memberest that thy brother hath aught against thee;
> Leave there thy gift before the altar, and go thy way; first be reconciled to thy brother, and then come and offer thy gift.
> Agree with thine adversary quickly, whiles thou art in the way with him; lest at any time the adversary deliver thee to the judge, and the judge deliver thee to the officer, and thou be cast into prison.
> Verily I say unto thee, Thou shalt by no means come out thence, till thou hast paid the uttermost farthing.

Until we actually reach oneness with God, it is of course quite natural that we should have misunderstandings and quarrels with one another. But we must not let our resentments stay with us, or they will eat into our hearts like cancer. Christ, who like all truly spiritual teachers was a great psychologist, taught that we must be reconciled as soon as possible with our brother, even before we offer our gift to God. Anyone who has practiced meditation will immediately understand how sound this teaching is.

Suppose someone has wronged you, and you feel irritated. When you begin to meditate, what happens? Prayer and meditation concentrate the mind and intensify the emotions. Consequently, the molehill of irritation becomes a mountain of anger. You start to imagine terrible things about the person who has wronged you. You find yourself unfit to pray and meditate, unable to come to God, until you are sincerely reconciled with your brother. There is only one way to feel sincerely reconciled, and that is to try to see God in all beings, and to love him in all. If you have been angry with your brother, pray for him as you pray for yourself—pray that both of you may grow in understanding and devotion to God. At once, you will gain spiritually. But if you keep your anger in your heart, you will hurt yourself as well as your brother.

It is taught in Buddhism and in Vedanta that it is a man's duty to pray for others before he prays for himself. He is asked to send a thought of good will toward all beings before he offers himself to God. Such a practice is a significant step toward the attainment of love for our neighbor and for God.

"Agree with thine adversary quickly, whiles thou art in the way with him . . ." Christ is teaching us that we must not waste our time and energy on quarrels and resentment but should re-establish ourselves as quickly as possible in the thought of God. To realize God is our purpose in life; therefore we should try to maintain ourselves in his consciousness with as few and as short interruptions as possible. "Give up all vain talk," the Upanishads tell us. "Know the Atman alone."

The desire to argue and quarrel is a sign of ego. If you want to find God, you must suppress the ego and humble yourself—not before your adversary, but before God within him. Never submit to a powerful adversary because you fear the consequences of disagreement; that would be cowardice. But discriminate between principles and opinions. There is a Hindi saying: "Say 'yea, yea' to everyone, but keep your own seat firm." Do not compromise on ideals and principles. But when it comes to opinions, appreciate views differing from yours, and accept them when they merit it. Swami Turiyananda used to say: "Stubbornness is not strength. Stubbornness merely hides one's weakness. Strong is he who is flexible like steel and does not break. Strong is he who can live in harmony with many people and heed opinions other than his own." If you are intolerant of the opinions of others and stubbornly insist on having your own way, you will suffer the consequences until you have "paid the uttermost farthing."

Ye have heard that it was said by them of old time, Thou shalt not commit adultery:

But I say unto you, That whosoever looketh on a woman to lust after her hath committed adultery with her already in his heart.

And if thy right eye offend thee, pluck it out, and cast it from thee: for it is profitable for thee that one of thy members should perish, and not that thy whole body should be cast into hell.

And if thy right hand offend thee, cut it off, and cast it from thee: for it is profitable for thee that one of thy members should perish, and not that thy whole body should be cast into hell.

It hath been said, Whosoever shall put away his wife, let him give her a writing of divorcement:

But I say unto you, That whosoever shall put away his wife, saving for the cause of fornication, causeth her to commit adultery: and whosoever shall marry her that is divorced committeth adultery.

Here Jesus is speaking of the necessity for self-mastery, for mental control of the passions, particularly lust. Merely refraining from lustful actions is not enough; lustful thoughts must be checked, too.

There are, of course, many teachers who would say: "Yes, indeed, we agree, an inner check on the passions is certainly necessary. Our young people must use self-control." But very few of those teachers could answer *why* self-control is needed. That is why young people today question them, and even begin to suspect that the teachers hate pleasure for its own sake because they are too old to take part in it themselves. "What does it matter what we do," say the young, "as long as we don't harm anyone else?" They are perfectly honest and sincere about this.

It is no use telling them that their pleasures are wicked, or that it is wrong to be happy, because they will never believe you: their instincts tell them that you are lying. When you talk about sin, they will disregard you. But if you stop telling them that they are sinful, and begin to tell them that God is inside each one of them; if you hold up the ideal of God-realization, and show them that the struggle for self-discipline is hard but exciting, like training for athletics; if you show them that by dissipating themselves they are cutting themselves off from the greatest joy in life, a joy far greater than all their worldly pleasures—then you will be talking a language they can understand. They may be skeptical, but some of them, at least, will want to try spiritual life for themselves.

The ideal of continence has been so misrepresented in this country that nearly everybody thinks of it as something negative, as a "don't." Don't be incontinent, the churches tell us; it is a sin. In this way, for the great majority of people, who instinctively hate "don'ts," the idea of continence has become unattractive, and associated with repression, gloom, and cowardice; while the idea of incontinence becomes more and more attractive, and is associated with freedom, fun, and courage. This terrible and destructive misunderstanding, if not corrected, will eventually poison the whole national life. Unless boys and girls can be taught the vital connection between continence and spiritual life, they will gradually waste their powers, they will lose the possibility of spiritual growth and with it much of their creativeness, and awareness.

Continence is *not* repression; it stores up energy and applies that energy to better uses. It is not an end in itself but an indispensable means of freeing the mind from distracting passions and keeping it in the consciousness of God. Sex-energy controlled becomes spiritual energy. To one who is continent, spiritual growth comes quickly and easily.

Many people think that by being continent they will lose the greatest pleasure the world has to offer: but the strange fact is that they will not really lose anything. As the sex-energy is conserved and as it becomes transformed, they will find a new and much more intense pleasure growing inside themselves; and that is the joy of coming closer and closer to union with God.

In the Bhagavad-Gita, the state of mind of the self-controlled man is described as follows:

Water flows continually into the ocean
But the ocean is never disturbed:
Desire flows into the mind of the seer
But he is never disturbed.

The seer knows peace:
The man who stirs up his own lusts
Can never know peace.
He knows peace who has forgotten desire.
He lives without craving:
Free from ego, free from pride.

The worldly person may think that the peace of the seer is like the peace of the grave. On the contrary, it is an experience of supreme and abiding joy, compared to which the short-lived satisfactions known in the sense-life appear insipid and worthless. If we wish to find lasting peace and happiness, we must turn to God. The more we devote ourselves to him, the more the desire for sense-gratification will leave us; and chastity and other virtues will naturally unfold in our lives.

Complete lifelong continence is for those who have a special dedication to God, as did Christ's disciples. They were monks, and their Master was training them to become teachers of men. Therefore he used emphatic words to remind them that they must preserve continence in thought, word, and deed. They must root out every obstacle in their path, every craving in their minds, and renounce every object of temptation. But because Christ knew that his teaching of total renunciation could not be followed universally, he said (Matthew 19:12): "All men cannot receive this saying, save they to whom it is given. For there are some eunuchs, which were so born from their mother's womb: and there are some eunuchs, which were made eunuchs of men: and there be eunuchs, which have made themselves eunuchs for the kingdom of heaven's sake. He that is able to receive it, let him receive it."

Lust is in the mind and must be overcome by controlling the mind, but not in a negative way. Thinking lustful thoughts while outwardly observing continence is not self-control. It is nothing but repression. Nor will whipping oneself purify the mind; it only weakens the body. True self-mastery, or inner control, is gained only if men make themselves eunuchs "for the kingdom of heaven's sake"; if they practice continence because they know worldly pleasures to be tasteless and empty compared to the joy of God.

Again, ye have heard that it hath been said by them of old
time, Thou shalt not forswear thyself, but shalt perform
unto the Lord thine oaths:
But I say unto you, Swear not at all; neither by heaven; for
it is God's throne:
Nor by the earth; for it is his footstool: neither by Jerusalem; for it is the city of the great King.
Neither shalt thou swear by thy head, because thou canst
not make one hair white or black.
But let your communication be, Yea, yea; Nay, nay: for
whatsoever is more than these cometh of evil.

Sri Ramakrishna used to say that God laughs on two occasions.
He laughs when two brothers divide land between them, asserting,
"This side belongs to me, and that side to you." God laughs, thinking to himself, "This whole universe is mine; and they say about one
little lump of earth, 'This side belongs to me, and that side to you!' "
God laughs again when the doctor says to the mother weeping because of her child's severe illness, "Don't worry. I shall cure your
child." The doctor does not realize that no one can save the child if
God wills that it should die.
    Christ here is telling us the same thing. Although man cannot
make "one hair white or black," in his ignorance he thinks himself
the doer. He asserts his ego, forgetting that the power he is using in
every thought and every action is the power of God, and that it is
God's heaven, God's throne, God's earth that he is trying to usurp.
Christ therefore tells us, "Swear not at all," for when we swear we
assert the ego.
    Truly spiritual people never plan, "I will do this, I will do
that." Having surrendered the ego to God, their first thought is, "If
the Lord wills . . ." Their humility stems from the realization that
God and his power are working through us—that God is the doer and
we are his instruments. This is an actual experience in the lives of
saints. A holy man once told me that he lived for some time in a state
of consciousness in which he vividly felt that each step he took was
guided by the power of God.
    "Not I, not I, but thou, O Lord!" The more we become estab-
lished in this idea, the more we renounce the thought of self, the
greater will be our attainment of peace.

3. ALDOUS HUXLEY:
INTRODUCTION TO THE SONG OF GOD: BHAGAVAD-GITA

One of the most important motifs of Neo-Vedanta, both in India and in the West, may be termed "universal mysticism," that is, an affirmation that the great mystics, of all religions and all times and places, have experienced and realized much the same thing. That "thing" was, needless to say, clearly expounded in the Vedanta classics, but it is important to see that it can be located in many other spiritual texts as well. Universal mysticism is, in fact, often called the "Perennial Philosophy," for it recurs century after century, even in the most seemingly barren soil, according to its advocates.

Few writers have expressed its essential tenets more eloquently than the noted novelist Aldous Huxley (1894–1963), both in his book The Perennial Philosophy (1946), and in the brief summation here presented. Author of such celebrated novels as Antic Hay (1923) and Brave New World (1932), Huxley, from a distinguished British scientific family, moved steadily toward a deeper interest in mysticism and Vedanta philosophy as his life advanced. After settling in the United States in 1937, he was affiliated with the Vedanta Society of Southern California.

More than twenty-five centuries have passed since that which has been called the Perennial Philosophy was first committed to writing; and in the course of those centuries it has found expression, now partial, now complete, now in this form, now in that, again and again.* In Vedanta and Hebrew prophecy, in the Tao Teh King and the Platonic dialogues, in the Gospel according to St. John and Mahayana theology, in Plotinus and the Areopagite, among the Persian Sufis and the Christian mystics of the Middle Ages and the Renaissance—the Perennial Philosophy has spoken almost all the languages of Asia and Europe and has made use of the terminology and traditions of every one of the higher religions. But under all this confusion of tongues and myths, of local histories and particularist doctrines, there remains a Highest Common Factor, which is the Perennial Philosophy in what may be called its chemically pure state. This final

---

*From Introduction by Aldous Huxley to Swami Prabhavananda and Christopher Isherwood, *The Song of God: Bhagavad-Gita*. Copyright © 1944, 1951 by The Vedanta Society of Southern California. Reprinted by permission.

purity can never, of course, be expressed by any verbal statement of the philosophy, however undogmatic that statement may be, however deliberately syncretistic. The very fact that it is set down at a certain time by a certain writer, using this or that language, automatically imposes a certain sociological and personal bias on the doctrines so formulated. It is only in the act of contemplation, when words and even personality are transcended, that the pure state of the Perennial Philosophy can actually be known. The records left by those who have known it in this way make it abundantly clear that all of them, whether Hindu, Buddhist, Hebrew, Taoist, Christian or Mohammedan, were attempting to describe the same essentially indescribable Fact.

The original scriptures of most religions are poetical and unsystematic. Theology, which generally takes the form of a reasoned commentary on the parables and aphorisms of the scriptures, tends to make its appearance at a later stage of religious history. The Bhagavad-Gita occupies an intermediate position between scripture and theology; for it combines the poetical qualities of the first with the clear-cut methodicalness of the second. The book may be described, writes Ananda K. Coomaraswamy in his admirable *Hinduism and Buddhism,* 'as a compendium of the whole Vedic doctrine to be found in the earlier Vedas, Brahmanas and Upanishads, and being therefore the basis of all the later developments, it can be regarded as the focus of all Indian religion.' But this 'focus of Indian religion' is also one of the clearest and most comprehensive summaries of the Perennial Philosophy ever to have been made. Hence its enduring value, not only for Indians, but for all mankind.

At the core of the Perennial Philosophy we find four fundamental doctrines.

First: the phenomenal world of matter and of individualized consciousness—the world of things and animals and men and even gods—is the manifestation of a Divine Ground within which all partial realities have their being, and apart from which they would be nonexistent.

Second: human beings are capable not merely of knowing *about* the Divine Ground by inference; they can also realize its existence by a direct intuition, superior to discursive reasoning. This immediate knowledge unites the knower with that which is known.

Third: man possesses a double nature, a phenomenal ego and

an eternal Self, which is the inner man, the spirit, the spark of divinity within the soul. It is possible for a man, if he so desires, to identify himself with the spirit and therefore with the Divine Ground, which is of the same or like nature with the spirit.

Fourth: man's life on earth has only one end and purpose: to identify himself with his eternal Self and so to come to unitive knowledge of the Divine Ground.

In Hinduism the first of these four doctrines is stated in the most categorical terms. The Divine Ground is Brahman, whose creative, sustaining and transforming aspects are manifested in the Hindu trinity. A hierarchy of manifestations connects inanimate matter with man, gods, High Gods and the undifferentiated Godhead beyond.

In Mahayana Buddhism the Divine Ground is called Mind or the Pure Light of the Void, the place of the High Gods is taken by the Dhyani-Buddhas.

Similar conceptions are perfectly compatible with Christianity and have in fact been entertained, explicitly or implicitly, by many Catholic and Protestant mystics, when formulating a philosophy to fit facts observed by super-rational intuition. Thus, for Eckhart and Ruysbroeck, there is an Abyss of Godhead underlying the Trinity, just as Brahman underlies Brahma, Vishnu and Shiva. Suso has even left a diagrammatic picture of the relations subsisting between Godhead, triune God and creatures. In this very curious and interesting drawing a chain of manifestation connects the mysterious symbol of the Divine Ground with the three Persons of the Trinity, and the Trinity in turn is connected in a descending scale with angels and human beings. These last, as the drawing vividly shows, may make one of two choices. They can either lead the life of the outer man, the life of separative selfhood; in which case they are lost (for, in the words of the Theologia Germanica, 'nothing burns in hell but the self'). Or else they can identify themselves with the inner man, in which case it becomes possible for them, as Suso shows, to ascend again, through unitive knowledge, to the Trinity and even, beyond the Trinity, to the ultimate Unity of the Divine Ground.

Within the Mohammedan tradition such a rationalization of the immediate mystical experience would have been dangerously unorthodox. Nevertheless, one has the impression, while reading certain Sufi texts, that their authors did in fact conceive of *al haqq*, the Real, as being the Divine Ground or Unity of Allah, underlying the active and personal aspects of the Godhead.

The second doctrine of the Perennial Philosophy—that it is possible to know the Divine Ground by a direct intuition higher than discursive reasoning—is to be found in all the great religions of the world. A philosopher who is content merely to know about the ultimate Reality—theoretically and by hearsay—is compared by Buddha to a herdsman of other men's cows. Mohammed uses an even homelier barnyard metaphor. For him the philosopher who has not realized his metaphysics is just an ass bearing a load of books. Christian, Hindu and Taoist teachers wrote no less emphatically about the absurd pretensions of mere learning and analytical reasoning. In the words of the Anglican Prayer Book, our eternal life, now and hereafter, 'stands in the knowledge of God'; and this knowledge is not discursive but 'of the heart,' a super-rational intuition, direct, synthetic and timeless.

The third doctrine of the Perennial Philosophy, that which affirms the double nature of man, is fundamental in all the higher religions. The unitive knowledge of the Divine Ground has, as its necessary condition, self-abnegation and charity. Only by means of self-abnegation and charity can we clear away the evil, folly and ignorance which constitute the thing we call our personality and prevent us from becoming aware of the spark of divinity illuminating the inner man. But the spark within is akin to the Divine Ground. By identifying ourselves with the first we can come to unitive knowledge of the second. These empirical facts of the spiritual life have been variously rationalized in terms of the theologies of the various religions. The Hindus categorically affirm that thou art That—that the indwelling Atman is the same as Brahman. For orthodox Christianity there is not an identity between the spark and God. Union of the human spirit with God takes place—union so complete that the word 'deification' is applied to it; but it is not the union of identical substances. According to Christian theology, the saint is 'deified,' not because Atman *is* Brahman, but because God has assimilated the purified human spirit into the divine substance by an act of grace. Islamic theology seems to make a similar distinction. The Sufi, Mansur, was executed for giving to the words 'union' and 'deification' the literal meaning which they bear in the Hindu tradition. For our present purposes, however, the significant fact is that these words are actually used by Christians and Mohammedans to describe the empirical facts of metaphysical realization by means of direct, super-rational intuition.

In regard to man's final end, all the higher religions are in complete agreement. The purpose of human life is the discovery of Truth, the unitive knowledge of the Godhead. The degree to which this unitive knowledge is achieved here on earth determines the degree to which it will be enjoyed in the posthumous state. Contemplation of truth is the end, action the means. In India, in China, in ancient Greece, in Christian Europe, this was regarded as the most obvious and axiomatic piece of orthodoxy. The invention of the steam engine produced a revolution, not merely in industrial techniques, but also and much more significantly in philosophy. Because machines could be made progressively more and more efficient, western man came to believe that men and societies would automatically register a corresponding moral and spiritual improvement. Attention and allegiance came to be paid, not to Eternity, but to the Utopian future. External circumstances came to be regarded as more important than states of mind about external circumstances, and the end of human life was held to be action, with contemplation as a means to that end. These false and, historically, aberrant and heretical doctrines are now systematically taught in our schools and repeated, day in, day out, by those anonymous writers of advertising copy who, more than any other teachers, provide European and American adults with their current philosophy of life. And so effective has been the propaganda that even professing Christians accept the heresy unquestioningly and are quite unconscious of its complete incompatibility with their own or anybody else's religion.

These four doctrines constitute the Perennial Philosophy in its minimal and basic form. A man who can practise what the Indians call Jnana yoga (the metaphysical discipline of discrimination between the Real and the apparent) asks for nothing more. This simple working hypothesis is enough for his purposes. But such discrimination is exceedingly difficult and can hardly be practised, at any rate in the preliminary stages of the spiritual life, except by persons endowed with a particular kind of mental constitution. That is why most statements of the Perennial Philosophy have included another doctrine, affirming the existence of one or more human Incarnations of the Divine Ground, by whose mediation and grace the worshipper is helped to achieve his goal—that unitive knowledge of the God-head, which is man's eternal life and beatitude. The Bhagavad-Gita is one such statement. Here, Krishna is an Incarnation of the Divine Ground in human form. Similarly, in Christian and Buddhist theology, Jesus and Gotama are Incarnations of divinity. But whereas in Hinduism and Buddhism more than one Incarnation of the Godhead is possible (and is regarded as having in fact taken place), for Christians there has been and can be only one.

An Incarnation of the Godhead and, to a lesser degree, any theocentric saint, sage or prophet is a human being who knows Who he is and can therefore effectively remind other human beings of what they have allowed themselves to forget: namely, that if they choose to become what potentially they already are, they too can be eternally united with the Divine Ground.

Worship of the Incarnation and contemplation of his attributes are for most men and women the best preparation for unitive knowledge of the Godhead. But whether the actual knowledge itself can be achieved by this means is another question. Many Catholic mystics have affirmed that, at a certain stage of that contemplative prayer in which, according to the most authoritative theologians, the life of Christian perfection ultimately consists, it is necessary to put aside all thoughts of the Incarnation as distracting from the higher knowledge of that which has been incarnated. From this fact have arisen misunderstandings in plenty and a number of intellectual difficulties. Here, for example, is what Abbot John Chapman writes in one of his admirable Spiritual Letters: 'The problem of *reconciling* (not merely uniting) mysticism with Christianity is more difficult. The Abbot (Abbot Marmion) says that St John of the Cross is like a sponge full of Christianity. You can squeeze it all out, and the full mystical theory remains. Consequently, for fifteen years or so, I hated St John of the Cross and called him a Buddhist. I loved St Teresa, and read her over and over again. She is first a Christian, only secondarily a mystic. Then I found that I had wasted fifteen years, so far as prayer was concerned.' And yet, he concludes, in spite of its 'Buddhistic' character, the practice of mysticism (or, to put it in other terms, the realization of the Perennial Philosophy) makes good Christians. He might have added that it also makes good Hindus, good Buddhists, good Taoists, good Moslems and good Jews.

The solution to Abbot Chapman's problem must be sought in

the domain, not of philosophy, but of psychology. Human beings are not born identical. There are many different temperaments and constitutions; and within each psycho-physical class one can find people at very different stages of spiritual development. Forms of worship and spiritual discipline which may be valuable for one individual may be useless or even positively harmful for another belonging to a different class and standing, within that class, at a lower or higher level of development. All this is clearly set forth in the Gita, where the psychological facts are linked up with general cosmology by means of the postulate of the *gunas*. Krishna, who is here the mouthpiece of Hinduism in all its manifestations, finds it perfectly natural that different men should have different methods and even apparently different objects of worship. All roads lead to Rome—provided, of course, that it is Rome and not some other city which the traveller really wishes to reach. A similar attitude of charitable inclusiveness, somewhat surprising in a Moslem, is beautifully expressed in the parable of Moses and the Shepherd, told by Jalaluddin Rumi in the second book of the Masnavi. And within the more exclusive Christian tradition these problems of temperament and degree of development have been searchingly discussed in their relation to the way of Mary and the way of Martha in general, and in particular to the vocation and private devotion of individuals.

We now have to consider the ethical corollaries of the Perennial Philosophy. 'Truth,' says St Thomas Aquinas, 'is the last end for the entire universe, and the contemplation of truth is the chief occupation of wisdom.' The moral virtues, he says in another place, belong to contemplation, not indeed essentially, but as a necessary predisposition. Virtue, in other words, is not the end, but the indispensable means to the knowledge of divine reality. Shankara, the greatest of the Indian commentators on the Gita, holds the same doctrine. Right action is the way to knowledge; for it purifies the mind, and it is only to a mind purified from egotism that the intuition of the Divine Ground can come.

Self-abnegation, according to the Gita, can be achieved by the practice of two all-inclusive virtues—love and non-attachment. The latter is the same thing as that 'holy indifference,' on which St François de Sales is never tired of insisting. 'He who refers every action to God,' writes Camus, summarizing his master's teaching, 'and has no aims save His Glory, will find rest everywhere, even amidst the

most violent commotions.' So long as we practise this holy indifference to the fruits of action, 'no lawful occupation will separate us
from God; on the contrary, it can be made a means of closer union.'
Here the word 'lawful' supplies a necessary qualification to a teaching which, without it, is incomplete and even potentially dangerous.
Some actions are intrinsically evil or inexpedient; and no good in-
tentions, no conscious offering of them to God, no renunciation of
the fruits can alter their essential character. Holy indifference re-
quires to be taught in conjunction not merely with a set of com-
mandments prohibiting crimes, but also with a clear conception of
what in Buddha's Eightfold Path is called 'right livelihood.' Thus,
for the Buddhist, right livelihood was incompatible with the making
of deadly weapons and of intoxicants; for the mediæval Christian,
with the taking of interest and with various monopolistic practices
which have since come to be regarded as legitimate good business.
John Woolman, the American Quaker, provides a most enlightening
example of the way in which a man may live in the world, while
practising perfect non-attachment and remaining acutely sensitive to
the claims of right livelihood. Thus, while it would have been profitable and perfectly lawful for him to sell West Indian sugar and rum
to the customers who came to his shop, Woolman refrained from
doing so, because these things were the products of slave labour.
Similarly, when he was in England, it would have been both lawful
and convenient for him to travel by stage coach. Nevertheless, he
preferred to make his journeys on foot. Why? Because the comforts
of rapid travel could only be brought at the expense of great cruelty
to the horses and the most atrocious working conditions for the post-
boys. In Woolman's eyes, such a system of transportation was intrinsically undesirable, and no amount of personal non-attachment
could make it anything but undesirable. So he shouldered his knap-
sack and walked.

In the preceding pages I have tried to show that the Perennial
Philosophy and its ethical corollaries constitute a Highest Common
Factor, present in all the major religions of the world. To affirm this
truth has never been more imperatively necessary than at the present
time. There will never be enduring peace unless and until human
beings come to accept a philosophy of life more adequate to the
cosmic and psychological facts than the insane idolatries of nation-
alism and the advertising man's apocalyptic faith in Progress towards

a mechanized New Jerusalem. All the elements of this philosophy are present, as we have seen, in the traditional religions. But in existing circumstances there is not the slightest chance that any of the traditional religions will obtain universal acceptance. Europeans and Americans will see no reason for being converted to Hinduism, say, or Buddhism. And the people of Asia can hardly be expected to renounce their own traditions for the Christianity professed, often sincerely, by the imperialists who, for four hundred years and more, have been systematically attacking, exploiting and oppressing, and are now trying to finish off the work of destruction by 'educating' them. But happily there is the Highest Common Factor of all religions, the Perennial Philosophy which has always and everywhere been the metaphysical system of the prophets, saints and sages. It is perfectly possible for people to remain good Christians, Hindus, Buddhists or Moslems and yet to be united in full agreement on the basic doctrines of the Perennial Philosophy.

The Bhagavad-Gita is perhaps the most systematic scriptural statement of the Perennial Philosophy. To a world at war, a world that, because it lacks the intellectual and spiritual prerequisites to peace, can only hope to patch up some kind of precarious armed truce, it stands pointing, clearly and unmistakably, to the only road of escape from the self-imposed necessity of self-destruction. For this reason we should be grateful to Swami Prabhavananda and Mr Isherwood for having given us this new version of the book—a version which can be read, not merely without that dull æsthetic pain inflicted by all too many English translations from the Sanskrit, but positively with enjoyment.

4. PARAMAHANSA YOGANANDA: THE SCIENCE OF RELIGION

Yogananda, founder of the Self-Realization Fellowship, was a teacher of deep psychological interests. In his celebrated Autobiography of a Yogi, he offers a stunning account of the "cosmic consciousness" reached on the upper levels of yogic practice, and numerous interesting perspectives on human nature from the yogic and Vedantic points of view. Here, in a typical argument, at once rational yet full of the mystic's insight, he shows that God in the form of Bliss is the true goal of human endeavor.

Bliss depends upon no particular condition, external or internal. *It is a native state of the Spirit.* Therefore it has no fear of being contradicted by any other condition. It will flow on continually forever, in defeat or success, in health or disease, in opulence or poverty.*

*   *   *

I remarked at the outset that if we made a close observation of the actions of men, we should see that the one fundamental and universal motive for which man acts is the avoidance of pain and the consequent attainment of Bliss, or God. The first part of the motive, i.e., the avoidance of pain, is something we cannot deny, if we observe the motives of all the good and bad actions performed in the world.

Take the case of a person who wishes to commit suicide, and that of a truly religious man who has dispassion for the things of the world. There can be no doubt about the fact that both of these men are trying to get rid of the pain which is troubling them. Both are trying to put an end to pain permanently. Whether they are successful or not is a different question, but so far as their motives are concerned there is unity.

But are all actions in this world *directly* prompted by the desire for the attainment of permanent Bliss, or God, the second part of the common motive for all actions? Does the evildoer have for his immediate motive the attainment of Bliss? Hardly. The reason for this was pointed out in the discussion about pleasure and Bliss. We found that because of the identification of the Spiritual self with the body it has fallen into the habit of indulging in desires and the consequent creation of wants. These desires and wants lead to pain, if not fulfilled—and to pleasure, if fulfilled—by objects.

But here occurs a fatal error on the part of man. When a want is fulfilled, man gets a pleasurable excitement and, through a sad mistake, fixes his eye solely upon the objects which create this excitement, and supposes them to be the main causes of his pleasure.

---

*From Paramahansa Yogananda, *The Science of Religion*, pp. 38–58. Copyright © 1953, 1982, by The Self Realization Fellowship. Reprinted by permission.

He entirely forgets that he had formerly an excitation in the form of desire or want in his own mind, and that later he had another excitation in his mind superseding the first one, in the form of pleasure which the coming of objects seems to produce. So, as a matter of fact, one excitation arose in the mind and was superseded by another in the same mind.

Outward objects are only the occasions—they are not causes. A poor person's desire for delicacies may be satisfied by an ordinary sweetmeat, and this fulfillment will give rise to pleasure. But the desire for delicacies on the part of a rich person may perhaps be satisfied only by the best of pastries, and the fulfillment will also give the *same amount of pleasure. Then does pleasure depend on outward objects, or on the state of mind? Surely the latter.*

But pleasure, as we said, is an excitation. Therefore it is never justifiable to drive away the excitation in desire by another excitation, viz., that felt in pleasure. Because we do this our excitations never end, and so our pain and misery never cease.

What we should do is to *set at rest* the excitation that is in desire and not to fan or continue it by excitation in pleasure. This setting at rest is rendered possible, in an effective way, only by Bliss-consciousness, which is not callousness but a superior stage of indifference to both pain and pleasure.

Every human being is seeking to attain Bliss by fulfilling desire, but he mistakenly stops at pleasure, and so his desires never end, and he is swept away into the whirlpool of pain.

Pleasure is a dangerous will-o'-the-wisp. And yet it is this pleasurable association that becomes our motive for future actions. This has proved to be as deceptive as the mirage in a desert. Since pleasure, as was said before, consists of an excitation-consciousness plus a contrast-consciousness that the pain is now no more, we prepare ourselves, when we aim at it instead of at Bliss, for running headlong into that cycle of ignorant existence which brings pleasure and pain in never-ending succession. We fall into terrible distress because of the change in our angle of vision from Bliss to pleasure.

Thus we see that though the true aim of mankind is the avoidance of pain and the attainment of Bliss, yet owing to a fatal error man, though trying to avoid pain, *pursues a deluding something named pleasure, mistaking it for Bliss.*

That the attainment of Bliss and not pleasure is the universal and highest necessity is indirectly proved by the fact that man is never satisfied with one object of pleasure. He always flies from one to another. From money to dress, from dress to property, thence to conjugal pleasure—there is a restless continuity.

And so he is constantly falling into pain, even though he wishes to avoid it by the adoption of what he deems proper means. Yet an unknown and unsatisfied craving seems ever to remain in his heart.

But a religious man (the second example which I proposed to show) always wishes to adopt proper religious means by which he can come in contact with Bliss, or God.

Of course when I say that God is Bliss, I mean also that He is ever-existent and that He is also *conscious* of His blissful existence. And when we wish Eternal Bliss or God, it is implied that with Bliss we also wish eternal, immortal, unchangeable, ever-conscious existence. That all of us, from the highest to the lowest, desire to be in Bliss has been proved *a priori,* and by a consideration of the motives and acts of men.

To repeat the argument in a slightly different way: suppose some Higher Being should come to us and say to all people of the earth, "You creatures of the world! I will give you eternal sorrows and misery along with eternal existence; will you take that?" Would any one like the prospect? Not one. All want eternal Bliss (*Ananda*) along with eternal existence (*Sat*). As a matter of fact, consideration of the motives of the world also shows there is no one but would like to have Bliss.

Similarly, no one likes the prospect of annihilation; if it is suggested, we shudder at the idea. All desire to exist permanently (*Sat*). But if we were given eternal existence without the *consciousness* of that existence, we would reject that. For who is there that would embrace existence in sleep? None. We all want conscious existence.

Furthermore, we want eternal *blissful conscious existence: Sat-Chit-Ananda* (Existence-Consciousness-Bliss). That is the Hindu name for God. But for a pragmatical consideration only, we emphasize the Blissful aspect of God and our motive for Bliss, leaving out the aspects of *Sat* and *Chit,* i.e., *conscious existence* (also other aspects of Him not dwelt on here).

Now, what is God? If God be something other than Bliss, and His contact produces in us no Bliss, or produces in us only pain, or if His contact does not drive pain away from us, should we want

Him? No. If God is something useless to us, we want Him not. What is the use of a God who remains always unknown and whose presence is not *inwardly* manifest to us in at least some circumstances in our life?

Whatever conception of God we form by the exercise of reason (such as: "He is transcendent" or "He is immanent") will always remain vague and indistinct unless really felt as such. In fact, we keep God at a safe distance, conceiving Him sometimes as a mere Personal Being, and then again *theoretically* thinking of Him as being within us.

It is because of this vagueness in our idea and experience concerning God that we are not able to grasp the real necessity for Him and the pragmatical value of religion. This colorless theory or idea fails to bring conviction to us. It does not change our lives, influence our conduct in an appreciable way, or *make us try to know God*.

What does Universal Religion say about God? It says that the *proof of the existence of God lies in ourselves*. It is an inner experience. You can surely recall at least one moment in your life when, in prayer or worship, you felt that the trammels of your body had nearly vanished, that the duality of experience—pleasure and pain, petty love and hate, and so on—had receded from your mind. Pure Bliss and tranquillity had welled up in your heart and you enjoyed an unruffled calm—Bliss and contentment.

Though this kind of higher experience does not often come to all, yet there can be no doubt that all men, at some time or other, in prayer or in a mood of worship or meditation, have enjoyed a few moments of unalloyed Peace.

Is this not a proof of the existence of God? *What other direct proof than the existence of Bliss in ourselves in real prayer or worship can we give of the existence and nature of God?* Though there is the cosmological proof of the existence of God—from effect we rise to cause, from the world to the World-Maker. And there is the teleological proof as well—from the *telos* (plan, adaptation) in the world, we rise to the Supreme Intelligence that makes the plan and adaptation. There is also the moral proof—from conscience and the sense of perfection we rise to the Perfect Being to whom our responsibility is due.

Still, we should admit that these proofs are more or less the products of inference. We cannot have full or direct knowledge of

God through the limited powers of the intellect. Intellect gives only a partial and indirect view of things. To view a thing intellectually is not to see it by being one with it: it is to view a thing by being apart from it.

But intuition, which we shall later explain, is the direct grasp of truth. It is in this intuition that Bliss-consciousness, or God-consciousness, is realized.

There is not a shadow of doubt as to the absolute identity of Bliss-consciousness and God-consciousness, because when we have that Bliss-consciousness we feel that our narrow individuality has been transformed and that we have risen above the duality of petty love and hate, pleasure and pain, and have attained a level from which the painfulness and worthlessness of ordinary consciousness become glaringly apparent.

And we also feel an inward expansion and all-embracing sympathy for all things. The tumults of the world die away, excitements disappear, and the "all in One and One in all" consciousness seems to dawn upon us. A glorious vision of light appears. All imperfections, all angularities, sink into nothingness. We seem to be translated into another region, the fountainhead of perennial Bliss, the starting point of one unending continuity. Is not Bliss-consciousness, then, the same as God-consciousness, in which the above states of realization appear?

It is evident, therefore, that God cannot be better conceived than as Bliss if we try to bring Him within the range of every one's calm experience. No longer will God be a supposition then, to be theorized over. Is this not a nobler conception of God? He is perceived as manifesting Himself in our hearts in the form of Bliss in meditation—in prayerful or worshipful mood.

If we conceive of God in this way, i.e., as Bliss, then and then only may we make religion universally necessary. For no one can deny that he wishes to attain Bliss and, if he wishes to achieve it in the proper way, he is going to be religious through approaching and feeling God, who is described as very close to his heart as Bliss.

This Bliss-consciousness or God-consciousness can pervade all our actions and moods, if we but let it. If we can get a firm hold on this, we shall be able to judge the relative religious worth of man's every action and motive on this earth.

If we are once convinced that the attainment of this Bliss-consciousness is our religion, our goal, our ultimate end, then all doubts as to the meaning of multifarious teachings, injunctions, and prohibitions of the different faiths of the world will disappear. Everything will be interpreted in the light of the stage of growth for which it is prescribed.

Truth will shine out, the mystery of existence will be solved, and a light will be thrown upon the details of our lives, with their various actions and motives. We shall be able to separate the naked truth from the outward appendages of religious doctrines and to see the worthlessness of the conventions that so often mislead men and create differences between them.

Furthermore, if religion is understood in this way, there is no man in the world—whether boy, youth, or an old person—who cannot practice it, whatever may be the station of life to which he belongs, whether that of student, laborer, lawyer, doctor, carpenter, scholar, or philanthropist. If to abolish the sense of want and attain Bliss is religion, who is there that is not trying to be religious and that will not try to be so in a greater degree, if proper methods are pointed out to him?

Herein does not arise the question of the variety of religions—that of Christ, of Mohammed, or of Sri Krishna. Every one in the world is inevitably trying to be religious, and can seek to be more completely so by the adoption of proper means. There is no distinction here of caste or creed, sect or faith, dress or clime, age or sex, profession or position. For this religion is universal.

If you said that all the people of the world ought to acknowledge Sri Krishna as their Savior, would all the Christians and Mohammedans accept that? If you asked every one to take Jesus as their Lord, would all the Hindus and Mohammedans do that? And if you bade all to accept Mohammed as their Prophet, would the Christians and Hindus agree to that?

But if you say, "Oh, my Christian, Mohammedan, and Hindu brethren, your Lord God is Ever-Blissful Conscious Existence (Being)," will they not accept this? Can they possibly reject it? Will they not demand Him as the only One who can put an end to all their miseries?

Nor may one escape this conclusion by saying that Christians, Hindus, and Mohammedans do not conceive Jesus, Krishna, and Mohammed respectively as the Lord God—they are thought to be only the standard-bearers of God, the human incarnations of divinity. What if one does think that way? It is not the physical bodies of Jesus, Krishna, and Mohammed that we are primarily interested in, nor are we so much concerned with the historical place they occupy.

Nor are they solely memorable to us because of their different and interesting ways of preaching truth. *We revere them because they knew and felt God.* It is that fact which interests us in their historical existence and in their manifold ways of expressing the truth.

Did not all of them realize God as Bliss and reveal real blessedness as true godliness? Is not that a sufficient bond of unity among them—let alone other aspects of Godhead and truth they may have realized and expressed? Should not a Christian, a Hindu, and a Mohammedan find interest in one another's prophets, inasmuch as all of them attained God-consciousness? As God unites all religions, it is the realization of Him as Bliss that unites the consciousness of the prophets of all religions.*

One should not think that this conception of God is too abstract, having nothing to do with our spiritual hopes and aspirations, which require the conception of God as a Personal Being. It is not the conception of an Impersonal Being, as commonly understood, nor that of a Personal Being, as narrowly conceived.

God is not a Person, as are we in our narrowness. Our being, consciousness, feeling, volition have but a shadow of resemblance to His Being (Existence), Consciousness, and Bliss. He is a Person in the transcendental sense. Our being, consciousness, and feeling are limited and empirical, His unlimited and transcendental. He has an Impersonal and Absolute aspect, but we should not think He is beyond the reach of all experience—even our inner one.

He comes within the calm experience of men. It is in Bliss-consciousness that we realize Him. There can be no other direct proof of His existence. It is in Him as Bliss that our spiritual hopes and aspirations find fulfillment—our devotion and love find an object.

---

*Bliss-consciousness is also stressed in so-called atheistic religions, such as Buddhism. The Buddhistic *Nirvana* is not, as mistakenly supposed by many Western writers, a "blowing out of light," an extinction of existence. It is rather the stage where narrow individuality is blotted out and transcendent calm in universality is reached. This is exactly what comes in higher Bliss-consciousness, though the name of God is not attached to it by the Buddhist.

A conception of a Personal Being who is nothing but ourselves magnified is not required. God may be or become anything—Personal, Impersonal, All-merciful, Omnipotent, and so forth. But we are not required to take note of these. *Whatever conception we have put forth exactly suits our purposes, our hopes, our aspirations, and our perfection.*

Nor should we think that this conception of God will make us dreamy idealists, severing our connection with the duties and responsibilities, joys and sorrows, of the practical world. If God is Bliss and if we seek Bliss to know Him, we may not neglect the duties and responsibilities of the world. In the performance of them we can still feel Bliss, for it is beyond them, and so they cannot affect it.

We transcend the joys and sorrows of the world in Bliss, but we do not transcend the necessity of performing our rightful duties in the world.

The man of Self-realization knows that God is the Doer—all power to perform actions flows into us from Him. He that is centered in his Spiritual self feels himself to be the *dispassionate seer* of all actions, whether he is seeing, hearing, feeling, smelling, tasting, or undergoing various other experiences on earth. Immersed in Bliss, such men live their lives in accordance with God's will.

When nonattachment is cultivated, narrow egoism vanishes. We feel that we are playing our appointed parts on the stage of the world, without being *inwardly affected* by the weal and woe, love and hate, that the playing of a part involves.

Verily, in all respects the world may be likened to a stage. The stage manager chooses people to help him in the enactment of a certain play. He allots particular parts to particular persons; all of them work according to his directions. One the stage manager makes a king, one a minister, one a servant, another the hero, and so on. One person has to play a sorrowful part, another a joyful role.

If each man plays his part according to the directions of the stage manager, then the play, with all its diversities of comical, serious, sorrowful parts, becomes successful. Even the insignificant parts have their indispensable places in the play.

The success of the play lies in the perfect acting out of each part. Each actor plays his role of sorrow or pleasure realistically, and to all outward appearances seems to be affected by it; but inwardly he remains untouched by it or by the passions he portrays—love, hate, desire, malice, pride, humility.

But if an actor, in the playing of a part, identified himself with a certain situation or a particular feeling expressed in the play and lost his own individuality, he would be thought foolish, to say the least. A story will bring out the latter point clearly.

Once in the house of a rich man the play of *Ramayan* was staged. In the course of the play it was found that the man who should play the part of *Hanuman* (a monkey), the attendant-friend of Ram, was missing. In his perplexity the stage manager seized upon an ugly simpleton, Nilkamal by name, and sought to make him enact the part of *Hanuman*.

Nilkamal at first refused, but was forced to appear on the stage. His ugly appearance excited loud laughter among the spectators and they began to shout in merriment, *"Hanuman, Hanuman!"*

Nilkamal could hardly bear this. He forgot that it was only a play, and bawled out in exasperation, "Why, sirs, do you call me *Hanuman?* Why do you laugh? I am not a *Hanuman*. The stage manager made me come out here this way."

In this complex world our lives are nothing but plays. But alas! we identify ourselves with the play, and hence feel disgust, sorrow and pleasure. We forget the direction and injunction of the Great Stage Manager. In the act of living our lives—playing our parts— we feel as real all our sorrows and pleasures, loves and hates—in a word, we become attached, affected.

This play of the world is without beginning and end. Everyone should play his part, as assigned by the Great Stage Manager, un-grudgingly; should play for the sake of the play only; should act sorrowful when playing sorrowful parts, or pleased when playing pleasurable parts, but should never be inwardly *identified with the play*.

Nor should one wish to play another's part. If everyone in the world portrayed the role of a king, the play itself would lose interest and meaning.

He that has attained Bliss-consciousness will *feel* the world to be a stage and will play out his part as best he can, remembering the Great Stage Manager, God, and knowing and feeling His plan and direction.

BHAKTI

Bhakti or devotionalism is of the greatest importance to the Hinduism of India. The worship of the average religious Hindu is more in the bhakti spirit than anything else, and bhakti is the soul of the most conspicuous religious art and verse. For bhakti is the way of devotional love, utilizing the most powerful of human passions to animate the greatest of all quests, for the divine.

Yet bhakti presents a different face of Hinduism than does Neo-Vedanta, and one until recently less well known outside India. Fervent where the latter tends to be cool and intellectual, prolific with images, ritual, even song and dance where Neo-Vedanta is restrained, bhakti is the Hinduism of the temple, the household shrine, and the heart aflame. Above all bhakti is theistic, rejoicing in a loving personal Deity when Advaita Vedanta seeks the impersonal Ground beyond the humanized face of God. Inevitably, bhakti is more culturally bound and less facilely universalistic than Neo-Vedanta. Some might have thought, in fact, that it could never be effectively transplanted outside India.

Nonetheless, a rich and deep devotional universalism is latent in bhakti. It has expressed itself not only in popular cults, but also in poetry wise in the subtle intertwinings of human and divine love, and in thought as sophisticated in its defense of love and personality as Advaita in its cause. Bhakti sages, for example, have cataloged the many stages of human love toward God, from that love which knows the Lord only as cosmic Creator or Master, to that which knows him as friend, as parent, or as spouse, to that poignant love which knows the Beloved most profoundly in those yearning moments when he seems to have withdrawn his face; for the way of love is never that of mere monistic identity with the Absolute, but is a way of intricate though invisible interplay, as between magnets, binding the human and the Supreme, and the lines of force love sets in motion are wholly alien to few humans. Nor is some ability to appreciate the charm of a bhakti god like Krishna—marvellous child, divine lover, and mature hero, with his fabulous paradises full of lotuses and peacocks, and with his earthly temples that in their opulence and color mirror something of that splendor—alien to human experience.

Bibliography

Daner, Francine. *The American Children of Krsna*. New York: Holt, Rinehart & Winston, 1976.

Gelberg, Steven J., ed. *Hare Krishna, Hare Krishna*. New York: Grove Press, 1983.

Goswami, Satsvarupa dasa. *Srila Prabhupada-lilamrta*, 6 vols. (Biography in English of Swami Bhaktivedanta.) Los Angeles: Bhaktivedanta Book Trust, 1980–1985.

Judah, J. Stillson. *Hare Krishna and the Counterculture*. New York: John Wiley, 1974.

I. SWAMI BHAKTIVEDANTA: KRISHNA CONSCIOUSNESS

Realizing the universal appeal of bhakti and Krishna was a task accomplished by A. C. Bhaktivedanta Swami Prabhupada, founder of the International Society for Krishna Consciousness. Bhaktivedanta represented the Caitanya tradition of the Vaisnava (Vishnuist) wing of bhakti. Caitanya (1486–1533), a great religious revivalist, advanced faith centered on Krishna as the supreme personal God, expressed through purity of life and ecstatic devotional song and dance. Krishna, resplendent with love and charm, who in his earthly life had been a winsome infant, a young lover, and the mature hero of the Bhagavad-Gita there revealed in all his cosmic power, was a wonderful lodestone for such devotion. In 1965, when he was nearly seventy, Bhaktivedanta brought Krishnaism to the United States. Reaching the "counterculture" at its crest, his joyous faith of chanting, colorful images, and utopian vision quickly took root in it, soon producing the organized "Hare Krishna" movement.

At the same time, Bhaktivedanta was a scholar and spiritual thinker of some distinction. He produced a massive translation and commentary on the Bhagavad-Gita, his movement's chief scripture, as well as commentaries on the works of Caitanya and many other books. The passage that follows is from a text directed toward occidental seekers.

Our Real Life*

The *Bhagavad-gītā* says that out of many thousands of human beings, one may try to make perfection of his life. Man is an animal, but he has one special prerogative, rational thought. What is that rational thought? Reasoning power, argument. Now, reasoning power is there in dogs and cats as well. Suppose a dog comes up to you; if you say, "Hut!" he'll understand. The dog will understand that you don't want him. So, he has some reasoning power. But what is the special reasoning power of the human being?

As far as the bodily necessities are concerned, the reasoning power is there even in the animal. If a cat wants to steal some milk from your kitchen, she has very nice reasoning power: she is always looking to see when the master is out and she can take. So, for the four propensities of animal life—eating, sleeping, mating and defending—there is reasoning power even in the beasts. Then, what is the special reasoning power of the human being, by which he is called the rational animal?

The special reasoning power is to inquire, "Why am I suffering?" This is special reasoning. The animals are suffering, but they do not know how to remedy the suffering. But human beings are making scientific advancement and philosophical advancement, cultural advancement, religious advancement—progress in so many lines—because they want to be happy. "Where is the point of happiness?" This reasoning power is especially given to the human being. Therefore, in the *Gītā*, Kṛṣṇa says, "Out of so many men, one may know Me."

Generally, the people are just like animals. They simply do not know anything beyond the necessities of the body: how to eat, how to sleep, how to mate and how to defend. And the *Bhagavad-gītā* says, out of many thousands, someone may develop this reasoning power: "Why am I suffering?" He asks this question: "Why am I suffering?" We do not want to suffer, but suffering is forced upon

*From His Divine Grace A. C. Bhaktivedanta Swami Prabhupada, *Krsna Consciousness: The Topmost Yoga System* (Los Angeles: Isckon Books, 1970). Copyright © 1970 by A. C. Bhaktivedanta Swami. Reprinted by permission of The Bhaktivedanta Book Trust.

us. We do not want too much cold, but too much cold and too much heat are forced upon us.

When there is some impetus to awaken this reasoning power, it is called *brahma-jijñāsā*. This is found in the *Vedānta-sūtra*. The first verse says that now, this human form of life is meant for asking the question of how to solve the problem of suffering.

So Krṣṇa says that this special prerogative of the human being is not awakened very easily, except by some good association. Just as we have this Krṣṇa conscious association. If we attain such association, where nice things are discussed, then that awakening of reason, that special prerogative of the human being, will come. As long as this question does not arise in one's mind, he should understand that whatever activities he is doing will lead to his defeat. He is simply leading an animal life. But, not when these questions arise: Why am I suffering? What am I? Am I meant for suffering? Am I meant for troubles?

I am undergoing troubles by nature's laws, and by the state's laws. So the question of freedom is how to become free from all these troubles. The *Vedānta-sūtra* also says that the soul, my actual self, is by nature joyful. Yet, I am suffering. Lord Krṣṇa further says that when these questions arise, gradually one comes to God. Those who have awakened to these questions are said to be on the path of perfection. And, when the question of God and our relationship with God comes, that is our final perfection of life.

Now, Krṣṇa says that out of many thousands of people, one may try to make perfection of this life; and out of many millions of such persons on the path of perfection, only one may understand Krṣṇa. So understanding Krṣṇa is not very easy. But it is also the easiest. It is not easy, but at the same time it is the easiest. It is the easiest if you follow the prescribed forms.

Lord Caitanya Mahāprabhu has introduced this chanting of Hare Krṣṇa. He has not exactly introduced it; it is in the scriptures. But He has especially propagated this formula. In this age this is the easiest method of self-realization. Simply chant Hare Krṣṇa. It can be done by everyone. In my classroom, I am perhaps the only Indian. My students are all Americans, and they are chanting and dancing. That means that, in any country, in any place, this can be performed. Therefore it is the easiest. You may not understand the philosophy of the *Bhagavad-gītā*. That is also not very difficult; but still, if you think that you cannot understand, you can still chant very easily: Hare Kṛṣṇa. Hare Kṛṣṇa.

If we want to understand God, Kṛṣṇa, this is the beginning. The easiest beginning—simply chanting. Now, there are many students of my ISKCON institution. This institution is open a little over a year;* but some of the students, by simply chanting, by the grace of Kṛṣṇa, have advanced in such a way that they can talk about the science of God, and they will very easily answer those human questions. So, this is the easiest method of transcendental meditation.

Kṛṣṇa says that out of many millions of people, one may understand Him. But, by chanting of this Hare Kṛṣṇa, as introduced by Lord Caitanya—chanting and dancing—you can understand Kṛṣṇa within a very short time. Knowledge begins not from Kṛṣṇa, but from things which we are accustomed to see every day.

Land is gross. If you touch it, you can feel its hardness. But, as soon as the land becomes still finer, it is water, and the touch is soft. And then again, from water to fire, still finer. After fire or electricity the air is still finer; and after air, the sky, ether, is finer still. Beyond ether, the mind is still finer; and beyond the mind, intelligence is still finer. And, if you go beyond intelligence to understand the soul, it is finer still. From these elements people have discovered so many sciences. There are many scientists, for example, who are soil experts; they can say, by analyzing a particular type of earth, what kind of minerals are there. Somebody seeks out silver, somebody seeks out gold, somebody seeks out mica. This is knowledge of gross things—the earth. If you go to finer substances, then you study water, or liquid things, such as petrol and alcohol. Go still finer, and from water you will go to fire and electricity. If you study electricity, you have to study all sorts of books. And, from this finer fire, you will come to air. We have so much advancement in our airplanes; we are studying how they move, how they are made—now sputniks and jets—so many things are being discovered.

Next comes the study of the ethereal: electronics, ethereal transformations from one thing to another. Then, finer still, is the mind—psychology and psychiatry. But for intelligence, rationalism, there

---

*This lecture was delivered in 1968 at ISKCON San Francisco, when that temple was in its second year.

is only a little philosophical speculation. And what about the soul? Is there any science of the soul? The materialists have none. Material science has advanced to the study of the ether, or the mind and intelligence, but there is no advancement beyond that. Beyond intelligence, they do not know what exists. But here in the *Bhagavad-gītā* you can find this.

The *Bhagavad-gītā* begins at the point after intelligence. When Arjuna was perplexed at the outset, his intelligence was perplexed—whether to fight or not to fight. Kṛṣṇa begins the *Gītā* from the point where intelligence fails. How does knowledge of the soul begin? It is just like a child is playing. You can understand this child's body is now so small, but one day this child will be grown up, like you or me. But the same soul will continue. So, by intelligence, you can understand that although the body is changed, the soul is there. The same soul which was existing in the body of the child is still continuing in the body of the old man. Therefore the soul is permanent, and only the body has changed. This is a very easy thing to understand. And the last change of this body is death. As at every moment, every second, every day, every hour, the body is changing, so the last change is when one cannot act with the body, and so he has to take another one. Just as, when my cloth is too worn out or old, I cannot put it on; I have to take a new cloth. It is similar with the soul. When the body is too old or unworkable, I have to change to another body. This is called death.

This is the beginning of the *Bhagavad-gītā,* when the preliminary knowledge of the soul is there. And you will find that there are only a few who can understand the existence of the soul as permanent, and of the body as changeable. Therefore Bhagavān, Lord Kṛṣṇa, says that, out of many, many millions of people, one may understand it. But still, the knowledge is there. If you want to understand it, it is not difficult. You can understand it.

Now, we should inquire into the existence of the ego, the finest material substance. What is ego? I am pure soul, but with my intelligence and mind I am in contact with matter, and I have identified myself with matter. This is false ego. I am pure soul, but I am identifying falsely. For example, I am identifying with the land, thinking that I am Indian, or that I am American. This is called *ahaṅkara.* *Ahaṅkara* means the point where the pure soul touches matter. That junction is called *ahaṅkara.* *Ahaṅkara* is still finer than intelligence.

Kṛṣṇa says that these are the eight material elements: earth, water, fire, air, ether, mind, intelligence and false ego. False ego means false identification. Our nescient life has begun from this false identification—thinking that I am this matter, although I am seeing every day, at every moment, that I am not this matter. Soul is permanently existing, while matter is changing. This misconception, this illusion, is called *ahaṅkara,* false ego. And your liberation means when you are out of this false ego. What is that status? *Aham brahmāsmi.* I am *Brahman,* I am spirit. That is the beginning of liberation.

Of course, one may be suffering from disease, from fever, and the temperature may come down to normal, 98.6 degrees. So he is now normal, but that is not the cure. Suppose for two days he has a 98.6 degree temperature, but with a slight change of diet, a slight change of behavior, the temperature rises immediately to 100. Relapse. Similarly, simply purifying the mind, rejecting this false *ahaṅkara* identification—I am not this body, I am not this matter; I am soul—this is not liberation. It is only the beginning of liberation. If you stick to this point, and continue—just as you might continue your activities and keep your temperature at 98.6 degrees—then you are a healthy man.

For example, in the West now there is some propaganda for taking intoxication. The people want to forget the bodily existence. But how long will you forget? There will be a relapse. You can forget for one hour or two, by intoxication, and think that I am not this body. But unless you are actually on the platform of understanding yourself by knowledge, it is not possible to continue. Still, everyone is trying to think, "I am not this body." They have experience that they are suffering so much on account of bodily identification, and so, "If only I could forget my bodily identification!"

This is only a negative conception. When you actually realize yourself, simply understanding that you are *Brahman* will not do. You have to engage in the activities of *Brahman.* Otherwise you will fall down. Simply flying very high is no solution to the problem of going to the moon. Nowadays the fools are trying to go to the moon, but they simply go 240,000 miles up from the Earth, touch the moon, and return. They are very proud. There is so much talk of aeronautics: crowds and meetings and conferences. But what have they done? What are 240,000 miles in that vast sky? If you go 240 million miles, still you are limited. So this will not do. If you want to go high, you must have permanent shelter. If you can take rest there, then you cannot fall down. But if you have no rest, then you will have to fall down. The airplane goes high, seven miles, eight miles up from the Earth, but it comes down immediately.

So, simply understanding *ahaṅkara* means no more than understanding the false identification. Simply understanding that I am not this matter, I am soul, is not perfection. The impersonalist, the void philosopher, simply thinks of the negative, that I am not this matter, I am not this body. This will not stay. You have to not only realize that you are not matter, but you have to engage yourself in the spiritual world. And that spiritual world means to be working in Kṛṣṇa consciousness. That spiritual world, that functioning of our real life, is Kṛṣṇa consciousness.

False ego I have already explained. It is neither matter nor spirit, but the junction—where the spirit soul comes into contact with matter and forgets himself. It is just as, in delirium, a man is diseased and his brain becomes puzzled, and gradually he forgets himself and becomes a madman. He is gradually forgetting. So there is the beginning of loss, and there is one point where he forgets. That beginning point is called *anaṅkara,* or false ego.

Chanting the *mahāmantra*—Hare Kṛṣṇa, Hare Kṛṣṇa, Kṛṣṇa Kṛṣṇa, Hare Hare/ Hare Rāma, Hare Rāma, Rāma Rāma, Hare Hare—is the process not merely of putting an end to this false conception of the self, but it goes beyond that, to the point where the pure spirit soul engages in his eternal, blissful, all-knowing activities in the loving service of God. This is the height of conscious development, the ultimate goal of all living entities now evolving through the cycles and species of material nature.

The Hare Kṛṣṇa Mantra

The transcendental vibration established by the chanting of HARE KṚṢṆA, HARE KṚṢṆA, KṚṢṆA KṚṢṆA, HARE HARE/ HARE RĀMA, HARE RĀMA, RĀMA RĀMA, HARE HARE is the sublime method for reviving our transcendental consciousness. As living spiritual souls, we are all originally Kṛṣṇa conscious entities, but due to our association with matter from time immemorial, our consciousness is now adulterated by the material atmosphere. The material atmosphere, in which we are now living, is called *māyā,* or illusion. *Māyā* means that which is not. And what is this illusion? The illusion is that we are all trying to be lords of material nature, while actually we are under the grip of her stringent laws. When a servant artificially tries to imitate the all-powerful master, it is called illusion. We are trying to exploit the resources of material nature, but actually we are becoming more and more entangled in her complexities. Therefore, although we are engaged in a hard struggle to conquer nature, we are ever more dependent on her. This illusory struggle against material nature can be stopped at once by revival of our eternal Kṛṣṇa consciousness.

Hare Kṛṣṇa, Hare Kṛṣṇa, Kṛṣṇa Kṛṣṇa, Hare Hare is the transcendental process for reviving this original pure consciousness. By chanting this transcendental vibration, we can cleanse away all misgivings within our hearts. The basic principle of all such misgivings is the false consciousness that I am the lord of all I survey.

Kṛṣṇa consciousness is not an artificial imposition on the mind. This consciousness is the original natural energy of the living entity. When we hear the transcendental vibration, this consciousness is revived. This simplest method of meditation is recommended for this age. By practical experience also, one can perceive that by chanting this *mahāmantra,* or the Great Chanting for Deliverance, one can at once feel a transcendental ecstasy coming through from the spiritual stratum. In the material concept of life we are busy in the matter of sense gratification as if we were in the lower animal stage. A little elevated from this status of sense gratification, one is engaged in mental speculation for the purpose of getting out of the material clutches. A little elevated from this speculative status, when one is intelligent enough, one tries to find out the supreme cause of all causes—within and without. And when one is factually on the plane of spiritual understanding, surpassing the stages of sense, mind and intelligence, he is then on the transcendental plane. This chanting of the Hare Kṛṣṇa *mantra* is enacted from the spiritual platform, and thus this sound vibration surpasses all lower strata of consciousness—namely sensual, mental and intellectual. There is no need, therefore, to understand the language of the *mantra,* nor is there any need for mental speculation nor any intellectual adjustment for chanting this *mahāmantra.* It is automatic, from the spiritual platform, and as such, anyone can take part in vibrating this transcendental sound without any previous qualification. In a more advanced stage, of course, one is not expected to commit offenses on grounds of spiritual understanding.

In the beginning, there may not be the presence of all transcendental ecstasies, which are eight in number. These are: 1) Being stopped as though dumb, 2) perspiration, 3) standing up of hairs on the body, 4) dislocation of voice, 5) trembling, 6) fading of the body, 7) crying in ecstasy, and 8) trance. But there is no doubt that chanting for a while takes one immediately to the spiritual platform, and one shows the first symptom of this in the urge to dance along with the chanting of the *mantra*. We have seen this practically. Even a child can take part in the chanting and dancing. Of course, for one who is too entangled in material life, it takes a little more time to come to the standard point, but even such a materially engrossed man is raised to the spiritual platform very quickly. When it is chanted by a pure devotee of the Lord in love, it has the greatest efficacy on hearers, and as such this chanting should be heard from the lips of a pure devotee of the Lord, so that immediate effects can be achieved. As far as possible, chanting from the lips of nondevotees should be avoided. Milk touched by the lips of a serpent has poisonous effects.

The word *Harā* is the form of addressing the energy of the Lord, and the words *Krsna* and *Rāma* are forms of addressing the Lord Himself. Both *Krsna* and *Rāma* mean the supreme pleasure, and *Harā* is the supreme pleasure energy of the Lord, changed to *Hare* (*Hah-ray*) in the vocative. The supreme pleasure energy of the Lord helps us to reach the Lord.

The material energy, called *māya,* is also one of the multi-energies of the Lord. And we the living entities are also the energy, marginal energy, of the Lord. The living entities are described as superior to material energy. When the superior energy is in contact with the inferior energy, an incompatible situation arises; but when the superior marginal energy is in contact with the superior energy, called *Harā,* it is established in its happy, normal condition.

These three words, namely *Harā, Krsna* and *Rāma,* are the transcendental seeds of the *mahāmantra.* The chanting is a spiritual call for the Lord and His energy, to give protection to the conditioned soul. This chanting is exactly like the genuine cry of a child for its mother's presence. Mother Harā helps the devotee achieve the Lord Father's grace, and the Lord reveals Himself to the devotee who chants this *mantra* sincerely.

No other means of spiritual realization is as effective in this age of quarrel and hypocrisy as the *mahāmantra:* Hare Kṛṣṇa, Hare Kṛṣṇa, Kṛṣṇa Kṛṣṇa, Hare Hare/ Hare Rāma, Hare Rāma, Rāma Rāma, Hare Hare.

How Bhakti-yoga Works

In the *Bhagavad-gītā* Kṛṣṇa tells His disciple, Arjuna, "I am disclosing a most confidential part of knowledge to you, because you are My dear friend." As is stated in the Fourth Chapter, the *Bhagavad-gītā* is spoken to Arjuna because of his one qualification: he was a devotee. The Lord says that the mystery of the *Bhagavad-gītā* is very confidential. Without being an unalloyed devotee you cannot know it. In India there are 645 different commentaries on the *Gītā.* One professor has proposed that Kṛṣṇa is a doctor and Arjuna is his patient, and has made his commentary in that way. Similarly, there are commentators and people who have taken it that everyone is perfect, and that they can interpret scripture in their own way. As far as we are concerned, we agree to read the *Bhagavad-gītā* according to the instructions given in the *Gītā* itself. This has to be taken through the *paramparā,* the system of disciplic succession. It is being taught by the Supreme Person because "you are My dear friend. I desire that you may become prosperous and happy. Therefore I speak to you." Kṛṣṇa wants everyone to be happy and peaceful and prosperous, but they do not want it. Sunshine is open to everyone, but if someone wishes to remain in darkness, what can the sunshine do for him? So the *Gītā* is open to everyone. There are different species of life, and lower and higher grades of understanding exist—that is a fact. But Kṛṣṇa says that this knowledge is for anyone. If one has lower birth or whatever, it doesn't matter. The *Bhagavad-gītā* offers transcendental subject matter everyone can understand provided he goes along with the principle as stated in the Fourth Chapter. That is, that the *Gītā* is coming down in disciplic succession: "I first of all instructed this *yoga* system to the sun-god Vivasvān, who taught it to Manu, who taught it to Ikṣvāku." From Kṛṣṇa the disciplic succession is coming down, but "in course of time the disciplic succession was broken." Arjuna is therefore made the new disciple. In the Second Chapter, Arjuna surrenders: "So far we have been talking as friends, but now I accept You as my spiritual master."

Anyone following the principle in this line accepts the *guru* as Kṛṣṇa, and the student must represent Arjuna. Kṛṣṇa is speaking as the spiritual master of Arjuna, and Arjuna says, "Whatever You are saying I accept." Read it like that—not: "I like this, so I accept it; this I don't like, and so I reject it." Such reading is useless nonsense.

The teacher must be a representative of Kṛṣṇa, a devotee, and the student must be like Arjuna. Then this Kṛṣṇa consciousness study is perfect. Otherwise it is a waste of time. In the *Śrīmad-Bhāgavatam* it is stated: "If anyone wants to understand the science of Kṛṣṇa, he should associate with pure devotees. When discussions take place among pure devotees, the potency of spiritual language is revealed." Scholarly discussion of the *Gītā* is futile. In the *Upaniṣads* it is stated: "To one who has firm faith in God, and similar faith in God's representative, all the import of Vedic language will be revealed." We must have the qualification of being a devotee. Become dear to God. My spiritual master used to say, "Don't try to see God. Act in such a way that God will see you." We have to qualify ourselves. By your qualification God Himself will come and see you.

If one can perceive God, he is transcendental to all material demands. We are always dissatisfied in the material world in circumstances that won't continue; happiness is temporary, and temporary plight also will not exist for much time. Cold, heat, duality—it is all coming and going. To get to the absolute stage is the process of Kṛṣṇa consciousness. Kṛṣṇa is seated in everyone's heart, and as you become purified He will show you the path. And in the end you will quit this body, and you will go to the spiritual sky.

"No one knows Me." Kṛṣṇa says, "My influence, My power and My extent. Even the *maharṣis* [the great thinkers] don't know. I am the origin of all demigods and the origin of all *ṛṣis*." There are so many forefathers we don't know of, and there are Brahmā and the demigods—what do we know? We can't reach to the platform where we can grasp God. We gather knowledge by limited senses, and Kṛṣṇa can't be reached by the mind, the center of the senses. Imperfect senses can't grasp perfect knowledge. Mind and sense manipulation can't reach Him. If you engage the senses in the service of the Lord, however, then He will reveal Himself through your senses.

People may say, "What is the use of understanding God? What is the use? Let Him stay in His place, let me stay in my place." But in the *śāstras*, the scriptures, it is stated that pious activities will raise us to beauty, knowledge and good birth; and that by impious (sinful) activities, we suffer. Suffering is always there, pious or impious, but a distinction is made. He who knows God, however, becomes freed from all possible sinful reactions, which no amount of piety can accomplish. If we reject God we can never be happy.

Not even considering human society, if you take the demigods who are more advanced and intelligent, they also don't know Krsna. The seven great sages whose planet is near the North Star also do not know. Krsna says: "I am the original, the source of all these demigods." He is the father of everything, not only the origin of demigods, but of the sages—and the universe. The *Srīmad-Bhāgavatam* describes how the universal form took place, and everything is emanating from Him. Also Krsna is the origin of *Paramātmā*, the Supersoul; and the impersonal *brahma-jyoti*, the shining effulgence, is in Him. Of everything, of every conception, "I am the source." The Absolute Truth may be realized in three phases, but is one nondual truth. *Brahman* (the glowing effulgence), localized Supersoul, and *Bhagavān*—the Supreme Person—are three features or aspects of God.

If no one knows the Supreme Personality of Godhead, how can He be known? He can be known when the Supreme Lord comes before you and reveals Himself to you. Then you can know. Our senses are imperfect, and they cannot realize the Supreme Truth. When you adopt a submissive attitude and chant, realization begins from the tongue. To eat and to vibrate sound is the business of the tongue. If you can control your tongue for *prasādam*, spiritual food, and make the sound vibration of the holy name, then by surrender of the tongue you can control all the other senses. If you cannot control your tongue, you cannot control your senses. Taste *prasādam* and become spiritually advanced. You can have this process at your home: offer vegetarian foods to Krsna, chant the Hare Krsna *mantra* and offer obeisances:

namo brahmanya-devāya
    go-brāhmana-hitāya ca
jagat-hitāya krsnāya
    govindāya namo namah.

Everyone can offer, and then take the food with friends. And chant before the picture of Krsna, and lead a pure life. Just see the result—the whole world will become Vaikuṇṭha, where there is no anxiety. All is anxious with us because we have accepted this material life. Just the opposite is so in the spiritual world. No one, however, knows how to get out of the material concept. Taking an intoxicant doesn't help; the same anxieties are there when you are finished being drunk. If you want to be free and want life eternal with bliss and knowledge, take to Kṛṣṇa. No one can know God, but there is this way: the process of Kṛṣṇa consciousness.

In the *Srīmad-Bhāgavatam* it is stated that no one can conquer Him or approach Him, but He becomes conquered. How? Let people remain in their own positions, but let them give up nonsense speculation through volumes of books. Thousands of books are printed and read, and after six months thrown away. This way and that—how can you know the Supreme by speculation on the information supplied by your blunt senses? Give up research—throw it away—just become submissive; acknowledge that you are limited and subordinate to material nature and to God. No one can be equal to or greater than God. So be submissive. Try to hear about the glories of the Supreme Lord from authorized sources. Such authority is handed over by disciplic succession. If we can understand by the same authority as Arjuna, that is real authority. God is always ready to reveal; you just become Kṛṣṇa conscious. Follow the path traversed by the great *ācāryas,* the devoted teachers, and then everything will be known. Although He is unconquerable and unknowable, He can be known in your home.

If you take to this process and follow the principles, what will be the result? As soon as you understand, you will know that the Supreme Lord is the cause of all causes, but that He is not caused by any other cause. And He is the master of all planets. This is not accepting blindly. God has given you the power of reason, the power of arguing—but don't argue falsely. If you want to know the transcendental science you must surrender. Surrender to authority and know Him by signs. Don't surrender to a fool or a rascal. Find one who is coming in disciplic succession, one who is fully convinced about the Supreme Absolute Truth. If you find such a person, surrender and try to please him, serve him and question him. Surrender unto Him is surrender to God. Question to learn, not to waste time.

The process is there, but if we waste time by intoxication we will never see Him, the unconquerable Lord. Follow the principles and slowly but surely, without doubt, you will know. "Yes, I'm making progress," you'll say. And it is very easy, and you can execute it and be in a happy mood. Study, take part with music, eat *prasādam*. And no one can cheat you by this process. But if you want to be cheated—go to the cheaters.

Try to understand it from the authoritative source and apply it in your life. Amongst the dying mortals, you will become the most intelligent because you are freed from sinful actions. If you act only for Kṛṣṇa, then you are freed from all reactions. You will have no anxiety over what is auspicious or inauspicious because you will be in touch with the most auspicious. This is the process. Ultimately, we can get in touch with Kṛṣṇa. Life will be successful. Anyone can adopt it, because it is very simple.

Here is a nice formula presented by Kṛṣṇa Himself: one should understand the position of Kṛṣṇa. He is unborn and without any cause. We have experience, all of us, that we are born, and we have a cause; our father is our cause. If someone poses himself as God, he has to prove that he is unborn and uncaused. Our practical experience is that we are born. Kṛṣṇa is not born. We have to understand this. Understanding this is to be firmly convinced He is the cause, but is not caused; and since He is not caused He is the proprietor of all manifestation. One who understands this simple philosophy is not illusioned.

We are generally illusioned. We are claiming ownership of the land. But before my birth the land was here, and after my death it will still be here. How long will I go on claiming, in body after body, "This is my land! This is my land!"? Is it not nonsense? One has to be out of illusion. We should know that whatever we are doing in the material concept of life is illusion. We have to understand whether we are illusioned or not. And all conditioned souls are illusioned. He who learns to be disillusioned gets free of all encumbrances. If we want freedom from all bonds, then we have to understand God. There is no neglecting this; it is our prime duty.

Out of millions of entities, one may be enlightened. Generally we are all born fools. As soon as I take birth I am nurtured by parents and educated to falsely claim a land as my own. National education means to make you more foolish. Am I not foolish? I am changing my body like a dress life after life. You have so many minds, so many dresses—who do you claim this one? Why don't you under-

stand: "This dress is nice, but next moment I may be in another."
You are in the grip of nature. You cannot say what dress you will
have: "Nature, make me American." No; material nature controls.
If you live like a dog—here, take a dog's dress. If you live a godly
life—here, take God.

Out of many fools someone tries to understand what I actually
am. Dog? American? Russian? This real inquiry goes on. If you inquire, you have to ask someone, not just yourself. When crossing
the street in a place you don't know, you have to ask the policeman
or some gentleman. For "what I am" you have to go to an authority
also. What is a spiritual master? He is a person conversant with the
science of Kṛṣṇa. Ordinarily nobody inquires; but if a man does, he
can make progress and come to this understanding: Kṛṣṇa is the cause
of all causes.

Four kinds of people, followers of scripture and higher authority, inquire about Kṛṣṇa. Those addicted to sinful activities can't inquire. They go on in intoxication. The righteous, pious man inquires
and goes to God. Facility is given to people in this process by the
authority—to make people happy, not to exploit people. The purpose
of ISKCON is, in this way, to understand the science of God. You
want happiness. Here it is. You are distressed by sinful reactions.
But if there is no sinful reaction there is no suffering. One who knows
Kṛṣṇa without doubt is relieved of all reactions. Kṛṣṇa says, "Come
to Me, and I will give you freedom from all reactions." Don't disbe-
lieve it. He can give you shelter; He has all power. If I give you such
a promise, because I have no such power I may break the promise.

If you associate yourself with Kṛṣṇa consciousness your dormant relationship with Kṛṣṇa will be evoked. We have a relationship
with Him. There is no question of disbelieving; it is simply foolish-
ness. The dormant relationship is there. We want to serve Kṛṣṇa, but
simply by the spell of illusion we think we have no connection with
Kṛṣṇa. We go on doing all "independent" nonsense, and we are always anxious. When we associate with these dormant feelings for
Kṛṣṇa, however, we will become engaged in Kṛṣṇa consciousness.

"God is unborn" indicates that He is different from the material
world. We have no such experience of the unborn. This city was
born—history is filled with dates. Spiritual nature, however, is unborn, and at once we can see the difference. The material nature is
born. You have to understand; if Kṛṣṇa is unborn then He is spiritual,

not like one of us. Kṛṣṇa is not some "extraordinary person who was also born." He is not born. So how can I decide He is an ordinary man? "Those who are fools and rascals think of Me as an ordinary man," Kṛṣṇa says in the *Gītā*. He is different from everything in this world. He is *anādi,* without cause.

Kṛṣṇa may be spiritual, but there are other spiritual bodies. We have spiritual bodies like Kṛṣṇa's, but they are born. They are not exactly born; it is like the sparks of the fire. The sparks are not born from the fire; they are actually there. We are also not born; we are sparks that come out of the original form. Even if we are not born, the spark comes out of Kṛṣṇa, so we are different; the sparks of the fire are fire, but they are not the original fire. As for quality, we are the same as Kṛṣṇa. It is like the difference between father and son. Father and son are different and nondifferent at the same time. The son is an expansion of the father, but he cannot claim that he is the father; that would be nonsense.

Because Kṛṣṇa is declaring Himself supreme proprietor, He is therefore different from anything. If I am the proprietor of New York State, I am still not New York State. In every step there is duality. No one can say we are completely one with God.

When you can understand Kṛṣṇa's and your own position in a nice analytical way, then at once you become free from sinful reactions. This process will help you. Chant Hare Kṛṣṇa and cleanse your mind, and you will receive the message. One has to be qualified. If you chant and hear, for no payment, you will approach God. All things will become clear and illuminated.

III

BUDDHISM

ZEN

Buddhism is above all the religion of enlightenment. It seeks to aid those who study and practice at its feet to break through all that can fetter or delude in the realm of conditioned reality, and become free in Nirvana, Unconditioned Reality. Buddhism does this by leading one to recognize the Four Noble Truths the Buddha himself discovered some twenty-five hundred years ago on the eve of his enlightenment. Beneath the numerous sectarian forms and rich accretions the faith of the Enlightened One has acquired in its journeys through many cultures and many centuries, Buddhism ultimately depends on these principles.

First, life as it is ordinarily lived is unsatisfactory, shot through with anxiety, suffering, and meaninglessness. Second, this state is the result of attachments or desires, for in a universe of continual flux and change, seeking to cling to anything—from the grossest passion to the subtlest idol of the mind to the notion of being a permanent separate self—can never bring anything but sorrow in the end. Third, the syndrome of suffering and desire can be struck at its point of origin; there can be an end to desire. Fourth, that can be achieved by following the Eightfold Path, which culminates in Right Concentration or Meditation. For meditation is the condition of mind that reverses the mind's ordinary outflow toward entangling objects of sensory or mental attachment.

The Zen school of Buddhism originated in China out of the commingling of Buddhism with the naturalism of Taoism, spreading

114

in the Middle Ages to Japan and other East Asian societies. It sought to actualize the Four Noble Truths in its own radical way, for it taught that enlightenment is available here and now, in the midst of ordinary life with its mix of suffering and joy. It is known by direct experience, hitting one as *satori,* surprise or shock. But the meditation of the Eightfold Path is an excellent way to prepare oneself for the realization. The very word *Zen* is a Japanese transliteration of the Sanskrit *dhyana,* meditation. Zen Buddhism has gathered about it a unique aura. The word evokes rows of monks rigidly seated in zazen in clean austere monasteries, their ranks patrolled by a proctor with a stick, and also the famous "Zen lunatics," outrageous men—half monk and half vagabond, half mad and half enlightened—whose pranks and poetry enliven the annals of China and Japan. Zen calls up special genres of art and verse, ink wash, tea ceremonies, *haiku* poetry, whose special genius is to portray nature just as it is, without theory or theology, yet so poignantly as to leave one deeply moved without being quite sure why.

Zen has been the best-known form of Buddhism in America. This is first of all because it has been fortunate in producing a remarkable series of exponents on these shores: Soyen Shaku, Nyogen Senzaki, above all D. T. Suzuki. That in turn owes to Zen's relative openmindedness and emphasis on humanistic culture and education in its homelands, and its relation to China and Japan's great tradition of arts and letters. But it is also no doubt true that no other version of Buddhism would have communicated itself quite so well to the American mind. Zen's boast of breaking through words and philosophies in favor of "direct pointing" and "immediate experience," its artistic simplicity and rapport with nature, all appealed to major strands of American consciousness. Senzaki, indeed, considered Zen none other than the American pragmatism of William James or John Dewey in another guise.

Yet that other guise was not without importance, for while Zen could hark to the American images of simplicity and self-reliance, it also offered entrée into another world of spiritual and cultural wonders, from the enigmatic Zen "riddles" or *koans* to the Zen-related martial arts. Zen's draw for Americans has lain first in its spiritual effectiveness, second in its combination of otherness and homeliness. Its greatest spokesman in the West, D. T. Suzuki, like his disciple Alan Watts, exploited the mix with a sure hand, offering the reader now a whiff of the exotic, now a reassuring correlation with a motif of the West.

Different aspects of Zen have appealed to various segments or generations of Americans. The age of Soyen Shaku and Senzaki Nyogen was, to judge from their own words, eager to hear of the reasonableness of Buddhism as well as its pointing to that beyond all reason. In the 1950s, the image of the ''Zen lunatic'' came to the fore in the work of such ''Beat'' writers as Jack Kerouac, who summed it all up in *The Dharma Bums*. The 1960s and 1970s, the era of the great Zen centers and the counterculture, was interested in Zen as a spiritual discipline and total, often communalistic, way of life. All through, still others, from poets like Gary Snyder to composers like John Cage, have been mainly interested in the relation of the Zen vision to artistic creativity. The tensions of these varying Zens are well expressed, and perhaps resolved, in the essay by Alan Watts here reproduced, *Beat Zen, Square Zen, and Zen*.

Whether in tragic conflict or immensely lucrative trade, seldom have two nations of such diverse cultural heritage been as deeply involved in one another's lives as have Japan and the United States in the twentieth century. The transmission of Zen to America, though but a tiny fragment of that exchange, helps reveal the spiritual dimensions, too seldom yet appreciated, of this momentous meeting.

Bibliography

In addition to the general books on Buddhism in America cited in the bibliography to the Introduction, the following may be of interest.

Ellwood, Robert, ed. *Zen in American Life and Letters*. Los Angeles: Undena Press, 1986.

Kapleau, Philip. *The Three Pillars of Zen*. Garden City, NY: Doubleday, 1965, rev. ed. 1980.

————. *Zen: Dawn in the West*. Garden City, NY: Doubleday, 1980.

Senzaki Nyogen and Ruth Strout McCandless. *The Iron Flute*. Rutland, Vt., and Tokyo: Charles E. Tuttle Co., 1961. Contains biographical material on Senzaki.

Tipton, Steven M. *Getting Saved from the Sixties.* Berkeley and Los Angeles: University of California Press, 1982. Long chapter on a major American Zen center.

Watts, Alan. *In My Own Way: An Autobiography.* New York: Random House, 1972.

Buddhist Selections

I. SOYEN SHAKU:
PIONEER OF ZEN IN AMERICA
A. ADDRESS AT THE WORLD'S
PARLIAMENT OF RELIGIONS

Of the several Buddhist speakers at the parliament, Anagarika Dharmapala of Ceylon, fiery and fluent in English, was the most charismatic and made the strongest immediate impression. The most lasting influence, however, was that of the Japanese Zen abbot Soyen Shaku, even though his brief and rather pedantic address had to be read for him in translation. But it was Shaku who best maintained a continuing relationship after the parliament with Americans interested in Buddhism, and above all it was Shaku who brought to America the spokesman for the Dharma destined to have the greatest impact of all in the West, his student D. T. Suzuki.

When the parliament was over, the German-American Dr. Paul Carus, editor of The Monist and of the Open Court Press and author of books on science and religion, invited Soyen Shaku to his home. In pursuance of his interest in the relation of science and religion, Carus had found himself drawn toward Buddhism, appreciating its apparent rationality and lack of dependence on miracle or faith. That appreciation was well supported by Soyen's talk on the Buddhist law of cause and effect. Carus proposed that Soyen help him in translating and editing a series of Oriental books. Soyen refused, but suggested D. T. Suzuki in his place. So it was that Suzuki stayed with Paul Carus and Open Court in LaSalle, Illinois, from 1897 to 1909, inaugurating a remarkable career of bringing Zen to the West.

Soyen Shaku's own address, while unspectacular, has a certain appeal in its logical clarity and its fine balance of a sense of quiet wonder at the diversity and marvel of the universe with a clear-eyed, rational look at its inner workings. In short compass it therefore strikes those notes that have always proved most effective in communicating the wisdom of the Enlightened One to the world, a well-tempered mix of wonder and reasonableness.

The Law of Cause and Effect, as Taught by Buddha*

If we open our eyes and look at the universe we observe the sun and moon and the stars on the sky; mountains, rivers, plants, ani-

---

*From J. W. Hanson, ed., *The World's Congress of Religions* (Chicago: J. W. Iliff, 1894), pp. 388–90.

mals, fishes and birds on the earth. Cold and warmth come alternately; shine and rain change from time to time without ever reaching an end. Again let us close our eyes and calmly reflect upon ourselves. From morning to evening we are agitated by the feelings of pleasure and pain, love and hate; sometimes full of ambition and desire, sometimes called to the utmost excitement of reason and will. Thus the action of mind is like an endless issue of a spring of water. As the phenomena of the external world are various and marvelous, so is the internal attitude of human mind. Shall we ask for the explanation of these marvelous phenomena? Why is the universe in a constant flux? Why do things change? Why is the mind subjected to a constant agitation? For these Buddhism offers only one explanation, namely, the law of cause and effect.

Now let us proceed to understand the nature of this law, as taught by Buddha himself:

First.   The complex nature of cause.
Second.   An endless progression of the causal law.
Third.   The causal law in terms of the three worlds.
Fourth.   Self-formation of cause and effect.
Fifth.   Cause and effect as the law of nature.

First.   The complex nature of cause. A certain phenomenon cannot arise from a single cause, but it must have several conditions; in other words, no effect can arise unless several causes combine together. Take for example a case of fire. You may say its cause is oil or fuel; but neither oil nor fuel alone can give rise to a flame. Atmosphere, space and several other conditions, physical or mechanical, are necessary for the rise of a flame. All these necessary conditions combined together can be called the cause of a flame. This is only an example for the explanation of the complex nature of cause, but the rest may be inferred.

Second.   An endless progression of the causal law. A cause must be preceded by another cause, and an effect must be followed by another effect. Thus, if we investigate the cause of a cause, the past of a past, by tracing back even to an eternity, we shall never reach the first cause. The assertion that there is the first cause is contrary to the fundamental principle of nature, since a certain cause must have an origin in some preceding cause or causes, and there is no cause which is not an effect. From the assumption that a cause is an effect of a preceding cause, which is also preceded by another, thus, ad infinitum, we infer that there is no beginning in the universe. As there is no effect which is not a cause, so there is no cause which is not an effect. Buddhism considers the universe has no beginning, no end. Since, even if we trace back to an eternity, absolute cause cannot be found, so we come to the conclusion that there is no end in the universe. Like as the waters of rivers evaporate and form clouds, and the latter changes its form into rain, thus returning once more into the original form of waters, the causal law is in a logical circle changing from cause to effect, effect to cause.

Third.   The causal law in terms of three worlds, namely, past, present and future. All the religions apply more or less the causal law in the sphere of human conduct, and remark that the pleasure and happiness of one's future life depend upon the purity of his present life. But what is peculiar to Buddhism is, it applies the law not only to the relation of present and future life, but also past and present. As the facial expressions of each individual are different from those of others, men are graded by the different degrees of wisdom, talent, wealth and birth. It is not education nor experience alone that can make a man wise, intelligent and wealthy, but it depends upon one's past life. What are the causes or conditions which produce such a difference? To explain it in a few words, I say, it owes its origin to the different quality of actions which we have done in our past life, namely, we are here enjoying or suffering the effect of what we have done in our past life. If you closely observe the conduct of your fellow beings, you will notice that each individual acts different from the others. From this we can infer that in future life each one will also enjoy or suffer the result of his own actions done in this existence. As the pleasure and pain of one's present actions, so the happiness or misery of our future world will be the result of our present action.

Fourth.   Self-formation of cause and effect. We enjoy happiness and suffer misery, our own actions being causes; in other words, there is no other cause than our own actions which make us happy or unhappy. Now let us observe the different attitudes of human life; one is happy and others feel unhappy. Indeed, even among the members of the same family, we often notice a great diversity in wealth and fortune. Thus various attitudes of human life can be explained by the self-formation of cause and effect. There is no one in the universe but one's self who rewards or punishes him. The diversity in future stages will be explained by the same doctrine. This is termed in Buddhism the "self-deed and self-gain," or "self-make and self-receive." Heaven and hell are self-made. God did not provide you with a hell, but you yourself. The glorious happiness of future life will be the effect of present virtuous actions.

Fifth.   Cause and effect as the law of nature. According to the different sects of Buddhism, more or less, different views are entertained in regard to the law of causality, but so far they agree in regarding it as the law of nature, independent of the will of Buddha, and much less of the will of human beings. The law exists for an eternity, without beginning, without end. Things grow and decay, and this is caused, not by an external power, but by an internal force which is in things themselves as an innate attribute. This internal law acts in accordance with the law of cause and effect, and thus appear immense phenomena of the universe. Just as the clock moves by itself without any intervention of any external force, so is the progress of the universe.

We are born in the world of variety; some are poor and unfortunate, others are wealthy and happy. The state of variety will be repeated again and again in our future lives. But to whom shall we complain of our misery? To none but ourselves. We reward ourselves; so shall we do in our future life. If you ask me who determined the length of our life, I say, the law of causality. Who made him happy and made me miserable? The law of causality. Bodily health, material wealth, wonderful genius, unnatural suffering are the infallible expressions of the law of causality which governs every particle of the universe, every portion of human conduct. Would you ask me about the Buddhist morality? I reply, in Buddhism the source of moral authority is the causal law. Be kind, be just, be humane, be honest, if you desire to crown your future. Dishonesty, cruelty, inhumanity, will condemn you to a miserable fall.

As I have already explained to you, our sacred Buddha is not the creator of this law of nature, but he is the first discoverer of the law who led thus his followers to the height of moral perfection. Who shall utter a word against him? Who discovered the first truth of the universe? Who has saved and will save by his noble teachings the millions and millions of the falling human beings? Indeed, too much approbation could not be uttered to honor his sacred name.

B.   TWO SERMONS BY SOYEN SHAKU

In 1905 Soyen Shaku returned to America for nearly two years. He first stayed at the spacious home of Mr. and Mrs. Alexander Russell, called "The House of Silent Light," on a cliff overlooking the sea south of San Francisco. The Russells were interested in the spiritual paths of the East, and Mrs. Russell, during Soyen's visit, was the first American seriously to practice zazen (Zen meditation) and koans (the famous Zen riddles). Soyen Shaku was joined for a time at the Russell home by two disciples, Senzaki Nyogen and D. T. Suzuki.

In 1906 Soyen Shaku embarked on a speaking tour in the United States, which included a visit with Paul Carus in Illinois. The two sermons following are among those preached on this tour; they were translated and edited by Suzuki, and published by Carus. They show obvious efforts to find common ground with Christianity, yet retain the same emphasis on Buddhist rationalism and naturalism, mingled with just a touch of exotic language and transcendent vision, as the parliament address. Yet in a sense their culminating insight is that radical, paradoxical, and characteristically Zen realization that the Path to Enlightenment is nothing other than "the normal state of mind."

Ignorance and Enlightenment*

The fundamental idea of Buddhism is "to disperse the clouds of ignorance in order to make the moon of enlightenment shine out in her glory."

By ignorance Buddhism understands the assertion of self-will, which is the root of all evil and misery in this world. Self-will is ignorance, because it is blind to the truth that the world is a relative existence, that the self separated from other fellow-selves is non-entity, and that individuals acquire their reality in proportion as they penetrate the foundation of existence. This truth is ignored by the principle of self-assertion. A man who is self-assertive pushes himself forward without any regard to the welfare of his brother creatures; he hails himself when he reaches the heights of self-

---

*From Soyen Shaku, *Zen for Americans*, trans. D. T. Suzuki (LaSalle, Ill.: Open Court Publishing Co., 1974). Reprint of 1913 ed., entitled *Sermons of a Buddhist Abbot*, copyright © 1906. Pp. 126–45.

aggrandizement; but unfortunately he fails to perceive that his success is but the road to his final destruction. For self-assertion really means self-annihilation. We live in fact in the oneness of things and die in isolation and singleness.

In Christian terminology, selfhood is the "flesh," or "the old man"; such is the meaning when Jesus exclaims that "the spirit is truly ready, but the flesh is weak" (Mark xiv, 38), or when Paul speaks of "the old man which is corrupt according to the deceitful lusts" (Eph. iv, 22), or when the flesh is spoken of as profiting nothing (John vi, 63), or allusion is made to its infirmity (Rom. vi, 19), or to its not pleasing God (Rom. viii, 8), or to its lusting against the spirit (Gal. v, 17). Christians are not so intellectual as Buddhists, and therefore, philosophically considered, the terminology of the former is not so definite and to the point as is that of the latter. Besides, the adoption of popular terms often suggests a wrong conception which is not intended; for instance, the distinction between the flesh and the spirit has a tendency to a dualistic interpretation of life. To conceive the nature of the flesh to be diametrically and radically opposed to that of the spirit is not in accord with the essentially monistic teaching of Buddhism. Those who are prone to asceticism and self-mortification are as much condemned by Buddha as the followers of hedonism for being ignorant and far from attaining the path of enlightenment.

When the ignorance of self-assertion is removed, Buddhism teaches, the enlightenment of universal lovingkindness takes its place; and the arrogance, tenacity, indefatigability, and impertinence which characterize egotistic impulses are all converted to do service for the general welfare of humanity, and they will then assume different names as most desirable virtues. As soon as the veil of ignorance is raised, the glory of enlightenment which is love is revealed, and we do no more hanker after self-gratification. Why? Because the Buddha-intelligence is universal and works in every one of us to bring out the consciousness of oneness underlying all individual phenomena. We as individuals are all different; mine is not thine and vice versa; and in this sense egoism is true, and the assertion of self-will is permissible to that extent. But we must never lose sight of "the same God that worketh all in all," and "in which we move and live and have our being," for he is the source of eternal life and the fountain of love. "Not what I will, but what thou wilt," is the most fundamental religious truth, not only in Christianity, but in Buddhism. Not the assertion of self-will, but the execution of the will of that being in which we are all one, constitutes the condition of enlightenment.

We must not, however, suppose that the divine will becomes manifest only when all the lust and passions of the flesh are destroyed. This is the teaching of anchorites and not of Buddhists. What the latter teach is to make the inclinations of the flesh those of the spirit, so that there will be left no hiatus between the two. What one wills, the other wills, and no discord or mutual exclusion is then allowed. To express this more Buddhistically, ignorance does not depart when enlightenment comes in, but ignorance itself becomes enlightenment; self-will is not annihilated in order to make room for the divine will, but self-will itself assumes divinity.

In the beginning of this discourse, I said that the fundamental idea of Buddhism is to disperse the clouds of ignorance in order to see the moon of enlightenment in her glory. This may suggest the thought that ignorance and enlightenment are fundamentally different and mutually contradicting, and that one thing called ignorance goes out and another thing called enlightenment comes in to take its place, as these two do not agree. But in truth I have there followed the popular dualistic conception of the matter; and therefore let me repeat that in Nirvâna, according to Buddhism, there is not such distinction as light and shade, ignorance and enlightenment, coming and going. If there is anything in Nirvâna, it is all enlightenment, all purity, and an unconditioned freedom from selfishness. Accordingly, when one attains Nirvâna, which is the realization of the Buddhist life, ignorance itself becomes enlightenment and self-will the divine will. What we thought ignorance is now enlightenment; where we located the final abode of the ego-soul, we have now the fount of divine will. This may sound somewhat sacrilegious, but the Buddhists are such consistent and never-yielding monists that they do not shrink from carrying out their logic to the end; they are not at all afraid of the charge of blasphemy or irreligiosity likely to be preferred by some pious Christians.

This purification or illumination of self-will, however, must not be confused with antinomianism or libertinism. The latter is given up to the wantonness of self-will and not to the free activity of the divine will. What the pure-hearted do is always pure, while whatever comes from a heart defiled with egoism is defiled and irrational. There are many points in the religious life which make it very difficult to distinguish the latter from the ethical life, for both are so closely related. But we could consider the subjectivity of religion as most characteristically contrasted to the objectivity of ethics. The distinction between the self-will and the divine will must be personally felt and individually experienced. This may sound vague and be considered as taking refuge in the maze of subjectivism; but the fact is that religion has its foundation in our subjective life, and anything that relates to it lacks in definition and exactitude so typical of things objective and intellectual. Religion, when devoid of this mystical element, loses its irresistible fascination. Of course, we must not make it abide always in the camera obscura of imagination and mysticism. We must take it out in the broad daylight of science and subject it to an intellectual scrutiny. But we cannot for all that ignore the fact that there is something in religion which defies or escapes the most penetrating searchlight of intellectual analysis. And in this something there lies its charm, its raison d'etre, and its power to remove vexation of spirit.

Whatever this be, Nirvâna, in which the spirituality of a human being is fully realized, can be attained only after most strenuous moral efforts on the part of the aspirant. Intellectual knowledge can be acquired through an outside agency; we of latter days may be far wiser in this particular respect than all our venerable moral and religious teachers of bygone ages, such as Socrates, Plato, Buddha, and Christ. But the spiritual region lies within, and each of us must strive, through our own inner and individual efforts and not through any outside agency, to unfold ourselves and bring about enlightenment. We may have high ideals, but let us remember that they can be realized only after long discipline and untiring exertion. Let those therefore forever strive—those that wish to follow the fundamental idea of Buddhism.

When the scholar driveth away sloth by earnestness,
He attaineth to the palace of wisdom,
Sorrowless in the sorrowing world,
And the wise one, he, looks upon the ignorant,
Even as one on the mountain-peak looks upon one on the
        ground.
                                        —*Dharmapada*, 28.

Spiritual Enlightenment

There are many characteristic points of divergence between religion and philosophy, though they have so much in common that some scholars, broadly speaking, take religion for practical philosophy and philosophy for speculative religion. The difference between the two, however, is not merely that of practicability and theorization. It is, in my judgment, more deeply rooted and fundamental. What is it, then? I believe that that which makes religion what it is in contradistinction to philosophy or ethics consists in the truth that it is essentially founded on facts of one's own spiritual experience, which is beyond intellectual demonstrability and which opens a finite mind to the light of universal effulgence. In short, spiritual enlightenment is indispensable in religion, while philosophy is mere intellection.

By spiritual enlightenment I mean a man's becoming conscious through personal experience of the ultimate nature of his inner being. This insight breaks as it were the wall of intellectual limitation and brings us to a region which has been hitherto concealed from our view. The horizon is now so widened as to enable our spiritual vision to survey the totality of existence. As long as we groped in the darkness of ignorance, we could not go beyond the threshold of individuation; we could not recognize the presence of a light whose most penetrating rays reveal all the mysteries of nature and mind. The spirit has found that the light is shining within itself even in its fullest glory, that it even partakes something of this universal light, that it blundered miserably in seeking its own ground outside of itself, that "Alpha and Omega, the beginning and the end, which is, and which was, and which is to come," is no more nor less than itself. And it is through this kind of enlightenment only that we fully satisfy our inmost spiritual yearnings and groanings. Without this, religion loses its significance, becoming merely an applied philosophy or system of metaphysics.

The enlightenment which thus constitutes the basis of the religious life is altogether spiritual and not intellectual. The intellect in its very nature is relative and cannot transcend its own limitations. It is dualistic no matter how high it may take a flight. It always needs an object with which to deal, and it never identifies itself with it, for it cannot do so without destroying itself. There must be the "I" and the "not-I" whenever intellection takes place. Self-alienation or keeping itself aloof from the object on which it exercises itself is the raison d'etre of intellect, being its strongest as well as its weakest point. Its strongest point is seen in science and philosophy, while its weakest point revealed in religion. For religion needs a synthetic faculty by which it can comprehend the realm of particulars, the realm of constant strivings and eternal contradictions. Religion wants to understand and preserve life as it is found, and not to "dissect and murder" it as is done by the intellect. Religion wants to see and not to demonstrate; to grasp directly with her own hands and not to rely upon a medium; to see intuitively and not discursively. What is therefore asked for by a religious spirit is fact and not representation, enlightenment and not reflection; and this will be supplied by no amount of speculation and imagination. We must advance one step further beyond the limits and boldly plunge into the abysmal depths of the Unknowable.

Can a mortal being with his limited consciousness have an insight into a field without its ken? No; as long as he relies solely upon his intellectual faculty, he is forever barred from so doing. For the intellect is really superficial and cannot penetrate through spatial and temporal relations, nor can she free herself from the bondage of logical sequence; and therefore the inner life of our being is altogether unknown to the intellect. We cannot be said to know an object thoroughly by merely becoming familiar with all its attributes, qualities, potentialities, and what not. All these can be understood through the senses and the reasoning faculty. There yet remains a certain feature of the object, the knowledge of which alone completes our understanding of it. Philosophy and science have done a great deal for the advancement of our knowledge of the universe, and there is a fair prospect of their further service for this end. But they are constitutionally incapable of giving rest, bliss, joy, and faith to a troubled spirit; for they do not provide us with a complete knowledge of existence, and are unable to lay bare the secrets of life. What they teach concerns the shell and husk of reality. In order to satisfy fully our religious yearnings we must not stop short at this; we must appeal to a different faculty, which will reveal to us the inmost life of the universe.

Fortunately, we are in possession of this peculiar faculty which might be called the religious sense, and through the exercise of which we come to realize the significance of our existence. How unbearable life would be, if we were not allowed to have this religious faculty and yet we had to raise those spirit-harassing questions which could not be solved by logic!

The faculty seems to have all the essential characteristics of the feeling. It is intuitive and does not analyze; it is direct and refuses a medium of any form. It allows no argument, it merely states, and its statement is absolute. When it says "yes," the affirmation has such a convincing force as to remove all doubts, and even skeptically disposed intellectual minds have to admit it as a fact and not a whim. It speaks as one with authority. True, it has only a subjective value, which, however, is just as ultimate and actual as sense-perception. Being immediate, there is no other way to test its validity than that each experience it personally, individually, and inwardly. The sun is risen on the horizon and all that have eyes see it and harbor not the shadow of a doubt as to its presence there. The inner sense which I have called religious faculty makes us feel the inmost life that is running through every vein and every artery of nature; and we are completely free from skepticism, unrest, dissatisfaction, and vexation of spirit. We never try to raise a doubt about the true nature of the feeling and ask ourselves whether it is merely a phenomenon of mental aberration or due to a calenture of the brain. We simply feel, and nothing more or less is to be asserted or denied. And this is what constitutes spiritual enlightenment.

Mere talking about or mere believing in the existence of God and his infinite love is nonsense as far as religion is concerned. Talking and arguing belong to philosophy, and believing in its ordinary sense is a sort of hypothesis, not necessarily supported by facts. Religion, however, wants above everything else solid facts and actual personal experience. If God exists, he must be felt. If he is love, it must be experienced and become the fact of one's inmost life. Without spiritual enlightenment, all is an idle talk, like a bubble which vanishes under the least pressure. Without the awakening of the religious sense or faculty, God is a shadow, the soul a ghost, and life a dream. In Buddhism, this faculty is known as *Prajñâ*.

If we distinguish faith from knowledge, the latter can be understood as simply intellectual, while the former is intuition gained through the exercise of the Prajñâ. In knowledge subject and object coexist and condition each other; in faith they become one, there is identity only and no mutuality. Transcending the reciprocity of the "I" and the "not-I," the Prajñâ beholds the universe in its ultimate oneness and feels all forms of life in their essential sameness. It knows that the impulse it feels is the quickening spirit of all existence, and that the pulsation of sympathy which beats in response to outside stimuli is the source of universal animation. Why? Because the Prajñâ feels so by reason of its own constitution.

The dictates of the Prajñâ are final and there is no higher faculty in our consciousness to annul them. Faith is absolute within its own limits and the office of the intellect is to explain or interpret it objectively. Speaking religiously, faith is fact and has to be reckoned with as such. It is only when it wants to express itself that intellection comes in, and individual culture or personal equation makes itself felt. To a great extent, I feel that differences or quarrels among the so-called religionists concerning their confession of faith are due to personal differences in esthetic taste, intellectual calibre, and the influence of environment, while the fact of faith as such remains fundamentally the same with Christians, Buddhists, or Taoists. As everybody endowed with sentiency feels the ice cold and the fire warm, so what the Prajñâ sees or feels in its inmost being must be universally the same. God, Allah, Dharmakâya, Tao, Holy Ghost, Brahma, and what not, are a mere verbal quibbling over the same fact which is felt in the deepest depths of our being. The inner reason of things which creates or destroys the three thousand worlds in the same breath must be smiling at the human trifling over naught.

Spiritual enlightenment must not be confused with trance, a state of consciousness in which there is nothing but blankness. Those who have had no spiritual experience or who have not come to recognize in the awakening of Prajñâ something altogether unique in our subjective life-phenomena frequently speak of enlightenment as an abnormal psychical condition, and try to explain it under the same category as hallucination, somnambulism, self-suggestion, and the like. But the fact is that enlightenment is not a special psychic state which excludes or suppresses the ordinary exercise of other mental faculties. Enlightenment goes and must go along with all psychological phenomena. If enlightenment is to be gained through the suspension of mentation, religion is false and faith is barren. Enlightenment is enlightenment because it enlightens all our motives, desires, whims, determinations, impulses, thoughts, etc. It does not stand separate from other states of consciousness, sending its commands from a certain vantage ground. In an enlightened mind a feeling or thought as it occurs is purified and free from the taints of ignorance and egotism. Enlightenment is constant and not sporadic. It permeates every mental fibre and works without rest. It is not something extraordinary that takes place by fits and starts. Spiritual enlightenment sheds light on the very reason of consciousness, for it is not a particular event of our psychical life.

When a Buddhist scholar was asked what was the Path, he answered, "The normal state of mind." In other words, spiritual enlightenment consists in following the natural course of human activity, for the enlightened find the ultimate reason of existence in their desire to drink or to eat according to their natural appetite, in their sympathy for the misery and suffering which are endured by the ignorant masses, in their aspiration to fathom the mysteries of nature and life, in their ever-assiduous attempt to realize the ideals of lovingkindness and universal brotherhood on this earth, in their ever-varying devices to let each creation fulfill its inherent mission and rest in its reason of existence. The religiously ignorant behave outwardly just as the enlightened, for as far as intellect and morals go there is no manifested difference between the ignorant and the enlightened. But, spiritually speaking, there is a wide gap dividing them, because one knows what he is striving after while the other is blindly feeling his way, and again because one finds an unspeakable bliss in all his doings and thinkings and feelings, while the other labors under a peculiar sensation of uneasiness and compulsion which he cannot well define but feels at the bottom of his heart.

A person may be very learned in all things, and his philosophical knowledge may be very profound. He has studied all the ancient lore of wisdom, and has even formulated his own system of metaphysics in which he has incorporated all the results of his erudition and speculation. But from the religious point of view he is yet far from enlightenment, for his study is like that of the artist who has painted a dragon and forgot to put the eyes in. His elaborate delineation and coloring in various hues of this huge mystic animal have miserably failed to produce the effect desired and attempted, for the eyes are blank and show no trace of the fiery animation which is possessed by the monster. The scholar has neglected the most important factor that is absolutely necessary in making up the complete knowledge of the universe. He thought that he knew everything under the sun when he exercised his intellectual power to its full extent and considered existence from all the possible standpoints which his understanding could grasp. But, as I stated before, the knowledge of an object is not complete unless its inner life or reason is felt; in other words, unless the duality of a knowing mind and a known object vanishes, and life is comprehended as it is and not in its intellectual mutilation. Buddhism says that even a blade of grass trembling in the evening breeze cannot be known so long as we cling to this form of individuation and are unable to merge our particular selves with the self of grass. Buddha, it is reported, once brought a flower before an assemblage of his disciples and showed it to them without any comments whatever, and the entire congregation was bewildered what to make of this strange behavior on the part of their master, except Kâshyapa, who, thoroughly understanding the import of this incident, softly smiled and nodded. Thereupon the Buddha solemnly proclaimed, "I am in possession of the Eye which penetrates into the depths of the Dharma and the mysteries of Nirvâna. I now give it to thee, O Kâshyapa, that thou mayest guard it well." What sort of eye could it have been which was transmitted from Buddha to Kâshyapa and which made the latter comprehend something incomprehensible in the flower in Buddha's hand?

In this we see the discrepancy between philosophy and religion more and more accentuated. It is sufficient for philosophy to know, but religion demands more than that. When the existence or non-existence of God is *proved,* philosophers are satisfied, for they have made the utmost use of the intellect, which is their sole weapon of attack and defense. In fact, they sometimes show a disposition to deride those who disagree with them. But as long as there is some unutterable yearning in the human heart for something more real, more vital, more tangible than mere abstraction, mere knowing, and mere "proving," we must conclude that our consciousness, however fractional, is capable of coming in touch with the inmost life of things in another way than intellection. The existence of Prajñâ, the organ of spiritual insight, therefore, is admitted by Buddhism, and their religious discipline is directed towards the awakening of this faculty, which is rightly designated "the mother of all Buddhas," and "the sharpest sword that cuts ignorance and egotism."

But one must not imagine that there is consciousness, there is

Prajñâ, and there is enlightenment. In point of fact, they are all one simultaneous act of the universal reason. We speak of them as if they were three different things: the sentient being is endowed with consciousness, and this consciousness has the faculty to become acquainted with its own reason of existence, and the resultant mental state constitutes what is called spiritual enlightenment. Intellectually, this distinction of course is inevitable, but as a man actually experiences it, the only fact he is conscious of is that he is, not as a particular being separate from others, but as simply existing and living. Buddhist scholars call this exalted state of spirituality *çûnyatâ* = emptiness, or *çânti* = tranquillity, or *samâdhi* = contemplation.

A few words may not be amiss here to explain these terms, which have been frequently misunderstood by the outsider. "Emptiness" may suggest a deprivation of all mental operations as in the trance, and "tranquillity" a dormant, sleeping, or "not-yet-awakened" state of mentality, while "contemplation" tends to indicate a withdrawal or suspension of all psychical functions; thus making spiritual enlightenment a synonym of death or annihilation. Such misinterpretations as these, however, ever prove the inherent one-sidedness of the understanding and consequently its inability to lead us to the final abode of eternal reason which has really "no-abode." Buddhists use the term "emptiness" to describe the "deep things of God" which are absolute and not relative. For when we say, "he is," it may be taken as meaning that he is as we individuals are.

By "All is empty, quiet, and abiding in eternal contemplation," Buddhists understand that the ultimate reason of the universe as manifested in all forms of animation and intelligence knows no disturbance, no commotion, no transgression, in the midst of all the stirring-up and moving-on of this phenomenal world. This, again, I have to state, guarding against misapprehension, does not mean that there is something within each existence which like the axle of a wheel or like the kernel of a seed forms its central part and remains quiet or alive even when the peripheral parts are whirling around or going to decay. Buddhism most emphatically condemns this sort of dualism as heretical and evil-breeding. The ultimate reason is absolutely quiet when it is moving on; it is perfectly empty when it is filled to the brim; it is eternally one when it is differentiating itself into myriads; it has no abode whatever where it finds itself located, housed, and roomed. And there is nothing paradoxical or enigmatic in this statement; it is plain as daylight and simple as the logical axiom $a = a$. But to realize its truth one must be spiritually enlightened, must go beyond the narrow limits of intellection, must drink directly from the well of eternal vitality and find out personally how it tastes, bitter or sweet.

Let philosophers and theologians say whatever they wish concerning the existence, nature, and activity of God; let them speculate as much as they wish on the theology of the universe and the destiny of mankind and many other abstruse problems of metaphysics; but let you who earnestly aspire to know what this life really means turn away from those wise men and reflect within, or look around yourselves with an open heart which watches and receives, and all the mysteries of the world will be revealed to you in the awakening of your Prajñâ.

2.   NYOGEN SENZAKI:
SELECTED SHORT SERMONS

Nyogen Senzaki, among the greatest of Buddhist missionaries to America, came to the Buddhist teaching of impermanence early, and its sorrow turning to joy stayed with him. He was born in Siberia, of a Japanese woman and a Chinese or Russian father, in 1876, and found by a Japanese monk as an infant lying on a road beside the frozen body of his mother. Brought to Japan, he was adopted by a shipbuilder named Senzaki, but largely educated by monks. In 1896 he entered Soyen Shaku's monastery, and despite severe ill health grew under him in the monastic life.

After joining Soyen in America in 1905, he remained in the United States until his death in 1958. For the first twenty years of his stay, he taught no Buddhism formally, but learned American life from the ground up in ways typical of Japanese immigrants in those days. He worked as hotel porter, clerk, and manager, as cook, waiter, houseboy, and finally teacher of the Japanese language. Beginning in the 1920s, he established Zen meditation centers in San Francisco and Los Angeles. He also acquainted himself with American intellectual history, finding in pragmatism, as we have seen, an ideal preparation for the simple but profound realizations of Zen, which shine far beyond words or theory. Through his students he established Zen centers from New York to Hawaii. The following short talks by Nyogen Senzaki well reveal the luminous pragmatism of his Zen, which sits rather loosely toward the rationalism of his teacher while, with a master's light but sure touch, directs the student to Zen as life itself, lived with freedom and joy.

Dharmakaya*

In eighteenth-century Japan there lived a Buddhist scholar by the name of Torei. Although he had studied all existing sutras, he had been unable to attain enlightenment, because his mind persisted in aimless wandering about the universe, still the victim of dualistic ideas. Even a great scholar like Torei continued to cling to the world of desire, of form and of no-form. While on a theoretical level he firmly believed that these aspects of the universe were nothing but *Mu,* on a practical level he was unable to enter deeply enough into meditation, and so could not attune himself with Dharmakaya—that is, unite himself with the universe in its actual nothingness.

One day—all of a sudden—he cast off his clinging ideas and entered at last into the region of absoluteness. His mind became like a naked body, and for him Nirvana was "visible and present, inviting all to come and see," just as the Buddha had said. He was enlightened; he attained realization. Like the smashing of a glass basin or the demolishing of a house of jade, he was awakened and entered into the palace of nothingness. He found Buddha within him; he saw his original nature face to face; he heard the sound of one hand. Looking up at the sky and laughing loudly, he exclaimed: "Oh how great is Dharmakaya! How great and immense that which exists forevermore!" He wrote a Chinese poem, which translated into English would be:

Dharmakaya, Dharmakaya!
I see you as a mountain leaning on the sky.
I see you as a rapid, constantly running cascade.
The teaching of Buddha is my own now.
I am the master of this flowery spring.

---

*From L. Nordstrom, ed., *Namu Dai Bosa: A Transmission of Zen Buddhism to America* (New York: Theatre Arts Books, 1976, for Zen Studies Society), pp. 27–29, 31–50, 56–61. Reprinted by permission of Zen Studies Society.

When Buddha was alive in this world, some of his disciples—those enthusiastic in meditation—acquired realization without difficulty. Others, chanting "Buddham saranam gacchami," worshiped Buddha as someone superhuman. These disciples neglected their own Buddhahood, which lies within the hearts of all, awaiting only our cultivation of it. For these disciples, Buddha's words and actions were merely external paradigms. Chanting "Dhamman saranam gacchami," they became homeless monks, establishing the Buddhist Order in accordance with the laws and regulations Buddha had formulated. Having found a harmonious life in this way, they chanted "Sangham saranam gacchami."

After Buddha passed away, those monks who had forgotten their own inner treasure erected images of him and worshiped them as their teacher, chanting "Buddham saranam gacchami." Though beautiful of heart, these monks were blind to the higher wisdom; chanting "Dhamman saranam gacchami," they clung to the words of the Buddha, worshiping the sutras instead of their own Buddha-nature. Thinking that as long as they stayed within the Order they were leading a pure and happy life, they chanted "Sangham saranam gacchami."

Even today, in Ceylon, Siam and Burma, such monks can be found. They are keeping the Three Treasures, but theirs are merely historical treasures. They fail to realize that there is a real Buddha—Dharmakaya, the substance of the universe; that there are many millions of unwritten sutras in this world, manifesting the truth of this universe; and that there are many ideal stages of life that emerge in the course of human struggle. Although these monks call themselves Buddhists, in my eyes they are completely petrified, with no spirit, no life, no active power within them.

Bodhisattvas, you have chosen to be Zen Buddhists—that is, rational and practical Buddhists. Though you chant in the name of the Three Treasures just as Ceylonese monks do, your Buddha is not an object of hero-worship; your Dharma is not reducible to written sutras; and your Sangha is more than merely a group of monks and nuns. Buddha said: "If you try to see me through my form, if you try to hear me through my voice, you will never reach me. Such a person is a stranger to my teaching."

When you, as Bodhisattvas, chant "Buddham saranam gacchami," you should try to attune yourself with the universe, until you are able to see its substance as your own. When you chant "Dhamman saranam gacchami," try to perceive the unwritten laws of the universe. And when you chant "Sangham saranam gacchami," try to realize that your everyday life is nothing but your emancipated mind in action. Remember always that you are Bodhisattvas, and as Bodhisattvas stand three thousand feet taller than the petrified monks and nuns of Ceylon!

At the door of our Zendo in San Francisco hung a verse from a Chinese poem, the translation of which is:

> Who said Buddha passed away from us?
> If you enter into deep meditation,
> You will see him every day.

Once I saw a kakemono written by Tessu Yamaoka, a well-known Zen student who, though only an Upasaka or layman, almost reached the stage of Zen master. The English translation would be:

> Falling blossoms lie scattered on the ground.
> No one tries to sweep them up.
> Birds are singing the melody of spring.
> Undisturbed, the guest is at rest in his land of dreams.

Isn't this the picture of true calmness itself? Nirvana beckons from this verse. Of what use are millions of gold pieces in this land of calmness? What can you do with the trash of book-learning in this fairyland of everlastingness? Your fame, your beauty, all your so-called power and strength—these are merely the toys of a nightmare of the past. Unless you enter once into this world of nothingness, you will miss something. The gate of the palace of realization may be entered while sipping tea. Yes, in a cup of tea you may be fortunate enough to find Zen. Let's have some tea!

Realization

I have been asked to explain what realization is, but if it could be explained it would not be realization. While you are kneading the dough of your thoughts, you cannot enjoy the bread of realization.

Confucius said:

My friends, do you think I was hiding it from you?
No! I would never do such a thing!
It was only that you were unable to see it.

Walking through the forest of many thoughts, just keep on
walking until you find yourself cornered in a place that admits neither
of advance nor retreat. Here your knowledge will be of no avail.
Even your religion will be unable to rescue you. If you are really
eager to enter realization, just go straight ahead, holding tenaciously
to the question "What is realization?" March on bravely! Surrounded by enemies, use your own sword; in the center of the bat-
tlefield, carve out a way for yourself. There will come a time when
all of a sudden you will lose hold of your sword and at that moment—
behold! You will have gained your true self.

"All sacred books are like poor candles to the sun," said Ko-
sen, comparing them to his own realization. Jakushitsu once said:

Didn't I tell you it was there?
You could have found it without any trouble at all.
The south wind is warm;
The sun shines peacefully;
The birds warble their glad songs.
Spring blossoms in every treetop.

Zen is not a puzzle; it cannot be solved by wit. It is a spiritual
food for those who want to learn what life is and what our mission
is in this world. Mere scholarly pursuits will never lead to realization. Zen is not so much a religion as it is the essence of life itself,
the naked truth of the universe, which is none other than the experience of Mind.

He who feels uneasy in his inner life can come to Zen and find
clear understanding and real joy. Zen does not propagandize. There
is no need. All will come, sooner or later. Some will come from the
literary class, along with some deep thinkers. Sorrow and struggle
may lead others to Zen. But however you come, however you are
led to Zen, you must come with a clear conscience and a pure heart.
You must come with a desperate desire to see life as it really is; and
must not permit anything to keep you from this, no matter how many

blind alleys of religious creeds you may have stumbled into in the past.

You may read all the books in all the libraries in the world; you may write thousands upon thousands of pages of your own thoughts. But if your mind is not thoroughly clear; if your knowledge does not come from the real source—you will never know who you are, you will remain forever a stranger to your true self.

(undated)

In This Lifetime

I could show you my clenched fist and open it like this—and bid you all good night. Unfortunately, however, educated on this side of the Pacific, you Westerners are somewhat deficient in intuitive matters, and so I am forced to give as a substitute, dualistic explanations, though that's not at all the way to express Zen.

Man began by assuming that the things about which he wished to learn existed outside of himself. Wondering what *that* is, he established so-called "science," which is the study of thatness. Soon, however, he discovered that his science explained only *how* things are, not *what* they are, and so man turned inward. Seeking to understand what *this* is, he established psychology and epistemology. Together these constitute the study of thisness. But, paradoxically enough, when the mind itself thus became an object of study, it ceased being *this* and became *that*. The experience of true thisness had been rendered impossible by the very nature of man's science (which can only understand thatness).

Of course Zen monks in China and Japan do not traffic at all in thisness or thatness. Somehow they manage to live quite happily and peacefully, for all that! Do you want to know the trick? They dwell in the region of what is known as *suchness*. Here is a story:

One day Seppo, a Chinese Zen master, went to the forest to cut down some trees. His disciple Chosei accompanied him.

"Don't stop until your ax cuts the very center of the tree," said the teacher.

"I have cut it off!" answered the disciple.

Seppo said: "The old masters transmitted the teaching to their disciples from heart to heart. How is it in your own case?"

Chosei threw his ax to the ground and said, "Transmitted!"

The teacher suddenly took his walking stick and struck his beloved disciple.

See how intimate these two woodcutters are! Monks are by nature coworkers, whether meditating in a Zendo or laboring out of doors. Priests, on the other hand, are just like actors, cooperating beautifully onstage, but once offstage, fighting together like cats in the green room. This is why Buddha prescribed that a monk's life should be as simple as possible, and used his own life as the model. The two monks in this story are true followers of Buddha. Together they carry the lamp of Dharma, the wisdom of suchness. No doubt about it!

The teacher said: "Don't stop until your ax cuts the very center of the tree." He was an expert woodsman as well as Zen master. Many Americans are currently seeking Truth, visiting classes in philosophy one after another, and studying meditation under various Oriental teachers. But how many of these students are either willing or able to cut through to the tree's very core? Scratching halfheartedly around the surface of the tree, they expect someone else to cut the trunk for them. Such people should stay in church where they belong, praying to the Supreme Being so that It will do their work for them. Zen wants nothing to do with such mollycoddles!

Chosei had caught the sparkle of Zen before his teacher had even finished, and so he said, "I have cut it off!" He was such a quick worker that he thought, acted and spoke at the same moment. *This* is realization in this lifetime.

Seppo was pleased and said: "The old masters transmitted the teaching to their disciples from heart to heart. How is it in your own case?" Chosei threw his ax to the ground—now *that* should have been enough! I can't figure out why this upstart had to spoil everything by adding, "Transmitted!" The teacher's blow came in no time, and Chosei certainly deserved it. Man is destined to fall at the very moment he thinks he has attained the summit. Those who declare themselves as having attained something are not genuine Zen students. We say in Japan, "The mouth is the cause of all troubles." It sure is! When it takes in too much, it causes indigestion; when it speaks out too much, it hurts even a friend's feelings. Basho once wrote a haiku on this; here is an English translation:

When I say a word
Oh my lips shiver
In the cold wind of autumn.

Someone wrote a poem about this woodcutters' story; I will read it for you and so close my speech.

Chosei had a good ax.
It was sharp enough
To cut a stump in two
With a single stroke.
Seppo made his big stick
A whetstone to sharpen it even more.

Thank you.

(1949)

A Morning Talk

Three Zen monks, Seppo, Kinzan and Ganto, met one day in the temple yard. Seppo saw a water pail and pointed to it. Kinzan said, "The water is calm and the moon reflects its image." "No, no," said Seppo, "it is not water; it is not the moon." The third one, Ganto, turned over the water pail with his hands. The story ends here.

There is a gatha, which in translation might read:

The moon of the Bodhisattva,
Clear and cool,
Floats in the empty sky.
If the mind of a sentient being
Tranquilizes itself
And becomes like a calm lake,
The beautiful image of Bodhi
Will appear there in no time.

Kinzan was in the same mood as this gatha when Seppo pointed to the pail; so he said, "The water is calm and the moon reflects its image." What Seppo was pointing to, however, was not the pail so much as the Buddha-body itself, which pervades the whole universe. By pointing to the pail Seppo was drawing the curtains so the entire stage could be seen and so the play could begin. Thus he said, "No, no, it is not water; it is not the moon." What Seppo had in mind was noumenon, not phenomenon. Although Seppo improved upon Kinzan's response, Ganto wiped away all traces by turning over the water pail; his action vividly reveals the nature of true emancipation.

In the Vedanta one finds a pantheistic doctrine according to which Brahman is the ultimate reality, and all phenomena are real only in virtue of their relation to and unification with Brahman. From this point of view, nothing real exists outside Brahman. As it is expressed in the *Upanishads:* "There is One only, without Second." Seppo's view is similar to this Vedanta doctrine. Ganto's action goes beyond this kind of Vedanta monism by showing that ultimate reality admits of secondness as well; it is One in a sense which is not the opposite of Second, but is beyond the distinction between oneness and secondness. It has been said (I believe by Professor Takakusu):

> In Buddhism, a man does not join himself to Buddha to become one. He merely frees himself from his delusions and becomes Buddha. If a thousand persons attain realization, there are one thousand Buddhas.

This statement clarifies the Buddhist conception of oneness. D. T. Suzuki has said:

> To define exactly the Buddhistic notion of the highest being, it may be convenient to borrow the term coined by a German scholar, *panentheism,* according to which God is all and one and more than the totality of existence.

From a sermon of his teacher, Soyen Shaku, he quotes the following:

> Religion is not to go to God by forsaking the world, but to find Him in it. Our faith is to believe in our essential oneness with Him and not in our sensuous separateness. "God is in us and we in Him," must be made the most fundamental faith of all religions.

In this morning's story, when Kinzan says, "The water is calm and the moon reflects its image," one is reminded of the Gospel of John: "All mine are thine and thine are mine; and I am glorified in them." But these words carry with them the slight echo of separateness, and so Seppo insists, "No, no, it is not water; it is not the moon." For him, there is only One, without Second. But Ganto, having no patience with any form of conceptualization, overturns the pail to expose the thing itself! Such action is Zen in practical life.

Zen is not a sect or religion; nor is it a school of philosophy. Both Vedanta and pantheism would be better off if they had some Zen in them. Then they would be able to do better work for mankind. It is not enough to tell people that it is possible to become a Buddha. What Zen does is actually to produce Buddhas! One thousand realizations, one thousand Buddhas. I once asked Suzuki, "What is panentheism?" and he told me he had never used such a word—at least not as far as Zen is concerned. He thereby played the same trick Ganto did.

Genro wrote a poem about this story:

In the garden of willows and flowers,
On the tower of beautiful music,
Two guests are enjoying wine,
Holding their golden cups
Under the pale light of the moon.
A nightingale starts suddenly
From the branch of a tree,
Dew dropping from the twigs.

Fugai, Genro's disciple, comments: "Nightingale? No. It is a phoenix!"

(1952)

Moonlight Party

Every year on the full moon night in August, we have a meeting to commemorate Abe no Nakamaro, a Japanese youth who, for the first time in the history of Japan, went to study in China. His genius as a poet was recognized by the Emperor of China, and he was asked to stay, serving the royal family as a tutor. He stayed there thirty-four years, in this high and honorable position, associating with the men of letters of the era. He was a man of unselfish character. Even though he had left Japan when he was only sixteen years old, he still could not forget his mother country.

The Emperor was very much moved by his request to return and gave Nakamaro his consent with warm sympathy. Nakamaro gave away everything he had among his friends—even a sword he liked so much he carried it with him day and night. He took off his gorgeous robe and put on the plain blue dress of the student. To him, life in China had been only a dream now past; he was returning to the land of cherry blossoms with an empty hand and a pining soul. His friends saw him off at the seashore of Ming State; the beautiful moon rose above the vastness of the sea, casting its silvery light on the endless waves. He could not help expressing his feeling in native verse—even though he had not spoken his mother tongue in thirty-four years. The uta he composed would read in English:

Moon! Moon!
I see you now above the vast field of blue waves.
So, you are the same moon
I looked at in my home town of Kasuga,
Rising above Mikasa Mountain.
Though I have been getting older in this foreign country,
You still have the same beautiful face.

This poem remains in the memory of the people of Mikado's land, and will perhaps be remembered by them forever. Nakamaro's ship ran into a terrible storm that forced him back to China, where he remained for the rest of his life, without ever returning to his longed-for country of moonlight. Following Japanese custom, I have held these meetings commemorating Nakamaro on the evening of the full moon, and as a rule I tell stories about the moon.

I have a Zen poem for you, written by Jakushitsu, a Japanese Zen master of the fourteenth century:

No living soul comes near that water.
A vast sheet of water as blue as indigo!
When everything is quiet and calm, at midnight,
The moonlight alone penetrates into the waves

The moonlight alone penetrates into the waves
And reaches the bottom easily and freely.

Zen is something that must be experienced, not explained. Scientific knowledge is gained and developed by syllogism; but Zen, because it is based solely on intuition, has no need for such a roundabout method. For this reason I would like to call Zen the method of *monologism*, if I may invent such a word. While philosophical knowledge is based on relativity, Zen—and here I have in mind not some kind of theory, but a kind of dynamic action in the world—transcends relativity. Zen action, because it transcends space and time, belongs to the fifth dimension—actually, it is nondimensional altogether; and for this reason, it can be exemplified by any dimension, from the first to the fourth, and beyond.

We see the moon in the sky. Why do we call it "the moon"? Names mean nothing, after all. We could call it "a star" or "a small earth"; "a silver tray" or "a custard pie." Why not? Objectively, you say the moon occupies a certain portion of space, and time is a necessary condition of its being perceived. But *who* perceives the moon? The mind. But *what is this mind* that perceives the moon? Zen has a short-cut answer to this question. For the moment you formulate this question, you are already just a second too late. Thinking of the question, you are too late to find the answer. If you think and speak nothing, on the other hand, you are too early. So what can you do?

When your mind vibrates either positively or negatively, you are still far from the subject. Just look at the moon and get attuned with it. Then you will know your true self; you will know the whole universe. Nothing will be able to keep you from your true self.

In the West people love moonlight more than the moon itself. They thank "God" for having created it. In the East people love the moon itself so much they almost *drink* it. There is no harm in drinking the moon, is there? One Japanese poet once said:

Is the moon myself, or is myself the moon?
I know not.
The autumn night is clear
And the autumn wind is cool.

Buddha Shakyamuni was very fond of moonlit nights, and sometimes sat and meditated all night under moonlight. He preached in a great amphitheater, where everyone could enjoy the moonlight while listening to his teaching. He made a rule for his disciples, that they should organize their gatherings on the full moon night, to confess their wrongdoings to each other and discuss Dharma and Emancipation. These meetings were called Uposatha in Pali. Many sutras were preached under moonlight, among them the *Punnaka Sutra,* or *Sutra of the Full Moon.*

Zen masters, being successors to the Buddha, have always been fond of the moon too. Bodhidharma, the twenty-eighth successor of Buddha, has as his eighth successor a master named Baso. One evening Baso was enjoying the moonlight with three of his disciples.

The master asked: "What are you thinking of at this moment?"

The first one said, "Just praising the Buddha."

The second one said, "Just meditating."

The third one said nothing, leaving the room abruptly.

The master commented: "The first disciple has acquired the faith; the second is dwelling in the meditation; but the third transcends everything." Now, what are *you* thinking of at this moment?

Shelley speaks of "some world far from ours, where music and moonlight and feeling are one." It sounds beautiful—as far as it goes—but why seek elsewhere? We should be satisfied with our own world and with our own selves. Each one of us is standing at the center of the universe. The world belongs to everyone. My teacher, Soyen Shaku, wrote (and I translate):

> The whole universe will be cleared away as you sit in meditation. The silver moon rises above the mountain. The rich see it, and so do the poor. The wise do, and the stupid as well. But only Zen students understand the real light of the moon.

It is all very well and good to offer praise to the Enlightened One, but it is far better to cultivate your own inner self. Baso's first disciple had his own beautiful religion, the second, his own profound philosophy. But as for the third—what shall we say of him? Such silent eloquence! He certainly said a mouthful (without opening his mouth)! I cannot find suitable words of praise, so let us repeat Jakushitsu's poem. What is it talking about? It is up to you to find out by yourselves.

> No living soul comes near that water.
> A vast sheet of water as blue as indigo!
> When everything is quiet and calm, at midnight,
> The moonlight alone penetrates into the waves
> And reaches the bottom easily and freely.

(undated)

Three Pictured Fans

The first uta is "Searching for the Ox." My translation is:

> How and when it happened I do not know,
> But my Ox is gone!
> Searching for the stray Ox,
> I am now entering into the remote mountains of meditation.

Man recognizes in himself the loss of something precious. This is where the compilers of the Old Testament got the story of Paradise Lost. In Genesis, Christians blame the serpent's evil advice for Adam and Eve's expulsion from the Garden of Eden. But Buddhists blame nobody but themselves for their ignorance. Buddhists know it is their own lack of mindfulness that has caused the Ox to stray. Everyone of us is born with a wisdom that transcends all ideas and thoughts. This wisdom is symbolized in the Zen tradition by the Ox. For the Buddhist, the Tree of Knowledge is the dualistic mind. However, since the ground of this mind is nondualistic, is Mind itself, the Buddhist has no reason to condemn eating of this Tree, nor to blame dualism in general. Where it says in Genesis, "In sorrow shalt thou eat of it, all the days of thy life," Buddhism concurs, but with the significant qualification that if one succeeds in recovering his lost wisdom, sorrow ceases to exist. How man can recover this wisdom, which will enable him to live happily in the world, is what is depicted in these beautiful pictured fans.

The simple-minded student does not know how or when it happened, but he knows his Ox is gone, and feels a vague uneasiness at

the thought of its absence. The deeper his grief becomes, the higher
will his aspiration become. When his aspiration to recover his Ox
has been aroused, the pleasures of the six senses will no longer stay
him; temptations of wealth and fame will no longer sway his mind.
He will go onward, straightforwardly pursuing his lost Ox. Step by
step, the road of meditation will become more and more difficult.
There will be rocky hills to be climbed over. Above the valley a per-
ilous ledge awaits his attempt at passage. A dangerous wall of huge
rocks and stones threatens him. But he fears nothing, simply march-
ing on bravely, thinking neither of past, present or future, searching
for his Ox in an eternal present. Actually to experience this stage of
meditation is immediately to enter into the remote mountains of
Dhyana. Then one is a true Zen student, a hero of Zen. Having
passed the first koan in the Oxherding Series, one can dry his sweat
with the first fan.

The second uta is "Seeing the Traces." My translation goes:

Many a time I searched for the Ox
And wandered in the mountains.
At last I discovered the traces of the hoofs
Impressed here and there!

Not many persons search for the Ox. Among those who do,
only a fortunate few even discover its traces. In books or in actual
life, we may discover such impressions of the Ox, but often we
confuse these with traces of another sort. Many students wander
for years without seeing even traces of wisdom. Presuming to an-
nounce the Truth, the church bell invites all seekers. But the inside
of a church is the last place to find traces of the Ox! One has a
much better chance remaining outside, where one may detect shadows of the Ox passing through the crowd. You will never see the
Ox by going inside! In Rabindranath Tagore's translation of *The
Songs of Kabir* we read:

O servant, where dost thou seek me?
Lo! I am beside thee.
I am neither in the temple nor in the mosque.
I am neither in Kaaba nor in Kailash.

Neither am I in rites and ceremonies, nor in Yoga and
    renunciation.
If thou art a true seeker, thou shalt at once see me.
Thou shalt meet me in a moment's time.

Constant meditation gives one watchful eyes, ever ready to
catch a glimpse of the traces of truth. When the time comes—with
such eyes—one cannot fail to perceive, not only impressions of the
Ox, but the Ox itself.
    The third uta is:

At a spot in the spring field
Where the thready willow invited me
I discovered my long-lost Ox!

As with receiving tea, so with self-realization: you hold your
empty cup, you are ready; but you must wait for someone to pour
the tea. Self-realization, or bumping-squarely-into-your-true-self,
usually involves a so-called "karma-relation," in the same way that
drinking tea usually involves its being poured by someone.
    At the stage expressed by this third uta, one's meditation is ma-
ture. There is neither relativity nor absoluteness. You are now far
above both sameness and difference. You have nothing to receive
and there is nothing to receive you. There is no time—no space—
just one eternal *now*. The person in this uta had already entered into
this condition of readiness, but was still unable to attain realization,
until he came upon the weeping willow in the field. On the verge of
their awakening, some hear the sound of a temple bell; some glance
at a cloud in the sky. These are examples of karma-relation. Some
monks pass their koans under their master's beating whip; some attain it while washing their faces in the morning. No matter how hard
you try, however, you cannot find the karma-relation that will en-
lighten you by looking for it. Instead of seeking out this karma-relation, devote yourself to constant meditation, with no desire for attainment. Then the doors of the gateless gate will open for you by
themselves.

                                                                    (1939)

Buddha's Words, Buddha's Mind

Modern Buddhism may be divided into two parts: Buddha-Wacchana (Buddha's Words) and Buddha-Hridaya (Buddha's Mind).

Buddha Shakyamuni preached for forty-five years after having attained his realization. During the eight months of the dry season, he used to go from place to place, accompanied by a number of disciples, exhorting people and teaching them by parables and sermons. The time of the rainy season he always spent in one place, either the house of one of his disciples or in the gardens and groves bestowed upon the Sangha by some of the rich laymen or laywomen. Lay believers were called Upasakas or Upasikas, respectively, while monks were called Bhikshus, and the nuns, Bhikshunis. Some of these lay believers understood Buddha's teaching thoroughly and clearly, practicing what they had acquired in their everyday life without renouncing the world like monks and nuns. Such lay believers served their families, their communities and their countries, carrying the influence of Dharma into their worldly occupations.

Among these lay believers were philosophers, poets, statesmen and kings. The current of their thought assimilated other Indian philosophical ideas, and the product became the general body of Buddhism. There were great monks and nuns whose profound knowledge and unselfish deeds gave strength and power to this general body of teaching, helping it to progress in India. In the golden age of the teaching, the liberal and broad-minded Buddhists called themselves Mahayana Buddhists, calling those who were more conservative and narrow-minded, Hinayana Buddhists. *Mahayana* means "great vehicle," and *Hinayana* means "small vehicle." Mahayana Buddhism is positive and practical, while Hinayana Buddhism is negative and pessimistic. Mahayana Buddhism admits the possibility that everyone may become a Buddha in this life, while Hinayana Buddhism believes this must await some future life—at best, the next incarnation. The two currents of thought are both based on Buddha-Wacchana, Buddha's words.

Buddha-Hridaya is Buddha's Mind, the very mind of enlightenment he attained under the Bodhi Tree at the age of thirty-five. When one opens his inner eye, he will attain the original source of the teaching, and then both Mahayana and Hinayana teachings will become his own possession. For Buddhism is the teaching of realization, that in awakening lies man's only salvation. Unless you acquire your own enlightenment, the teachings of the thousands of Mahayana books will be for you mere speculation. And though you devote yourself to the Hinayana teaching, renouncing the world and living the rest of your life in a secluded monastery, unless you open your own inner gate by your own efforts, after your monkish body perishes you will have to start your endless travel in Samsara all over again—that is, you will remain in the world of birth and death, and be unable to enter Nirvana, the condition of true happiness.

There is no difference between Mahayana and Hinayana, man and woman, monk and nun; whoever strives hard enough will acquire the fruits of meditation. This is the teaching of Buddha-Hridaya.

Buddha-Wacchana and Buddha-Hridaya should work together, since obviously they are closely related to each other. For several hundred years after the death of the Buddha, the masters of Buddha-Wacchana were also masters of Buddha-Hridaya; but later on, this ceased to be the case, and the two became separated. Masters would specialize in one or the other, and so different lineages of scholars (Buddha-Wacchana) and patriarchs (Buddha-Hridaya) came into being. The speculations and arguments of the scholars, because unenlightened, tended at times to mislead their followers; but the patriarchs who carried the lamp of Dharma succeeded in preserving the pure teaching of Buddha Shakyamuni. There are now very few of these masters of Buddha-Hridaya left; they are the true teachers of meditation, and we call them Zen masters.

(1931)

Ripe, Unripe Fruit

Our seclusion week is nearing its close—there are only two days left. Faithful coworkers in Zen meditation, you have encouraged me throughout the past few days, and I appreciate this very much. Confucius said: "There are three friendships which are advantageous, and three which are injurious. Friendship with the upright, with the discerning, and with the sincere—these are advantageous; friendship with the man of specious airs, with the insinuatingly soft, and with the glib-tongued—these are injurious." A Buddhist Sangha is a group of friends whose friendships are advantageous, in the sense Confucius has so well defined. I am thankful for the privilege of being one of these Sangha friends, and for being able to keep myself free from injurious friendships.

As the good old Buddhist Shinran said: "I am not a teacher, but a member of this group of harmonious friends. I have neither disciples nor pupils of my own." Buddhist monks have no concept of home, but when good friends like you gather around me, I begin to feel as if I had indeed found a home. Like Hotei-San, I am a very happy monk. Have you ever seen a statue of a fat Chinese monk carrying a linen sack and smiling happily? In Chinatown the storekeepers call him "Happy Chinaman." That is Hotei-San. Someday I will tell you more about him. Actually, since you're talking right now to one of his cousins, you really don't need to hear much more! Instead, I will tell you a few stories about some other Chinese monks.

Whenever the great master Baso was asked, "What is Buddha?" he would reply: "That mind of yours is Buddha." If you ask me, I will make the same reply. Baso's answer should not be interpreted as some kind of philosophical idealism, however. He is not saying that the Buddha has no real existence; that it exists only in your mind. You have no mind you can claim as your own anyway! The reality of the Buddha could not derive from the reality of your mind, since in fact there is no such reality. What is your mind? It is not sensation, it is not perception, it is not consciousness—it is not any of the constituents associated with it. So when Baso said, "That mind of yours is Buddha," what could he have meant? What did he really mean? This is your koan, or theme for meditation. The other day I wrote an uta; I will translate it for you into English:

What is Buddha?
You should have looked before you asked.

Although Baso answered "That mind of yours is Buddha" no matter what the question or who the questioner, he was not one of those modern ministers who give the same canned—almost playful—response, "God is Love," no matter what they are asked. The difference is that with his words Baso was able to open the heart of anyone who questioned him; he was able actually and directly to touch the hinges of that person's mind. And, like a good sculptor, he did not need many tools.

Eighty masters were produced from among Baso's disciples. One of these was called Daibai. Upon having heard his master's words, Daibai put off his heavy burdens and retired to live in the mountains for many years, where he could enjoy and deepen his attainment. Like a true scholar, Daibai was in no hurry to market his knowledge or wisdom. Zen masters used to hide themselves in remote parts of the world, meditating in the deep mountains among trees and rocks, with monkeys and rabbits for companions. They did so not because they were misanthropic, but because they wanted to guard their Dharma against the dust of glory and fame. Modern students of religion are altogether too impatient. Without waiting for the fruit to ripen, they open up their stores and begin to sell their wares. Such unripened fruit is unhealthy, and may cause injury to those who do not know the difference.

Daibai was not one of these quick sellers. One day in the mountains a friend from his old monastery found him and was asked by Daibai: "What answer does our master give these days when asked 'What is Buddha'?" The visitor said: "Our teacher changed his answer recently. Now he says, 'That mind of yours is not Buddha.' " To this Daibai replied: "No matter what my old teacher says, I say: 'This mind of mine is the Buddha.' " I want all of you to think this one over.

The visiting monk returned to the monastery and told Baso what Daibai had said. Then Baso remarked: "I see now that big fruit has ripened." He must have been very pleased indeed to have uttered such admiring words.

Afterward, a monk asked Baso why he had begun saying, "That mind of yours is Buddha" in the first place. Baso said: "I wanted the children to stop their crying." The questioner continued: "When the children had stopped their crying, what would you say then?"

Baso answered: "That mind of yours is not Buddha."

"Suppose one neither cries nor wishes candy, then what would you say?"

The master rejoined: "There is nothing."

The questioner then asked: "If there were someone who neither cried, nor needed candy, nor clung to nothingness, what would you propose to him?"

The master replied: "Such a person would be a master already and could handle all situations by himself. What would I have to say to him!"

When Baso was very sick and nearing death, an attendant, greatly concerned, asked him how he felt. "Sun-faced Buddha, Moon-faced Buddha," was the reply. It is said that the Sun-faced Buddha lives for 1800 years, the Moon-faced Buddha only one night. So Baso was saying: "Some Buddhas have lived for one thousand eight hundred years, and some for only one night. What difference does it make if I die tomorrow?" Now while I certainly don't want any of you to die before you are very old, I do want you all to die like Buddhas—peacefully and calmly. We are performing birth-and-death every minute, every hour, every day and every year. Whether you make yourself a three-minute Buddha or a ten-year Buddha is up to you. Only two more days remain of this seclusion week. Make yourselves at least two-day Buddhas!

(undated)

Zen and American Life

Like a living current of vivid thought, Zen flows throughout our everyday life. You can touch it in ordinary conversation as well as in scholarly books. Sometimes a mere word expresses Zen almost too much; sometimes a silent mood speaks Zen quite loudly. When you sip tea smilingly, your cup may be brimful of Zen; when you have a spring breeze for your companion, you meet Zen face to face under the window. We have all had Zen from the very beginning; but unless the hinges of our minds turn gracefully to open our hearts, so that I can see myself in you and you yourself in me, there will be no Zen at all—no matter how long I speak, nor how patiently you listen.

Some of you may think of Zen as a sort of mysticism, but it is not at all a strange cult. In it there is neither miracle nor hokus-pokus. It is a way of life that all of you can experience. He who studies Zen controls his surroundings and never is controlled by them—that's all there is to it! I carry my nyoi the way an Englishman carries his cane. The word *nyoi* means "obedient servant"—it never complains, no matter how hot or cold it gets; it follows me wherever I go; it always meditates with me, and never engages in noisy argumentation. If I speak of entering into this nyoi, you would probably classify me as one of those Indian fakirs, or wonder how a stout monk like me could perform such a feat. In the Zen sense, I enter the nyoi when there is no nyoi separate from me, and when I am no longer separate from it. Unification is the key with which to unlock the door of Zen.

Here is a story to help make my meaning clearer. There once was a man who had a beard fifteen inches long. He was very proud of it and was always smoothing it down and caressing it. One day a friend asked him whether he slept with his beard outside or inside of the bedclothes. He was unable to answer. That night he experimented, first with his beard outside, then with it inside, but he could not remember where he kept it; nor could he decide which would be the best way! The beard he had been so proud of became a troublesome burden, and he was unable to sleep because of it.

When the mind functions smoothly, one is unaware of its functioning. An expert golfer forgets he is playing golf; a true poet forgets he has pen in hand, allowing the beautiful thoughts that flood his mind to weave their own brocade upon the page. Zen will make you an expert in the game of life. Thinking rightly, without hesitation, you will be able to live rightly, without embarrassment.

Zen is not a religion based on faith; nor is it some sort of speculative philosophy. It is the actualization of the unselfish life. The German scholar Rudolf Otto has said: "Zen monks are practical mystics. Their work is their religion and their religion is their work." In this regard, they are much like the Benedictine monks of the Middle Ages in Europe, who combined worship with labor as well.

Zen is not restricted to monasteries; it pervades everyday life and is found particularly in the area of the artistic. In Japanese culture it is everywhere—in chanoyu (the art of tea); in ikebana (the art of flower arrangement); in literature; in arts and crafts; in the military arts; and even in so-called physical culture too. It is not at all something unusual in Japan. Even boys and girls of high-school age practice Zen. This mind training will be continued throughout college and in their careers as well.

American ministers have tried in vain to convert young Japanese to modern clerical Christianity. They are wasting their time and labor! The reason for this has been well put by D. T. Suzuki in "Is Zen a Religion?"

> It is not a religion in the sense that the term is popularly understood. For there is in Zen no god to worship, no ceremonial rites to observe, no future abode where the dead are destined to, and, last of all, no soul whose welfare is to be looked after by somebody else. Zen is free from all these dogmatic and religious encumbrances.

This is why Zen students make such tough customers for Christian missionaries!

Confucius said:

> At fifteen I had my mind bent on learning. At thirty I stood firm. At forty I had no doubts. At fifty I knew the decrees of heaven. At sixty my ear was an obedient organ for the reception of truth. At seventy I could follow what my heart desired without transgressing what was right.

Buddhists don't want to wait until they are seventy before accomplishing their mind training. As Buddha said:

> If you are brave enough to strip off your delusions, you will be Buddha at that moment; but if you cling to the lukewarm teachings to which you are attracted because of your own selfish ideas, and walk back and forth in the blind alleys of faiths and beliefs of various kinds, you will never be able to get your emancipation.

The true aim of Buddhism is realization and nothing else. In the course of time, however, Buddhism degenerated and became like other religions: an elaborate church system was formed, and strange, impure elements came to be introduced which distorted the original teaching. Modern Japanese Buddhist sects exhibit this tendency to stray from the mainstream. But Zen is the only one that preserves the essence of Buddhism, which is none other than the fact of Buddha's

Enlightenment. So I dare say, if you wish to study Japanese Buddhism, study Zen first!

In general, "pious" Christians are unable to enter the gate of Zen, because they cling too much to religious conventions. Of course, there have been exceptions—Richard of St. Victor, for example, who said: "If thou wishest to search out the deep things of God, search out the depths of thine own spirit." The French novelist Victor Hugo expressed the same idea by saying: "The way to ascend to God is to descend into oneself." These quotations express the first stage of Zen. In Meister Eckhardt's "The eye with which I see God is the eye with which God sees me," we get a glimpse of still higher stages of Zen (which Meister Eckhardt was able to enter into without difficulty). So apparently it is not impossible for Christians to understand Zen—just very difficult. . . .

When I first came to this country I was told that America had no philosophy of its own; that its thought was a merely derivative reflection of the thought of other countries and cultures. But I have found out that this is not wholly true. America has had philosophers as well as original thinkers who were true makers of history, even though their influence may not have extended abroad. In particular, I have in mind the American freethinkers, from Thomas Paine to Robert Ingersoll, whose books I enjoy reading very much. I also admire a great deal the American Transcendentalism of Ralph Waldo Emerson. It was after having read these writers and philosophers that I at last came upon William James's Pragmatism—the philosophy of practicality, the gospel of energy, whose chief criterion is success. Zen and American Pragmatism have much in common. Just as Pragmatism, according to James, was a new name for an old thought, so I say Zen is an old name for a new thought!

Americans in general are lovers of freedom and equality; for this reason, they make natural Zen students. There are eight aspects of American life and character that make America fertile ground for Zen:

1. American philosophy is practical.
2. American life does not cling to formality.
3. The majority of Americans are optimists.
4. Americans love nature.

5. They are capable of simple living, being both practical and efficient.
6. Americans consider true happiness to lie in universal brotherhood.
7. The American conception of ethics is rooted in individual morality.
8. Americans are rational thinkers.

Pragmatism is truly an indigenous American philosophy. At the same time, however, it is but another name for one manifestation of the sparkling rays of Zen in the actual, practical world.

A Thursday Night Lecture

It gives me great pleasure to meditate with you all, on this the first night of the New Year.

A Zen student should be someone of very few words—the fewer the better. I could open my hands like this and close the meeting silently. But since our aim at meetings like this is to interpret Zen rather than actually to show it in action, I shall do my best to explain in words this peculiar subject called "Zen Buddhism."

I have here a Zen poem by Jakushitsu; the English translation goes:

Didn't I tell you it was there?
You could have found it without trouble, after all.
The south wind is warm;
The sun shines peacefully;
The birds warble their glad songs.
Spring blossoms in the treetops.

Once more—I know you like it. (He repeats the poem.) But now let's translate this poem into simpler, up-to-the-minute San Francisco language: "Happy New Year to you all!" This is what it's saying, right?

Once upon a time a student of Buddhism asked his master: "What is the one straight passage to Buddhism?" The master replied with a Chinese word meaning "most intimate." Very simple dialogue, no? In another anecdote, a master was asked: "What is

Buddhism?'' The master answered with a word meaning ''Walk on!'' or ''Go on!'' Or in good old American slang—''Beat it!''

Another master was asked, ''Where is your Buddhism?'' and he answered, ''Everywhere.'' So you see Buddhism always expresses itself in the shortest way possible—*no word at all* would be best of all. As I said before, I could open my hands like this and bid you all good night. But this would be to imitate another master's method of teaching, and—perhaps unfortunately for me—this is not allowed in Buddhism. You must create your own thought and express it in your own words. What you say must come directly from your own inner self.

The most intimate relative of yours is *you*. One cannot get rid of oneself. You may estrange your friends; forget your brothers and sisters; drive away your children; run away from your parents; divorce your wife or husband. But how in the world can you get rid of yourself! One must solve one's own problems and work out one's own emancipation by oneself. The only way to open the gate of Buddhism is to use your own working mind as the precious key.

Buddhism does not believe in the existence of some ''Supreme Being.'' It worships nothing but the inner self of each and every one of us. A student of Buddhism should not ask anyone for help in acquiring enlightenment. If he works hard and strives constantly, he cannot but attain emancipation. Is this not the most intimate, the most straightforward passage for everyone?

Buddhism is the most bold and radical form of all freethinking. In Buddhism, thought, word and action are one. It is no wonder, then, that the master said, ''Walk on!'' when asked ''What is Buddhism?'' A thought without action is a wasted corpse; a word without thought and action is a dead, useless word.

Man is like a bicyclist: He is safe from falling only as long as he keeps on going. If we hold our will like an iron wall against all kinds of trouble; if our breathing is in harmony with the rhythm of right-mindedness, every action of ours will become part of the progressive current of the universe, and we will see Buddhism around us wherever we are. Then if anyone asks us where our Buddhism is, we can reply: ''Our Buddhism is everywhere.''

(undated)

3. ALAN WATTS:
BEAT ZEN, SQUARE ZEN, AND ZEN

Alan Watts (1915–1973) was a potent presence in the American East-
ern spiritual scene from the forties through the sixties, and through his
widely popular books the presence has lingered past his death. Born and
educated in England, in the 1930s he encountered such English Buddhists
as Christmas Humphreys, who introduced him to D. T. Suzuki on the lat-
ter's visit to London in 1936. On the eve of World War II, having married
an American woman (the daughter of Ruth Fuller, later Ruth Fuller Sasaki,
an important Zennist in her own right), Watts came to America.

Despite his Eastern interests, Watts undertook study for the Episcopal
priesthood, being ordained in 1945. He then served for five years as Epis-
copal chaplain at Northwestern University; during this period his wrestlings
with the reconciliation of Buddhism and Christianity produced a couple of
highly original, and in their own way brilliant, works of religious philos-
ophy, Behold the Spirit (1947) and The Supreme Identity (1950). By 1950,
however, his first marriage and his vocation to the priesthood both had
soured. He left them, reconstructing a life in the San Francisco area as
teacher, lecturer, and writer. While he never formally embraced Zen, in the
1950s he was identified with the Zen, largely influenced by Suzuki, then in
vogue among intellectuals and Beat writers. His book The Way of Zen
(1957) was an important exposition of Zen in the Suzuki tradition, stressing
less rigorous practice than Zen as a concept-shattering awareness linked to
aesthetic sensitivity and inner freedom.

At the same time, Watts held back from fully endorsing the way of
the Beat Zennists, supremely portrayed in Jack Kerouac's highly autobio-
graphical novel The Dharma Bums. This book centers on the figure of Gary
Snyder, thinly disguised in the novel as Japhy Ryder, the later Pulitzer
Prize–winning poet who is here represented as the consummate American
Zen Buddhist, virtually a bodhisattva. Watts yields to no one in his admi-
ration of Snyder. (Indeed, in his autobiography, In My Own Way, he pays
him what must be one of the most remarkable tributes in all literature: "I
can only say that a universe which has manifested Gary Snyder could never
be called a failure.") Yet he contended that the spiritually sensitive but un-
even Kerouac had drawn only an imperfect portrait of the roughneck saint
that was Snyder, wrongly making him patron of a hedonistic Beat caricature
of Zen as unbalanced in its way as the rulebook "Square" Zen of the mon-
asteries is in its.

Sorting this out is the burden of the pamphlet by Alan Watts here re-
produced. While its immediate reference is to the fifties scene, Beat Zen,
Square Zen, and Zen remained in print for decades after its first publication.

It beautifully delineates for the Western novice various strands of Zen, and the appeal of that Eastern path in the West, while helping one to find a way between its extremes—or to jump into an extreme if that is what one wants. At the same time, it illustrates the literary grace that very seldom failed Watts in his many books on the convoluted trails of the spirit.

Beat Zen, Square Zen, and Zen*

It is as difficult for Anglo-Saxons as for the Japanese to absorb anything quite so Chinese as Zen. For though the word "Zen" is Japanese and though Japan is now its home, Zen Buddhism is the creation of T'ang dynasty China. I do not say this as a prelude to harping upon the incommunicable subtleties of alien cultures. The point is simply that people who feel a profound need to justify themselves have difficulty in understanding the viewpoints of those who do not, and the Chinese who created Zen were the same kind of people as Lao-tzu, who, centuries before, had said, "Those who justify themselves do not convince." For the urge to make or prove oneself right has always jiggled the Chinese sense of the ludicrous, since as both Confucians and Taoists—however different these philosophies in other ways—they have invariably appreciated the man who can "come off it." To Confucius it seemed much better to be human-hearted than righteous, and to the great Taoists, Lao-tzu and Chuang-tzu, it was obvious that one could not be right without also being wrong, because the two were as inseparable as back and front. As Chuang-tzu said, "Those who would have good government without its correlative misrule, and right without its correlative wrong, do not understand the principles of the universe."

To Western ears such words may sound cynical, and the Confucian admiration of "reasonableness" and compromise may appear to be a weak-kneed lack of commitment to principle. Actually they reflect a marvelous understanding and respect for what we call the balance of nature, human and otherwise—a universal vision of life

*From Alan Watts, *Beat Zen, Square Zen, and Zen* (San Francisco: City Lights Books). Copyright © Alan Watts, 1959. Reprinted by permission of Mary Jane Watts.

as the Tao or way of nature in which the good and the evil, the creative and the destructive, the wise and the foolish are the inseparable polarities of existence. "Tao," said the *Chung-yung,* "is that from which one cannot depart. That from which one can depart is not the Tao." Therefore wisdom did not consist in trying to wrest the good from the evil but in learning to "ride" them as a cork adapts itself to the crests and troughs of the waves. At the roots of Chinese life there is a trust in the good-and-evil of one's own nature which is peculiarly foreign to those brought up with the chronic uneasy conscience of the Hebrew-Christian cultures. Yet it was always obvious to the Chinese that a man who mistrusts himself cannot even trust his mistrust, and must therefore be hopelessly confused.

For rather different reasons, Japanese people tend to be as uneasy in themselves as Westerners, having a sense of social shame quite as acute as our more metaphysical sense of sin. This was especially true of the class most attracted to Zen, the *samurai.* Ruth Benedict, in that very uneven work *Chrysanthemum and Sword,* was, I think, perfectly correct in saying that the attraction of Zen to the *samurai* class was its power to get rid of an extremely awkward self-consciousness induced in the education of the young. Part-and-parcel of this self-consciousness is the Japanese compulsion to compete with oneself—a compulsion which turns every craft and skill into a marathon of self-discipline. Although the attraction of Zen lay in the possibility of liberation from self-consciousness, the Japanese version of Zen fought fire with fire, overcoming the "self observing the self" by bringing it to an intensity in which it exploded. How remote from the regimen of the Japanese Zen monastery are the words of the great T'ang master Lin-chi:

> In Buddhism there is no place for using effort. Just be ordinary and nothing special. Eat your food, move your bowels, pass water, and when you're tired go and lie down. The ignorant will laugh at me, but the wise will understand.

Yet the spirit of these words is just as remote from a kind of Western Zen which would employ this philosophy to justify a very self-defensive Bohemianism.

There is no single reason for the extraordinary growth of Western interest in Zen during the last twenty years. The appeal of Zen arts to the "modern" spirit in the West, the work of Suzuki, the war with Japan, the itchy fascination of "Zen-stories," and the attraction of a nonconceptual, experiential philosophy in the climate of scientific relativism—all these are involved. One might mention, too, the affinities between Zen and such purely Western trends as the philosophy of Wittgenstein, Existentialism, General Semantics, the metalinguistics of B. L. Whorf, and certain movements in the philosophy of science and in psychotherapy. Always in the background there is our vague disquiet with the artificiality or "antinaturalness" of both Christianity, with its politically ordered cosmology, and technology, with its imperialistic mechanization of a natural world from which man himself feels strangely alien. For both reflect a psychology in which man is identified with a conscious intelligence and will standing apart from nature to control it, like the architect-God in whose image this version of man is conceived. The disquiet arises from the suspicion that our attempt to master the world from outside is a vicious circle in which we shall be condemned to the perpetual insomnia of controlling controls and supervising supervision *ad infinitum.*

To the Westerner in search of the reintegration of man and nature there is an appeal far beyond the merely sentimental in the naturalism of Zen—in the landscapes of Ma-yuan and Sesshu, in an art which is simultaneously spiritual and secular, which conveys the mystical in terms of the natural, and which, indeed, never even imagined a break between them. Here is a view of the world imparting a profoundly refreshing sense of wholeness to a culture in which the spiritual and the material, the conscious and the unconscious, have been cataclysmically split. For this reason the Chinese humanism and naturalism of Zen intrigue us much more strongly than Indian Buddhism or Vedanta. These, too, have their students in the West, but their followers seem for the most part to be displaced Christians—people in search of a more plausible philosophy than Christian supernaturalism to carry on the essentially Christian search for the miraculous. The ideal man of Indian Buddhism is clearly a superman, a *yogi* with absolute mastery of his own nature, according perfectly with the science-fiction ideal of "men beyond mankind." But the Buddha or awakened man of Chinese Zen is "ordinary and nothing special"; he is humorously human like the Zen tramps portrayed by Mu-chi and Liang-k'ai. We like this because here, for the first time, is a conception of the holy man and sage who is not impossibly remote, not superhuman but fully human, and, above all, not a solemn and sexless ascetic. Furthermore, in Zen the *satori* experience of awakening to our "original inseparability" with the universe seems, however elusive, always just round the corner. One has even met people to whom it has happened, and they are no longer mysterious occultists in the Himalayas nor skinny *yogis* in cloistered *ashrams*. They are just like us, and yet much more at home in the world, floating much more easily upon the ocean of transience and insecurity.

Above all, I believe that Zen appeals to many in the post-Christian West because it does not preach, moralize, and scold in the style of Hebrew-Christian prophetism. Buddhism does not deny that there is a relatively limited sphere in which human life may be improved by art and science, reason and good-will. However, it regards this sphere of activity as important but nonetheless subordinate to the comparatively limitless sphere in which things are as they are, always have been, and always will be—a sphere entirely beyond the categories of good and evil, success and failure, and individual health and sickness. On the one hand, this is the sphere of the great universe. Looking out into it at night, we make no comparisons between right and wrong stars, nor between well and badly arranged constellations. Stars are by nature big and little, bright and dim. Yet the whole thing is a splendor and a marvel which sometimes makes our flesh creep with awe. On the other hand, this is also the sphere of human, everyday life which we might call existential.

For there is a standpoint from which human affairs are as much beyond right and wrong as the stars, and from which our deeds, experiences, and feelings can no more be judged than the ups and downs of a range of mountains. Though beyond moral and social valuation, this level of human life may also be seen to be just as marvelous and uncanny as the great universe itself. This feeling may become particularly acute when the individual ego tries to fathom its own nature, to plumb the inner sources of its own actions and consciousness. For here it discovers a part of itself—the inmost and greatest part—which is strange to itself and beyond its understanding and control. Odd as it may sound, the ego finds that its own center and nature is beyond itself. The more deeply I go into myself, the more I am not myself, and yet this is the very heart of me. Here I find my own inner workings functioning of themselves, sponta- neously, like the rotation of the heavenly bodies and the drifting of the clouds. Strange and foreign as this aspect of myself at first seems to be, I soon realize that it *is* me, and much more me than my su- perficial ego. This is not fatalism or determinism, because there is no longer anyone being pushed around or determined; there is noth- ing that this deep "I" is not doing. The configuration of my nervous- system, like the configuration of the stars, happens of itself, and this "itself" is the real "myself."

From this standpoint—and here language reveals its limitations with a vengeance—I find that I cannot help doing and experiencing, quite freely, what is always "right," in the sense that the stars are always in their "right" places. As Hsiang-yen put it,

There's no use for artificial discipline,
For, move as I will, I manifest the ancient Tao.

At this level, human life is beyond anxiety, for it can never make a mistake. If we live, we live; if we die, we die; if we suffer, we suffer; if we are terrified, we are terrified. There is no problem about it. A Zen "master" was once asked, "It is terribly hot, and how shall we escape the heat?" "Why not," he answered, "go to the place where it is neither hot nor cold?" "Where is that place?" "In summer we sweat; in winter we shiver." In Zen one does not feel guilty about dying, or being afraid, or disliking the heat. At the same time, Zen does not insist upon this point of view as something which one *ought* to adopt; it does not preach it as an ideal. For if you don't understand it, your very not understanding is also IT. There would be no bright stars without dim stars, and, without the sur- rounding darkness, no stars at all.

The Hebrew-Christian universe is one in which moral urgency, the anxiety to be right, embraces and penetrates everything. God, the Absolute itself, is good as against bad, and thus to be immoral or in the wrong is to feel oneself an outcast not merely from human society but also from existence itself, from the root and ground of life. To be in the wrong therefore arouses a metaphysical anxiety and sense of guilt—a state of eternal damnation—utterly disproportionate to the crime. This metaphysical guilt is so insupportable that it must eventually issue in the rejection of God and of his laws—which is just what has happened in the whole movement of modern secularism, materialism, and naturalism. Absolute morality is profoundly destructive of morality, for the sanctions which it invokes against evil are far, far too heavy. One does not cure the headache by cutting off the head. The appeal of Zen, as of other forms of Eastern philosophy, is that it unveils behind the urgent realm of good and evil a vast region of oneself about which there need be no guilt or recrimination, where at last the self is indistinguishable from God.

But the Westerner who is attracted by Zen and who would understand it deeply must have one indispensable qualification: he must understand his own culture so thoroughly that he is no longer swayed by its premises unconsciously. He must really have come to terms with the Lord God Jehovah and with his Hebrew-Christian conscience so that he can take it or leave it without fear or rebellion. He must be free of the itch to justify himself. Lacking this, his Zen will be either "beat" or "square," either a revolt from the culture and social order or a new form of stuffiness and respectability. For Zen is above all the liberation of the mind from conventional thought, and this is something utterly different from rebellion against convention, on the one hand, or adapting foreign conventions, on the other.

Conventional thought is, in brief, the confusion of the concrete universe of nature with the conceptual things, events, and values of linguistic and cultural symbolism. For in Taoism and Zen the world is seen as an inseparably interrelated field or continuum, no part of which can actually be separated from the rest or valued above or below the rest. It was in this sense that Hui-neng, the Sixth Patriarch, meant that "fundamentally not one thing exists," for he realized that things are *terms* not entities. They exist in the abstract world of thought, but not in the concrete world of nature. Thus one who actually perceives or feels this to be so no longer feels that he is an ego, except by definition. He sees that his ego is his *persona* or social role, a somewhat arbitrary selection of experiences with which he has been taught to identify himself. (Why, for example, do we say "I think" but not "I am beating my heart"?) Having seen this, he continues to play his social role without being taken in by it. He does not precipitately adopt a new role or play the role of having no role at all. He plays it cool.

The "beat" mentality as I am thinking of it is something much more extensive and vague than the hipster life of New York and San Francisco. It is a younger generation's nonparticipation in "the American Way of Life," a revolt which does not seek to change the existing order but simply turns away from it to find the significance of life in subjective experience rather than objective achievement. It contrasts with the "square" and other-directed mentality of beguilement by social convention, unaware of the correlativity of right and wrong, of the mutual necessity of capitalism and communism to each other's existence, of the inner identity of puritanism and lechery, or of, say, the alliance of church lobbies and organized crime to maintain laws against gambling.

Beat Zen is a complex phenomenon. It ranges from a use of Zen for justifying sheer caprice in art, literature, and life to a very forceful social criticism and "digging of the universe" such as one may find in the poetry of Ginsberg, Whalen and Snyder, and, rather unevenly, in Kerouac, who is always a shade too self-conscious, too subjective, and too strident to have the flavor of Zen.

When Kerouac gives his philosophical final statement, "I don't know. I don't care. And it doesn't make any difference"—the cat is out of the bag, for there is a hostility in these words which clangs with self-defense. But just because Zen truly surpasses convention and its values, it has no need to say "To hell with it," nor to underline with violence the fact that anything goes.

It is indeed the basic intuition of Zen that there is an ultimate standpoint from which "anything goes." In the celebrated words of the master Yun-men, "Every day is a good day." Or as is said in the *Hsin-hsin Ming:*

> If you want to get the plain truth,
> Be not concerned with right and wrong.
> The conflict between right and wrong
> Is the sickness of the mind.

But this standpoint does not exclude and is not hostile towards the distinction between right and wrong at other levels and in more limited frames of reference. The world is seen to be beyond right and wrong when it is not framed: that is to say, when we are not looking at a particular situation by itself—out of relation to the rest of the universe. Within this room there is a clear difference between up and down; out in interstellar space there is not. Within the conventional limits of a human community there are clear distinctions between good and evil. But these disappear when human affairs are seen as part and parcel of the whole realm of nature. Every framework sets up a restricted field of relationships, and restriction is law or rule.

Now a skilled photographer can point his camera at almost any scene or object and create a marvelous composition by the way in which he frames and lights it. An unskilled photographer attempting the same thing creates only messes, for he does not know how to place the frame, the border of the picture, where it will be in relation to the contents. How eloquently this demonstrates that as soon as we introduce a frame anything does *not* go. But every work of art involves a frame. A frame of some kind is precisely what distinguishes a painting, a poem, a musical composition, a play, a dance, or a piece of sculpture from the rest of the world. Some artists may argue that they do not want their works to be distinguishable from the total universe, but if this be so they should not frame them in galleries and concert halls. Above all they should not sign them nor sell them. This is as immoral as selling the moon or signing one's name to a mountain. (Such an artist may perhaps be forgiven if he knows what he is doing, and prides himself inwardly, not on being a poet or painter, but a competent crook.) Only destructive little boys and vulgar excursionists go around initialling the trees.

Today there are Western artists avowedly using Zen to justify the indiscriminate framing of simply anything—blank canvases, totally silent music, torn up bits of paper dropped on a board and stuck where they fall, or dense masses of mangled wire. The work of the composer John Cage is rather typical of this tendency. In the name of Zen, he has forsaken his earlier and promising work with the "prepared piano," to confront audiences with eight Ampex tape-recorders simultaneously bellowing forth random noises. There is, indeed, a considerable therapeutic value in allowing oneself to be deeply aware of any sight or sound that may arise. For one thing, it brings to mind the marvel of seeing and hearing as such. For another, the profound willingness to listen to or gaze upon anything at all frees the mind from fixed preconceptions of beauty, creating, as it were, a free space in which altogether new forms and relationships may emerge. But this is therapy; it is not yet art. It is on the level of the random ramblings of a patient on the analyst's couch: very important indeed as therapy, though it is by no means the aim of psychoanalysis to substitute such ramblings for conversation and literature. Cage's work would be redeemed if he framed and presented it as a kind of group session in audio-therapy, but as a concert it is simply absurd. One may hope, however, that *after* Cage has, by such listening, set his own mind free from the composer's almost inevitable plagiarism of the forms of the past, he will present us with the new musical patterns and relationships which he has not yet uttered.

Just as the skilled photographer often amazes us with his lighting and framing of the most unlikely subjects, so there are painters and writers in the West, as well as in modern Japan, who have mastered the authentically Zen art of controlling accidents. Historically this first arose in the Far-East in the appreciation of the rough texture of brush-strokes in calligraphy and painting, and in the accidental running of the glaze on bowls made for the tea-ceremony. One of the classical instances of this kind of thing came about through the shattering of a fine ceramic tea-caddy, belonging to one of the old Japanese tea-masters. The fragments were cemented together with gold, and its owner was amazed at the way in which the random network of thin gold lines enhanced its beauty. It must be remembered, however, that this was an *objet trouvé*—an accidental effect *selected* by a man of exquisite taste, and treasured as one might treasure and exhibit a marvelous rock or a piece of driftwood. For in the Zen-inspired art of *bonseki* or rock-gardening, the stones are selected with infinite care, and though the hand of man may never have changed them it is far from true that any old stone will do. Furthermore, in calligraphy, painting, and ceramics, the accidental effects of running glaze or of flying hair-lines of the brush were only accepted and presented by the artist when he felt them to be fortuitous and unexpected marvels within the context of the work as a whole.

What governed his judgement? What gives *certain* accidental effects in painting the same beauty as the accidental outlines of clouds? According to Zen feeling there is no precise rule, no rule, that is to say, which can be formulated in words and taught systematically. On the other hand, there is in all these things a principle of order which in Chinese philosophy is termed *li,* and which Joseph Needham has translated "organic pattern." *Li* originally meant the markings in jade, the grain in wood, and the fiber in muscle. It designates a type of order which is too multi-dimensional, too subtly interrelated, and too squirmingly vital to be represented in words or mechanical images. The artist has to know it as he knows how to grow his hair. He can do it again and again, but can never explain how. In Taoist philosophy this power is called *te,* or "magical virtue." It is the element of the miraculous which we feel both at the stars in heaven and at our own ability to be conscious.

It is the possession of *te,* then, which makes all the difference between mere scrawls and the "white writing" of Mark Tobey which admittedly derived its inspiration from Chinese calligraphy. It was by no means a purely haphazard drooling of paint or uncontrolled wandering of the brush, for the character and taste of such an artist is visible in the grace (a possible equivalent of *te*) with which his strokes are formed even when he is not trying to represent anything except strokes. It is also what makes the difference between mere patches, smudges, and trails of black ink and the work of such Japanese moderns as Sabro Hasegawa and Onchi, which is after all in the *haboku* or "rough style" tradition of Sesshu. Anyone can write absolutely illegible Japanese, but who so enchantingly as Ryokwan? If it is true that "when the wrong man uses the right means, the right means work in the wrong way," it is often also true that when the right man uses the wrong means, the wrong means work in the right way.

The real genius of Chinese and Japanese Zen artists in their use of controlled accidents goes beyond the discovery of fortuitous beauty. It lies in being able to express, at the level of artistry, the realization of that ultimate standpoint from which "anything goes" and at which "all things are of one suchness." The mere selection of any random shape to stick in a frame simply confuses the metaphysical and the artistic domains; it does not express the one in terms of the other. Set in a frame, any old mess is at once cut off from the totality of its natural context, and for this very reason its manifestation of the Tao is concealed. The formless murmer of night noises in a great city has an enchantment which immediately disappears when formally presented as music in a concert hall. A frame outlines a universe, a microcosm, and if the contents of the frame are to rank as art they must have the same quality of relationship to the whole and to each other as events in the great universe, the macrocosm of nature. In nature the accidental is always recognized in relation to what is ordered and controlled. The dark *yin* is never without the bright *yang*. Thus the painting of Sesshu, the calligraphy of Ryok-wan, and the ceramic bowls of the Hagi or Karatsu schools reveal the wonder of accidents in nature through accidents in a context of highly disciplined art.

The realization of the unswerving "rightness" of whatever happens is no more manifested by utter lawlessness in social conduct than by sheer caprice in art. As Zen has been used as a pretext for the latter in our times, its use as a pretext for the former is ancient history. Many a rogue has justified himself with the Buddhist formula, "Birth-and-death (*samsara*) is Nirvana; worldly passions are Enlightenment." This danger is implicit in Zen because it is implicit in freedom. Power and freedom can never be safe. They are dangerous in the same way that fire and electricity are dangerous. But it is quite pitiful to see Zen used as a pretext for license when the Zen in question is no more than an idea in the head, a simple rationalization. To some extent "Zen" is so used in the underworld which often attaches itself to artistic and intellectual communities. After all, the Bohemian way of life is primarily the natural consequence of artists and writers being so absorbed in their work that they have no interest in keeping up with the Joneses. It is also a symptom of creative changes in manners and morals which at first seem as reprehensible to conservatives as new forms in art. But every such community attracts a number of weak imitators and hangers-on, especially in the great cities, and it is mostly in this class that one now finds the stereotype of the "beatnik" with his phony Zen. Yet if Zen were not the pretext for this shiftless existence, it would be something else.

Is it, then, this underworld which is described in Kerouac's *Dharma Bums?* It is generally known that *The Dharma Bums* is not a novel but a flimsily fictionized account of the author's experiences in California in 1956. To anyone who knows the milieu described, the identity of each character is plain and it is no secret that Japhy Ryder, the hero of the story, is Gary Snyder.* Whatever may be said of Kerouac himself and of a few other characters in the story, it

---

*The names were changed at the last minute, and at one point "Gary" remains instead of "Japhy." The excerpt published in the Summer 1958 *Chicago Review* under the title "Meditation in the Woods" keeps the original names.

would be difficult indeed to fit Snyder into any stereotype of the Bohemian underworld. He has spent a year of Zen study in Kyoto, and
has recently (1959) returned for another session, perhaps for two
years this time. He is also a serious student of Chinese, having studied with Shih-hsiang Chen at the University of California, and su-
perbly translated a number of the poems of the Zen hermit Han
Shan.* His own work scattered through many periodicals, entitles
him to be regarded as one of the finest poets of the San Francisco
renaissance.

But Snyder is, in the best sense, a bum. His manner of life is a
quietly individualistic deviation from everything expected of a
"good consumer." His temporary home is a little shack without util-
ities on a hillside in Mill Valley, at the top of a steep trail. When he
needs money he goes to sea, or works as a firewatcher or logger.
Otherwise, he stays at home or goes mountain-climbing, most of the
time writing, studying, or practicing Zen meditation. Part of his
shack is set aside as a formal "meditation hall," and the whole place
is in the best Zen tradition of clean and uncluttered simplicity. But
this is not a Christian or Hinayana Buddhist style of asceticism. As
The Dharma Bums made plain, it combines a voluntary and rather
joyous poverty with a rich love-life, and for Western, and much Eastern, religiosity this is the touchstone of deviltry. This is not the place
to argue the complex problem of spirituality and sexuality,† but one
can only say, "So much the worse for such religiosity." This attitude
has seldom been a part of Zen, new or old, beat or square.

In *The Dharma Bums,* however, we are seeing Snyder through
Kerouac's eyes, and some distortions arise because Kerouac's own
Buddhism is a true beat Zen which confuses "anything goes" at the
existential level with "anything goes" on the artistic and social levels. Nevertheless, there is something endearing about Kerouac's personality as a writer, which comes out in the warmth of his admiration
for Gary, and in the lusty, generous enthusiasm for life which wells
up at every point in his colorful and wholly undisciplined prose. This
exuberent warmth makes it impossible to put Kerouac in the class of
the beat mentality described by John Clelland-Holmes—the cool,

---

*"Cold Mountain Poems," *Evergreen Review,* vol. 2, no. 6, 1958.
†For which see Part II of my *Nature, Man, and Woman,* New York, 1958.

fake-intellectual hipster searching for kicks, name-dropping bits of Zen and jazz jargon to justify a disaffiliation from society which is in fact just ordinary, callous exploitation of other people. In the North Beach, Greenwich Village, and elsewhere such characters may occasionally be found, but no one has ever heard of any of them, and their identification with the active artists and poets of these communities is pure journalistic imagination. They are, however, the shadow of a substance, the low-level caricature which always attends spiritual and cultural movements, carrying them to extremes which their authors never intended. To this extent beat Zen is sowing confusion in idealizing as art and life what should be kept to oneself as therapy.

One of the most problematic characteristics of beat Zen, shared to some extent both by the creative artists and their imitators, is the fascination for marijuana and peyote, and the notion that the states of consciousness produced by these substances have some affinity with *satori*. That many of these people "take drugs" naturally lays them wide open to the most extreme forms of righteous indignation, despite the fact that marijuana and peyote (or its derivative, mescaline) are far less harmful and habit-forming than whiskey or tobacco. But while it is true that these drugs induce states of great aesthetic insight and, perhaps, therapeutic value, the *satori*-experience is so startlingly different from anything of this kind that no one who had shared both could possibly confuse them. Both states of consciousness require an apparently paradoxical type of language to describe them, for which reason one might easily confuse the drug-induced states with written accounts of *satori*. But *satori* is always marked by a kind of intense clarity and simplicity from which complex imagery, jazzed-up sense perceptions, and the strange "turned-on" feeling invariably produced by these drugs are absent. It is not by chance that *satori* is called *fu-sho* or "unproduced," which means, among other things, that there is no gimmick whether psychological or chemical for bringing it about. *Satori* always remains inaccessible to the mind preoccupied with its own states or with the search for ecstasy.

Now the underlying protestant lawlessness of beat Zen disturbs the square Zennists very seriously. For square Zen is the Zen of established tradition in Japan with its clearly defined hierarchy, its rigid discipline, and its specific tests of *satori*. More particularly, it is the kind of Zen adopted by Westerners studying in Japan, who will before long be bringing it back home. But there is an obvious difference between square Zen and the common-or-garden squareness of the Rotary Club or the Presbyterian Church. It is infinitely more imaginative, sensitive and interesting. But it is still square because it is a quest for the *right* spiritual experience, for a *satori* which will receive the stamp (*inka*) of approval and established authority. There will even be certificates to hang on the wall.

If square Zen falls into any serious excess it is in the direction of spiritual snobbism and artistic preciousness, though I have never known an orthodox Zen teacher who could be accused of either. These gentlemen seem to take their exalted office rather lightly, respecting its dignity without standing on it. The faults of square Zen are the faults of any spiritual in-group with an esoteric discipline and degrees of initiation. Students in the lower ranks can get unpleasantly uppity about inside knowledge which they are not at liberty to divulge—"and you wouldn't understand even if I could tell you"—and are apt to dwell rather sickeningly on the immense difficulties and iron disciplines of their task. There are times, however, when this is understandable, especially when someone who is just goofing-off claims that he is following the Zen ideal of "naturalness."

The student of square Zen is also inclined at times to be niggling in his recognition of parallels to Zen in other spiritual traditions. Because the essentials of Zen can never be accurately and fully formulated, being an experience and not a set of ideas, it is always possible to be critical of anything anyone says about it, neither putting up nor shutting up. Any statement about Zen, or about spiritual experience of any kind, will always leave some aspect, some subtlety, unexpressed. No one's mouth is big enough to utter the whole thing. The Western follower of Zen should also resist the temptation to associate himself with an even worse form of snobbery, the intellectual snobbery so largely characteristic of Far-Eastern studies in American universities. In this particular field the fad for making humanistic studies "scientific" has gone to such wild extremes that even Suzuki is accused of being a "popularizer" instead of a serious scholar—presumably because he is a little unsystematic about footnotes and covers a vast area instead of confining himself with rigor to a single problem, *e.g.*, "An Analysis of Some Illegible and Archaic Character-forms in the Tun-huang Manuscript of the Sutra of

the Sixth Patriarch.'' There is a proper and honorable place in scholarship for the meticulous drudge, but when he is on top instead of on
tap his dangerous envy of real intelligence drives all creative scholars
from the field.*

In its artistic expression square Zen is often rather tediously
studied and precious, a fate which all too easily befalls a venerable
aesthetic tradition when its techniques are so highly developed that
it takes a lifetime to master any one of them. No one has then the
time to go beyond the achievements of the old masters, so that new
generations are condemned to endless repetition and imitation of
their refinements. The student of *sumi*-painting, calligraphy, *haiku*-
poetry, or tea-ceremony can therefore get trapped in a tiresomely
repetitious affectation of styles, varied only with increasingly esoteric allusions to the work of the past. When this comes to the point
of imitating the old masters' happy accidents in such a way that
''primitive'' and ''rough'' effects are produced by the utmost practice and deliberation, the whole thing becomes so painful that even
the wildest excesses of beat Zen art look refreshing. Indeed, it is possible that beat Zen and square Zen will so complement and rub
against one another that an amazingly pure and lively Zen will arise
from the hassle.

For this reason I see no really serious quarrel with either extreme. There was never a spiritual movement without its excesses
and distortions. The experience of awakening which truly constitutes
Zen is too timeless and universal to be injured. The extremes of beat
Zen need alarm no one since, as Blake said, ''the fool who persists
in his folly will become wise.'' As for square Zen, ''authoritative''
spiritual experiences have always had a way of wearing thin, and
thus of generating the demand for something genuine and unique
which needs no stamp.

I have known followers of both extremes to come up with per-

---

*Suzuki, incidentally, is a very rare bird among contemporary Asians—an
original thinker. He is no mere mouthpiece for any fixed tradition, and has come
forth with some ideas about comparative religion and the psychology of religion
which are of enormous importance, quite aside from what he has done to translate
and interpret the literature of Zen. But it is just for this reason that people in square
Zen and academic sinology have their qualms about accepting him.

fectly clear *satori* experiences, for since there is no real "way" to *satori* the way you are following makes very little difference.

But the quarrel *between* the extremes is of great philosophical interest, being a contemporary form of the ancient dispute between salvation by works and salvation by faith, or between what the Hindus called the ways of the monkey and the cat. The cat—appropriately enough—follows the effortless way, since the mother cat carries her kittens. The monkey follows the hard way, since the baby monkey has to hang on to its mother's hair. Thus for beat Zen there must be no effort, no discipline, no artificial striving to attain *satori* or to be anything but what one is. But for square Zen there can be no true *satori* without years of meditation-practice under the stern supervision of a qualified master. In seventeenth-century Japan these two attitudes were *approximately* typified by the great masters Bankei and Hakuin, and it so happens that the followers of the latter "won out" and determined the present-day character of Rinzai Zen.*

Satori can lie along both roads. It is the concomitant of a "nongrasping" attitude of the senses to experience, and grasping can be exhausted by the discipline of directing its utmost intensity to a single, ever-elusive objective. But what makes the way of effort and will-power suspect to many Westerners is not so much an inherent laziness as a thorough familiarity with the wisdom of our own culture. The square Western Zennists are often quite naive when it comes to an understanding of Christian theology or of all that has been discovered in modern psychiatry, for both have long been concerned with the fallibility and unconscious ambivalence of the will. Both have posed problems as to the vicious circle of seeking self-surrender or of "free-associating on purpose" or of accepting one's conflicts to escape from them, and to anyone who knows anything about either Christianity or psychotherapy these are very real problems. The interest of Chinese Zen and of people like Bankei is that

---

*Rinzai Zen is the form most widely known in the West. There is also Soto Zen which differs somewhat in technique, but is still closer to Hakuin than to Bankei. However, Bankei should not exactly be identified with beat Zen as I have described it, for he was certainly no advocate of the life of undisciplined whimsy despite all that he said about the importance of the uncalculated life and the folly of seeking Satori.

they deal with these problems in a most direct and stimulating way, and begin to suggest some answers. But when Herrigel's Japanese archery master was asked, "How can I give up purpose on purpose?" he replied that no one had ever asked him that before. He had no answer except to go on trying blindly, for five years.

Foreign religions can be immensely attractive and highly overrated by those who know little of their own, and especially by those who have not worked through and grown out of their own. This is why the displaced or unconscious Christian can so easily use either beat or square Zen to justify himself. The one wants a philosophy to justify him in doing what he pleases. The other wants a more plausible authoritative salvation than the Church or the psychiatrists seem to be able to provide. Furthermore the atmosphere of Japanese Zen is free from all one's unpleasant childhood associations with God the Father and Jesus Christ—though I know many young Japanese who feel just the same way about their early training in Buddhism. But the true character of Zen remains almost incomprehensible to those who have not surpassed the immaturity of needing to be justified, whether before the Lord God or before a paternalistic society.

The old Chinese Zen masters were steeped in Taoism. They saw nature in its total interrelatedness, and saw that every creature and every experience is in accord with the Tao of nature just as it is. This enabled them to accept themselves as they were, moment by moment, without the least need to justify anything. They didn't do it to defend themselves or to find an excuse for getting away with murder. They didn't brag about it and set themselves apart as rather special. On the contrary, their Zen was *wu-shih,* which means approximately "nothing special" or "no fuss." But Zen is "fuss" when it is mixed up with Bohemian affectations, and "fuss" when it is imagined that the only proper way to find it is to run off to a monastery in Japan or to do special exercises in the lotus posture for five hours a day. And I will admit that the very hullabaloo about Zen, even in such an essay as this, is also fuss—but a little less so.

Having said that, I would like to say something for all Zen fussers, beat or square. Fuss is all right, too. If you are hung on Zen, there's no need to try to pretend that you are not. If you really want to spend some years in a Japanese monastery, there is no earthly reason why you shouldn't. Or if you want to spend your time hopping freight cars and digging Charlie Parker, it's a free country.

> In the landscape of Spring there is neither better nor worse;
> The flowering branches grow naturally, some long, some
>   short.

TIBETAN BUDDHISM

The Buddhism of Tibet, Vajrayana or Tantric Buddhism, has long exercised a rich but shifting fascination for outsiders. For many centuries Indians regarded the Himalayan heights of Tibet, well-spring of the sacred Ganges, as the abode of gods and wizards. Many early Western explorers of the spiritual East, including Theosophists, were not far behind in regarding that virtually impenetrable land of monks and temples a Shangri-la of ancient wisdom and advanced adepts. As Tibet gradually yielded its secrets to the world in the past century or so, however, others have seen it in different lights: as a benighted land of rank superstition and priestly exploitation, as an interesting anthropological preserve.

Western religious interest in Tibetan Buddhism, however, has held up well under the impact of further information. The study and translation of more and more texts, and the investigation of more and more practices in this complex, highly ritualized, and deeply intellectual spiritual world, have convinced those drawn to it that here is a realm of strange but profound wisdom and power. Tibet fit well the spiritual mood of the sixties, with its colorful gods of virtually psychedelic beauty or horror, its ornate rituals and deep rumbling chants, its lore of superhuman psychic achievement. As we have seen, several Tibetan centers were founded around refugee lamas in that decade.

Bibliography

Numerous books on Tibetan Buddhism may be found, but little exists on it in the United States beyond the valuable information in the general books on Buddhism in America cited in the bibliography at the end of this volume, particularly those of Prebish and Fields. On Evans-Wentz, see Ken Winkler, *Pilgrim of the Clear Light: The Biography of Dr. Walter Y. Evans-Wentz* (Berkeley, Calif.: Dawnfire Books, 1982).

I.   W. Y. EVANS-WENTZ:
THE TIBETAN BOOK OF THE DEAD

*One ambassador of spiritual Tibet, however, long antedates the Ti-
betan centers and has undoubtedly influenced far more seekers than they.
That representative of the "Land of Snows" is a book, The Tibetan Book of
the Dead, edited by W. Y. Evans-Wentz. Originally published in 1927, this
classic has long remained in print through successive editions and revisions,
and experienced a boom in popularity in the 1960s. Needless to say, there
were those who compared its account of after-death experience on inner
planes to the psychedelic experience, but the book's appeal was wider than
that. It embodies at once the glamor of high wisdom in an exotic setting, and
more substantively a rich idealism that shows how the worlds in which we
live, together with heaven and hell, grow out of states of consciousness.*

*The Tibetan Book of the Dead (or Bardo Thodol, "Book of the Inter-
mediate States," as it is in Tibetan) does not begin to exhaust the plenitude
of Tibetan Buddhism. Indeed, the West has probably overestimated its importance in that tradition. But as a world spiritual classic it has come to have
a special place, in no small part because of the elaborate introductory ap-
paratus Evans-Wentz prepared for his editions of it, composed both by himself and by such distinguished guests as C. G. Jung and the German-born
Lama Govinda.*

*Before turning to Evans-Wentz's own introductions, however, let us
take a moment to review the world view underlying the book. The basic
concept is of three "levels" of reality, the trikaya or three "bodies" of the
Buddha-nature, or universal essence. The first of these is the Dharmakaya,
the pure essence of the universe itself, one with Nirvana or the Void of Buddhist philosophy since it is absolute Unconditioned Reality. The second is
the Sambhogakaya, the level of "perfect endowment" where the unconditioned essence takes those ideal forms familiar to faith and mystical experience, in a word, the heavens of religion. The third, the Nirmanakaya
or "incarnational" level, is the concrete world in which the Unconditioned
appears not as God in Heaven but as the historical Buddhas. One can, however, reach the second and even the first levels on various occasions: in the
womb before birth, in dreams and meditation, and above all after death in
the intermediate experience before one's next incarnation. The Tibetan
Book of the Dead, intended to be whispered in the ear of a dying person, is
a Baedeker of that experience.*

*It relates that one first experiences the Dharmakaya, the "Clear Light
of the Void." If one can recognize it as one's true nature, one can be liberated
right there. If, however, it is too bright and one turns away, one falls back to
the "Heaven" level, where one sees a series of resplendent cosmic buddhas,*

each embracing his female *"wisdom."* If one can accept any of them as one's true nature, one can be liberated through that one. If they are rejected, however, one confronts them again, now as horrendous *"terrifying deities"*; even here, though, one may be saved as it were through the *"shock therapy"* of confronting them as an aspect of one's own nature projected like the others against the Void. Finally, if nothing avails, one is blown by the high winds of karma into the world that past deeds have prepared the cosmic wanderer to enter, where one seeks the oblivion of a womb and rebirth.

The passages following from Evans-Wentz's Introduction to the book summarize this picture with more technical detail. As cluttered as it may sometimes seem, that vision has a transcendent sweep and a fundamentally simple underlying idealism that has proved richly illuminating to many. Not least of these was no doubt Evans-Wentz himself, who as a very young man had participated deeply in Theosophy, and who ended his quest with Swami Yogananda's Self-Realization Fellowship, without rejecting Theosophy or Tibet.

Walter Yeeling Evans-Wentz (1878–1965) was a native of Trenton, New Jersey, and was educated at Stanford and Oxford. His first mature interest was in Celtic folklore, eventuating in *The Fairy Faith in Celtic Countries (1911)*. A compulsive traveler, though, Evans-Wentz was soon in Asia. Never married, of independent income, he was the archetype of the reserved, mildly eccentric, and unworldly free-lance scholar who finds his way into odd corners of the world and discovers unusual things. It was in 1919 in Sikkim that he met the Lama Kazi Dewa-Samdup, who translated the *Bardo Thodol* in close collaboration with Evans-Wentz; who then also edited it and prepared the book for publication. Evans-Wentz, who himself did not know Tibetan, as he freely acknowledges, worked with Dewa-Samdup until the latter's death in 1922, and then with other associates, to produce an important pioneer series of Tibetan works: *Tibetan Yoga and Secret Doctrine, Tibet's Great Yogi Milarepa, The Tibetan Book of the Great Liberation*. While the scholarship may be dated in some particulars, their invaluable role in introducing the spiritual riches of the *"Land of Snows"* to the world will not be forgotten by those who have profited from those treasures.

The Wisdom Teachings*

Also involved in symbolical language there are, as fundamental occult doctrines of the *Bardo Thödol,* what the translator called The

---

*From *The Tibetan Book of the Dead* by W. Y. Evans-Wentz, pp. 10–18 and

Wisdom Teachings; and these—which are essential *Mahāyāna* doctrines—may be outlined as follows:

The Voidness.—In all Tibetan systems of *yoga,* realization of the Voidness (Tib. *Stong-pa-ñid*—pron. *Tong-pa-ñid:* Skt. *Shūnyatā*) is the one great aim; for to realize it is to attain the unconditioned *Dharma-Kāya,* or 'Divine Body of Truth' (Tib. *Chos-sku*—pron. *Chö-Ku*), the primordial state of uncreatedness, of the supramundane *Bodhic* All-Consciousness—Buddhahood. Realization of the Voidness (Pali, *Suññata*) is the aim of Theravādists too.

The Three Bodies.—The *Dharma-Kāya* is the highest of the Three Bodies (Tib. *Sku-gsum*—pron. *Kū-sum*: Skt. *Tri-Kāya*) of the Buddha and of all Buddhas and beings who have Perfect Enlightenment. The other two bodies are the *Sambhoga-Kāya* or 'Divine Body of Perfect Endowment' (Tib. *Longs-spyod-rzogs-sku*—pron. *Long-chöd-zo-ku*) and the *Nirmāna-Kāya* or 'Divine Body of Incarnation' (Tib. *Sprul-pahi-sku*—pron. *Tül-pai-ku*).

The *Dharma-Kāya* is symbolized—for all human word-concepts are inadequate to describe the Qualityless—as an infinite ocean, calm and without a wave, whence arise mist-clouds and rainbow, which symbolize the *Sambhoga-Kāya;* and the clouds, enhaloed in the glory of the rainbow, condensing and falling as rain, symbolize the *Nirmāna-Kāya.*

The *Dharma-Kāya* is the primordial, formless *Bohdi,* which is true experience freed from all error or inherent or accidental obscuration. In it lies the essence of the Universe, including both *Sangsāra* and *Nirvāna,* which, as states or conditions of the two poles of consciousness, are, in the last analysis, in the realm of the pure intellect, identical.

In other words, the *Dharma-Kāya* (lit. 'Law Body') being Essential Wisdom (*Bodhi*) unmodified, the *Sambhoga-Kāya* (lit. 'Compensation Body', or 'Adorned Body') embodies, as in the Five Dhyānī Buddhas, Reflected or Modified Wisdom, and the *Nirmāna-Kāya* (lit. 'Changeable Body', or 'Transformed Body') embodies, as in the Human Buddhas, Practical or Incarnate Wisdom.

The Uncreated, the Unshaped, the Unmodified is the *Dharma-*

Kāya. The Offspring, the Modification of the Unmodified, the manifestation of all perfect attributes in one body, is the *Sambhoga-Kāya*: 'The embodiment of all that is wise, merciful and loving in the *Dharma-Kāya*—as clouds on the surface of the heavens or a rainbow on the surface of the clouds—is said to be *Sambhoga-Kāya'*. The condensation and differentiation of the One Body as many is the *Nirmāna-Kāya,* or the Divine Incarnations among sentient beings, that is to say, among beings immersed in the Illusion called *Sangsāra,* in phenomena, in worldly existence. All enlightened beings who are reborn in this or in any other world with full consciousness, as workers for the betterment of their fellow creatures, are said to be *Nirmāna-Kāya* incarnates.

With the *Dharma-Kāya* Tantric Buddhism associates the Primordial Buddha Samanta-Bhadra (Tib. *Kün-tu-bzang-po*—pron. *Kün-tu-zang-po*), Who is without Beginning or End, the Source of all Truth, the All-Good Father of the Lāmaistic Faith. In this same highest Buddha realm Lāmaism places Vajra-Dhāra (Tib. *Rdorje-Chang*—pron. *Dorje-Chang*), 'The Holder of the *Dorje* (or Thunderbolt)', 'the Divine Expounder of the Mystic Doctrine called *Vajra Yāna* (Tib. *Rdorje Theg-pa*—pron. *Dorje Theg-pa*) or *Mantra Yāna*'; and also the Buddha Amitābha (Tib. *Hod-dpag-med*—pron. *Wod-pag-med*; . . .), the Buddha of Boundless Light, Who is the Source of Life Eternal. In the *Sambhoga-Kāya* are placed the Five Dhyānī Buddhas (or Buddhas of Meditation), the Lotus Herukas, and the Peaceful and Wrathful Deities, all of whom will appear in the *Bardo* visions. With the *Nirmāna-Kāya* is associated Padma Sambhava, who, being the first teacher in Tibet to expound the *Bardo Thödol,* is the Great *Guru* for all devotees who follow the *Bardo* teachings.

The opinion commonly held by men not initiated into the higher *lāmaic* teachings, that Northern Buddhism recognizes in the Primordial or Ādi-Buddha a Supreme Deity, is apparently erroneous. The translator held that the Ādi-Buddha, and all deities associated with the *Dharma-Kāya,* are not to be regarded as personal deities, but as Personifications of primordial and universal forces, laws, or spiritual influences, which sustain—as the sun sustains the earth's physical life—the divine nature of all sentient creatures in all worlds, and make man's emancipation from all *sangsāric* existences possible:

In the boundless panorama of the existing and visible universe, whatever shapes appear, whatever sounds vibrate,
whatever radiances illuminate, or whatever conscious-
nesses cognize, all are the play or manifestation of the *Tri-
Kāya,* the Three-fold Principle of the Cause of All Causes,
the Primordial Trinity. Impenetrating all, is the All-Pervading Essence of Spirit, which is Mind. It is uncreated,
impersonal, self-existing, immaterial, and indestructible.
(Lāma Kazi Dawa-Samdup.)

Thus, the *Tri-Kāya* symbolizes the Esoteric Trinity of the
higher Buddhism of the Northern School; the Exoteric Trinity being,
as in the Southern School, the *Buddha,* the *Dharma* (or Scriptures),
the *Saṅgha* (or Priesthood). Regarded in this way—the one trinitar-
ian doctrine as esoteric, the other as exoteric—there are direct correspondences   between   the   two   Trinities.   Detailed   and
comprehensive understanding of the *Tri-Kāya* Doctrine, so the *lāmas*
teach, is the privilege of initiates, who, alone, are fitted to grasp and
to realize it.

The translator himself regarded the *Tri-Kāya* Doctrine as having
been transmitted by a long and unbroken line of initiates, some Indian, some Tibetan, direct from the days of the Buddha. He considered that the Buddha, having re-discovered it, was merely its
Transmitter from preceding Buddhas; that it was handed on orally,
from *guru* to *guru,* and not committed to writing until comparatively
recent times, when Buddhism began to decay, and there were not
always sufficient living *gurus* to transmit it in the old way. The theory of Western scholars, that simply because a doctrine is not found
recorded before a certain time it consequently did not exist previously, he—as an initiate—laughed at; and the rather strenuous efforts of Christian apologists to claim for the *Tri-Kāya* Doctrine a
Christian origin he held, likewise, to be wholly untenable. He had
been a close and sympathetic student of Christianity; and, as a young
man, he had been much sought after by Christian missionaries, who
looked upon him, with his remarkable learning and superior social
standing, as an unusually desirable subject for conversion. He care-
fully examined their claims, and then rejected them, on the ground
that, in his opinion, Christianity, as presented by them, is but an imperfect Buddhism, that the Aṣokan Buddhist missionaries to Asia

Minor and Syria, as to Alexandria, must have profoundly influenced Christianity through some such probable connecting link as the Essenes, that, if Jesus were an historical character, He, being—as the Lāma interpreted the Jesus of the *New Testament* clearly to be—a Bodhisattva (i.e. a Candidate for Buddhahood), was, undoubtedly, well acquainted with Buddhist ethics, and taught them, as in the Sermon on the Mount.

The Doctrine of the Three Bodies conveys the esoteric teachings concerning the Path of the Teachers, their descent from the Higher to the Lower, from the threshold of *Nirvāna* to the *Sangsāra;* and progression from the Lower to the Higher, from the *Sangsāra* to *Nirvāna,* is symbolized by the Five Dhyānī Buddhas, each personifying a universal divine attribute. Contained in the Five Dhyānī Buddhas lies the Sacred Way leading to At-one-ment in the *Dharma-Kāya,* to Buddhahood, to Perfect Enlightenment, to *Nirvāna*—which is spiritual emancipation through Desirelessness.

The Five Wisdoms.—As the All-Pervading Voidness, the *Dharma-Kāya* is the shape (which is shapelessness) of the Body of Truth; the Thatness constituting it is the *Dharma-Dhātu* (Tib. *Chös-kyi-dvyings*—pron. *Chö-kyi-ing*), the Seed or Potentiality of Truth; and this dawns on the First Day of the *Bardo* as the glorious blue light of the Dhyānī Buddha Vairochana, the Manifester, 'He Who in Shapes Makes Visible' [the universe of matter]. The *Dharma-Dhātu* is symbolized as the Aggregate of Matter. From the Aggregate of Matter arise the creatures of this world, as of all worlds, in which animal stupidity is the dominant characteristic; and the *māra* (or illusion of shape) constitutes in all realms of the *Sangsāra*—as in the human kingdom where *manas* (or mind) begins to operate—the Bondage, emancipation from which is *Nirvāna.* When in man, made as perfect as human life can make him, the stupidity of his animal nature and the illusion of shape, or personality, are transmuted into Right Knowledge, into Divine Wisdom, there shines forth in his consciousness the All-Pervading Wisdom of the *Dharma-Dhātu,* or the Wisdom born of the Voidness, which is all-pervading.

As the Aggregate of Matter, dawning in the *Bardo* of the First Day, produces physical bodies, so the Water-Element, dawning on the Second Day, produces the life-stream, the blood; Anger is the obscuring passion, consciousness is the aggregate, and these, when transmuted, become the Mirror-like Wisdom, personified in Vajra-Sattva (the *Sambhoga-Kāya* reflex of the Dhyānī Buddha Akṣhobhya), the 'Triumphant One of Divine Heroic Mind'.

The Earth-Element of the Third Day, producing the chief solid constituents of the human form, and of all physical forms, gives rise to the passion of Egoism, and the aggregate is Touch; and these, when divinely transmuted, become the Wisdom of Equality, personified in Ratna-Sambhava, the 'Gem-born One', the Beautifier.

The Fire-Element of the Fourth Day, producing the animal-heat of embodied human and animal beings, gives rise to the passion of Attachment, or Lust, and the Aggregate of Feelings. Herein the transmutation gives birth to the All-Discriminating Wisdom, which enables the devotee to know each thing separately, yet all things as one; personified in the Dhyānī Buddha Amitābha, 'He of Boundless Light', the Illuminator, or Enlightener.

The Element Air, of the Fifth Day, produces the breath of life. Its quality, or passions, in man is Envy, or Jealousy. Its aggregate is Volition. The transmutation is into the All-Performing Wisdom, which gives perseverance and unerring action in things spiritual, personified in Amogha-Siddhi, the 'Almighty Conqueror', the Giver of Divine Power.

[As explained above, in Section IV,] the last Element, Ether, which produces the mind, or Knower, and the desire-body of the dwellers in the Intermediate State, does not dawn for the deceased, because—as the text tells us—the Wisdom Faculty of the Consciousness, that is to say, the supramundane Buddha (or *Bodhic*) consciousness, has not been developed in the ordinary humanity. To it is related—as in our text—Vajra-Sattva and the Mirror-like Wisdom and the Aggregate of *Bodhic* Wisdom, Vajra-Sattva being then synonymous, esoterically, with Samanta-Bhadra (who, in turn, is often personified in Vairochana, the Chief of the Five Dhyānī Buddhas), the Ādi-Buddha, the Primordial, the Unborn, Unshaped, Unmodified *Dharma-Kāya*.

When the perfection of the Divine Body-Aggregate is attained by man, it becomes the unchanging, immutable Vajra-Sattva. When the perfection of the Divine Speech-Principle is attained, with it comes the power of divine speech, symbolized by Amitābha. The perfection of the Divine Thought-Principle brings divine infallibility, symbolized by Vairochana. The perfection of the Divine Qualities of Goodness and Beauty is the realization of Ratna-Sambhava, their producer. With the perfection of Divine Actions comes the realization of Amogha-Siddhi, the Omnipotent Conqueror.

To one after another of these divine attributes, or principles, innate in every human being, the deceased is introduced, as though in a symbolic drama of initiation, to test him and discover whether or not any part of his divine (or *bodhic*) nature has been developed. Full development in all the *bodhic* powers of the Five Dhyānī Buddhas, who are the personifications of them, leads to Liberation, to Buddhahood. Partial development leads to birth in one of the happier states: *deva-loka,* the world of the *devas* or gods; *asura-loka,* the world of the *asuras* or titans; *nara-loka,* the world of mankind.

After the Fifth Day the *Bardo* visions become less and less divine; the deceased sinks deeper and deeper into the morass of *sangsāric* hallucinations; the radiances of the higher nature fade into the lights of the lower nature. Then—the after-death dream ending as the Intermediate State exhausts itself for the percipient, the thought-forms of his mental-content all having shown themselves to him like ghostly spectres in a nightmare—he passes on from the Intermediate State into the equally illusionary state called waking, or living, either in the human world or in one of the many mansions of existence, by being born there. And thus revolves the Wheel of Life, until the one who is bound on it breaks his own bonds through Enlightenment, and there comes, as the Buddha proclaims, the Ending of Sorrow.

In Sections I to V, above, the more prominent occult teachings underlying the *Bardo Thödol* have been briefly expounded. In Sections VI to XII, which are to follow, the chief *Bardo* rites and ceremonies, the *Bardo* psychology, and other of the *Bardo* doctrines will be explained and interpreted. The last Sections, XIII to XV, will be devoted to a consideration of our manuscript, its history, the origin of the *Bardo Thödol* texts, and our translating and editing.

In addition to these fifteen sections, there are, as Addenda (see pp. 211–41), six complementary sections, addressed chiefly to the student, who, more than the ordinary reader, will be interested in certain of the more abstruse doctrines and problems which arise from a careful study of the translation and its annotations.

* * *

The *Bardo* or After-Death State

From the moment of death and for three and one-half or sometimes four days afterwards, the Knower, or principle of consciousness, in the case of the ordinary person deceased, is believed to be thus in a sleep or trance-state, unaware, as a rule, that it has been separated from the human-plane body. This period is the First *Bardo,* called the *Chikhai Bardo* (Tib. *Hchi-khahi Bar-do*), or 'Transitional State of the Moment of Death', wherein dawns the Clear Light, first in primordial purity, then the percipient, being unable to recognize it, that is to say, to hold on to and remain in the transcendental state of the unmodified mind concomitant with it, perceives it *karmically* obscured, which is its secondary aspect. When the First *Bardo* ends, the Knower, awakening to the fact that death has occurred, begins to experience the Second *Bardo,* called the *Chönyid Bardo* (Tib. *Chös-nyid Bar-do*), or 'Transitional State of [the Experiencing or Glimpsing of] Reality'; and this merges into the Third *Bardo,* called the *Sidpa* (or *Sidpai*) *Bardo* (Tib. *Srid-pahi Bar-do*), or 'Transitional State of [or while seeking] Rebirth', which ends when the principle of consciousness has taken rebirth in the human or some other world, or in one of the paradise realms.

The passing from one *Bardo* to another is analogous to the process of birth; the Knower wakes up out of one swoon or trance state and then another, until the Third *Bardo* ends. On his awakening in the Second *Bardo,* there dawn upon him in symbolic visions, one by one, the hallucinations created by the *karmic* reflexes of actions done by him in the earth-plane body. What he has thought and what he has done become objective: thought-forms, having been consciously visualized and allowed to take root and grow and blossom and produce, now pass in a solemn and mighty panorama, as the consciousness-content of his personality.

In the Second *Bardo,* the deceased is, unless otherwise enlightened, more or less under the delusion that although he is deceased he still possesses a body like the body of flesh and blood. When he comes to realize that really he has no such body, he begins to develop an overmastering desire to possess one; and, seeking for one, the *karmic* predilection for *sangsāric* existence naturally becoming all-determining, he enters into the Third *Bardo* of seeking Rebirth, and eventually, with his rebirth in this or some other world, the after-death state comes to an end.

For the commonality, this is the normal process; but for those very exceptional minds, possessed of great *yogīc* knowledge and enlightenment, only the more spiritual stages of the *Bardo* of the first few days will be experienced; the most enlightened of *yogīs* may escape all of the *Bardo,* passing into a paradise realm, or else reincarnating in this world as soon as the human body has been discarded, maintaining all the while unbroken continuity of consciousness. As men think, so are they, both here and hereafter, thoughts being things, the parents of all actions, good and bad alike; and, as the sowing has been, so will the harvest be.

If escape from the Intermediate State is not achieved, through rebirth into some other state—that of Hell being possible for the very exceptional evil-doer, though not for the ordinary person, who expiates normal moral delinquencies upon being reborn as a human being—within the symbolic period of Forty-nine Days, a period whose actual duration is determined by *karma,* the deceased remains subject to all the *karmic* illusions of the *Bardo,* blissful or miserable as the case may be, and progress is impossible. Apart from liberation by gaining *Nirvāṇa* after death—thus cutting asunder for ever the *karmic* bonds of worldly or *sangsāric* existence in an illusionary body of propensities—the only hope for the ordinary person of reaching Buddhahood lies in being reborn as a human being; for birth in any other than the human world causes delay for one desirous of reaching the Final Goal.

The Psychology of the *Bardo* Visions

Definite psychological significance attaches to each of the deities appearing in the *Bardo Thödol;* but, in order to grasp it, the student must bear in mind that—as suggested above—the apparitional visions seen by the deceased in the Intermediate State are not visions of reality, but nothing more than the hallucinatory embodiments of the thought-forms born of the mental-content of the percipient; or, in other words, they are the intellectual impulses which have assumed personified form in the after-death dream-state.

Accordingly, the Peaceful Deities (Tib. *Z'i-wa*) are the personified forms of the sublimest human sentiments, which proceed from the psychic heart-centre. As such, they are represented as the first to dawn, because, psychologically speaking, the heart-born impulses precede the brain-born impulses. They come in peaceful aspect to control and to influence the deceased whose connexion with the human world has just been severed; the deceased has left relatives and friends behind, works unaccomplished, desires unsatisfied, and, in most cases, he possesses a strong yearning to recover the lost opportunity afforded by human embodiment for spiritual enlightenment. But, in all his impulses and yearnings, *karma* is all-masterful; and, unless it be his *karmic* lot to gain liberation in the first stages, he wanders downwards into the stages wherein the heart-impulses give way to brain-impulses.

Whereas the Peaceful Deities are the personifications of the feelings, the Wrathful Deities (Tib. *T'o-wo*) are the personifications of the reasonings and proceed from the psychic brain-centre. Yet, just as impulses arising in the heart-centre may transform themselves into the reasonings of the brain-centre, so the Wrathful Deities are the Peaceful Deities in a changed aspect.

As the intellect comes into activity, after the sublime heart-born impulses subside, the deceased begins to realize more and more the state in which he is; and with the supernormal faculties of the *Bardo*-body which he begins to make use of—in much the same manner as an infant new-born in the human world begins to employ the human plane sense-faculties—he is enabled to think how he may win this or that state of existence. *Karma* is, however, still his master, and defines his limitations. As on the human plane the sentimental impulses are most active in youth and often lost in mature life, wherein reason commonly takes the place of them, so on the after-death plane, called the *Bardo,* the first experiences are happier than the later experiences.

From another aspect, the chief deities themselves are the embodiments of universal divine forces, with which the deceased is inseparably related, for through him, as being the microcosm of the macrocosm, penetrate all impulses and forces, good and bad alike. Samanta-Bhadra, the All-Good, thus personifies Reality, the Primordial Clear Light of the Unborn, Unshaped *Dharma-Kāya*. Vairochana is the Originator of all phenomena, the Cause of all Causes. As the Universal Father, Vairochana manifests or spreads forth as seed, or semen, all things; his *shakti,* the Mother of Great Space, is the Universal Womb into which the seed falls and evolves as the world-systems. Vajra-Sattva symbolizes Immutability. Ratna-Sambhava is the Beautifier, the Source of all Beauty in the Universe. Amitābha is Infinite Compassion and Love Divine, the *Christos.* Amogha-Siddhi is the personification of Almighty Power or Omnipotence. And the minor deities, heroes, *ḍākinīs* (or 'fairies'), goddesses, lords of death, *rākṣhasas,* demons, spirits, and all others, correspond to definite human thoughts, passions, and impulses, high and low, human and sub-human and superhuman, in *karmic* form, as they take shape from the seeds of thought forming the percipient's consciousness-content.

As the *Bardo Thödol* text makes very clear by repeated assertions, none of all these deities or spiritual beings has any real individual existence any more than have human beings: 'It is quite sufficient for thee [i.e. the deceased percipient] to know that these apparitions are [the reflections of] thine own thought-forms'. They are merely the consciousness-content visualized, by *karmic* agency, as apparitional appearances in the Intermediate State—airy nothings woven into dreams.

The complete recognition of this psychology by the deceased sets him free into Reality. Therefore is it that the *Bardo Thödol,* as the name implies, is The Great Doctrine of Liberation by Hearing and by Seeing.

The deceased human being becomes the sole spectator of a marvellous panorama of hallucinatory visions; each seed of thought in his consciousness-content *karmically* revives; and he, like a wonder-struck child watching moving pictures cast upon a screen, looks on, unaware, unless previously an adept in *yoga,* of the non-reality of what he sees dawn and set.

At first, the happy and glorious visions born of the seeds of the impulses and aspirations of the higher or divine nature awe the uninitiated; then, as they merge into the visions born of the corresponding mental elements of the lower or animal nature, they terrify him, and he wishes to flee from them; but, alas, as the text explains, they are inseparable from himself, and to whatsoever place he may wish to flee they will follow him.

It is not necessary to suppose that all the dead in the Intermediate State experience the same phenomena, any more than all the living do in the human world, or in dreams. The *Bardo Thödol* is merely typical and suggestive of all after-death experiences. It merely describes in detail what is assumed will be the *Bardo* visualizations of the consciousness-content of the ordinary devotee of the Red Hat School of Padma Sambhava. As a man is taught, so he believes. Thoughts being things, they may be planted like seeds in the mind of the child and completely dominate his mental content. Given the favourable soil of the will to believe, whether the seed-thoughts be sound or unsound, whether they be of pure superstition or of realizable truth, they take root and flourish, and make the man what he is mentally.

Accordingly, for a Buddhist of some other School, as for a Hindu, or a Moslem, or a Christian, the *Bardo* experiences would be appropriately different: the Buddhist's or the Hindu's thought-forms, as in a dream state, would give rise to corresponding visions of the deities of the Buddhist or Hindu pantheon; a Moslem's, to visions of the Moslem Paradise; a Christian's, to visions of the Christian Heaven, or an American Indian's to visions of the Happy Hunting Ground. And, similarly, the materialist will experience after-death visions as negative and as empty and as deityless as any he ever dreamt while in the human body. Rationally considered, each person's after-death experiences, as the *Bardo Thödol* teaching implies, are entirely dependent upon his or her own mental content. In other words, as explained above, the after-death state is very much like a dream state, and its dreams are the children of the mentality of the dreamer. This psychology scientifically explains why devout Christians, for example, have had—if we are to accept the testimony of Christian saints and seers—visions (in a trance or dream state, or in the after-death state) of God the Father seated on a throne in the New Jerusalem, and of the Son at His side, and of all the Biblical scenery and attributes of Heaven, or of the Virgin and Saints and Archangels, or of Purgatory and Hell.

In other words, the *Bardo Thödol* seems to be based upon verifiable data of human physiological and psychological experiences;

and it views the problem of the after-death state as being purely a psycho-physical problem; and is, therefore, in the main, scientific. It asserts repeatedly that what the percipient on the *Bardo* plane sees is due entirely to his own mental-content; that there are no visions of gods or of demons, of heavens or of hells, other than those born of the hallucinatory *karmic* thought-forms constituting his personality, which is an impermanent product arising from the thirst for existence and from the will to live and to believe.

From day to day the *Bardo* visions change, concomitant with the eruption of the thought-forms of the percipient, until their *karmic* driving force exhausts itself; or, in other words, the thought-forms, born of habitual propensities, being mental records comparable as has already been suggested to records on a cinema-film, their reel running to its end, the after-death state ends, and the Dreamer, emerging from the womb, begins to experience anew the phenomena of the human world.

The *Bible* of the Christians, like the *Koran* of the Moslems, never seems to consider that the spiritual experiences in the form of hallucinatory visions by prophet or devotee, reported therein, may, in the last analysis, not be real. But the *Bardo Thödol* is so sweeping in its assertions that it leaves its reader with the clear-cut impression that every vision, without any exception whatsoever, in which spiritual beings, gods or demons, or paradises or places of torment and purgation play a part, in a *Bardo* or any *Bardo*-like dream or ecstasy, is purely illusionary, being based upon *sangsāric* phenomena.

The whole aim of the *Bardo Thödol* teaching, as otherwise stated elsewhere, is to cause the Dreamer to awaken into Reality, freed from all the obscurations of *karmic* or *sangsāric* illusions, in a supramundane or *Nirvāṇic* state, beyond all phenomenal paradises, heavens, hells, purgatories, or worlds of embodiment. In this way, then, it is purely Buddhistic and unlike any non-Buddhist book in the world, secular or religious.

IV

TAOISM

The ancient Chinese spiritual tradition known as Taoism—the way of the Way—presents itself as the path of strength through yielding, of wisdom through stillness and unlearning, of leading through seeming not to lead, of accomplishing all things through not-doing. It is the way of water that seeks the downward course of least resistance yet in time wears away the hardest rock, of the sapling that though bent nearly to the ground will spring back upright again. It is fitting, then, that such a tradition should penetrate the American consciousness only in a subtle and inward way. Taoism came to America through no impassioned Vivekananda or enigmatic Blavatsky. Yet certain of its books have been read, and its attitudes—sometimes appropriately unrecognized by most—have entered American arenas from the philosophy of sport to cinema hits, and martial arts studios, where a taste at least of Taoist flavor can be savored, are far more common than Zen or Vedanta centers.

Taoism in China has generated a full-fledged religion, with a rich pantheon and elaborate rites, together with yogic and alchemical practices centering around the development of *ch'i,* spiritual energy, and immortality. The Taoist heavens and grottos of immortals have inspired a wonderful fairy tale–like literature some Westerners have enjoyed, and the concept of *ch'i* is basic to the martial arts. Even more, however, Westerners have appreciated the fundamental writings of philosophical Taoism, the *Tao te ching* of Lao Tzu (traditionally dated sixth century B.C.E.) and the book of Chuang Tzu (369–286 B.C.E.?). These books convey the essential Taoist themes of deep naturalism, inwardness, and gaining through giving. Fur-

195

ther, they sparkle with humor and humanity as they direct one's gaze to the folly of solemnity and the wisdom of folly.

Bibliography

There is unfortunately little work available on Taoism or Taoist influence in America. On Merton, on the other hand, a vast literature can be found. Perhaps the best biography is Michael Mott, *The Seven Mountains of Thomas Merton* (Boston: Houghton Mifflin, 1984), with extensive bibliography.

Taoist Selection

I. THOMAS MERTON:
THE WAY OF CHUANG TZU

Certainly it was this quality that attracted the well-known Trappist monk Thomas Merton to the old Taoist sage Chuang Tzu. Merton (1915–1968) was a convert to Roman Catholicism who entered the Abbey of Gethsemani in Kentucky in 1941, and in 1948 published a best-selling autobiography, The Seven Storey Mountain, which quickly made him the most famous monk in America. Subsequently, his faith developed new dimensions that deeply involved him in the changes his church underwent in the Vatican II era (1962–1965), opposition to the Vietnam War, and dialogue with the religions of the East. The last interest was reflected in several books, including Mystics and Zen Masters and Zen and the Birds of Appetite, as well as The Way of Chuang Tzu.

That book is a largely verse translation of selected passages from the Chinese philosopher, which Merton prepared with the help of the distinguished scholar John Wu. Merton wrote a long introduction, most of which is reproduced here. In it we can see what pulled Merton to his fellow contemplative of so many centuries before. He discusses, for example, the problem of the Ju, those earnest Confucianists who attempt to observe virtue and do good. From all their efforts they attain only mixed results and mixed happiness, for the very act of making the good something extraneous to be achieved creates a fatal division between it and oneself.

This does not mean one should do nothing, in the ordinary (not the Taoist) sense of doing nothing. Merton wrote about Chuang Tzu in the thick of engagement in the Vatican II controversies, the antiwar movement, and social-justice efforts. Yet he found help in Chuang Tzu precisely because, as a monk, he was coming to perceive that what effect he could have would come from his being a "marginal man," a "hidden" person so far as the ordinary structure of society was concerned, who could see and speak all the more clearly because he had the outsider's eye and the honesty of one with nothing to lose.

According to his biographer, Michael Mott, "The model for Merton of the hidden life was Chuang Tzu," and his version of him "became at once Merton's favorite among his own books." The convert Trappist become ecclesiastical reformer and social critic, as well as poet and mystic, acutely divined that what the America of the sixties, with its violent lurches forward and backward, its high-decibel protests and counterprotests, badly needed was someone like Chuang Tzu sitting in his grove looking at it all from another angle, talking about it with kindly chuckles and sardonic flashes.

This does not mean that the Catholic monk of nearly twenty-five years became a Taoist. Indeed, it would be almost contrary to the nature of Taoism to insist that anyone ought to "become" a Taoist. Rather, this passage is an example of the kind of influence Taoism can exercise, as well as being representative of a person important in the dialogue between Eastern and Western religion in America.

The Way of Chuang Tzu*

There is not much danger of confusing Chuang Tzu with Confucius or Mencius, but there is perhaps more difficulty in distinguishing him at first sight from the sophists and hedonists of his own time. For example, Yang Chu resembles Chuang Tzu in his praise of reclusion and his contempt for politics. He bases a philosophy of evasion, which is frankly egotistical, on the principle that the bigger and more valuable the tree is, the more likely it is to fall victim to the hurricane or to the lumberman's axe.

The avoidance of political responsibility was, therefore, essential to Yang's idea of personal happiness, and he carried this to such an extent that Mencius said of him, "Though he might have benefited the whole world by plucking out a single hair, he would not have done it." However, even in Yang Chu's hedonism we can find elements which remind us of our own modern concern with the person: for instance the idea that the life and integrity of the person remain of greater value than any object or any function to which the person may be called to devote himself, at the risk of alienation. But a personalism that has nothing to offer but evasion will not be a genuine personalism at all, since it destroys the relationships without which the person cannot truly develop. After all, the idea that one can seriously cultivate his own personal freedom merely by discard-

---

*From Thomas Merton, *The Way of Chuang Tzu*. Copyright © 1965 by the Abbey of Gethsemani, Inc. Reprinted by permission of New Directions Publishing Corporation.

The selection is from Merton's introduction, "A Study of Chuang Tzu," pp. 17–32.

ing inhibitions and obligations, to live in self-centered spontaneity, results in the complete decay of the true self and of its capacity for freedom.

Personalism and individualism must not be confused. Personalism gives priority to the *person* and not the individual self. To give priority to the person means respecting the unique and inalienable value of the *other* person, as well as one's own, for a respect that is centered only on one's individual self to the exclusion of others proves itself to be fraudulent.

The classic *Ju* philosophy of Confucius and his followers can be called a traditional personalism built on the basic social relationships and obligations that are essential to a humane life and that, when carried out as they should be, develop the human potentialities of each person in his relation to others. In fulfilling the commands of nature as manifested by tradition, which are essentially commands of love, man develops his own inner potential for love, understanding, reverence, and wisdom. He becomes a "Superior Man" or a "Noble Minded Man," fully in harmony with heaven, earth, his sovereign, his parents and children, and his fellow men, by his obedience to *Tao*.

The character of the "Superior Man" or "Noble Minded Man" according to *Ju* philosophy is constructed around a four-sided mandala of basic virtues. The first of these is compassionate and devoted love, charged with deep empathy and sincerity, that enables one to identify with the troubles and joys of others as if they were one's own. This compassion is called *Jen,* and is sometimes translated "human heartedness." The second of the basic virtues is that sense of justice, responsibility, duty, obligation to others, which is called *Yi.* It must be observed that Ju philosophy insists that both Jen and Yi are completely disinterested. The mark of the "Noble Minded Man" is that he does not do things simply because they are pleasing or profitable to himself, but because they flow from an unconditional moral imperative. They are things that he sees to be right and good in themselves. Hence, anyone who is guided by the profit motive, even though it be for the profit of the society to which he belongs, is not capable of living a genuinely moral life. Even when his acts do not conflict with the moral law, they remain amoral because they are motivated by the desire of profit and not the love of the good.

The other two basic virtues of Ju are necessary to complete this picture of wholeness and humaneness. *Li* is something more than exterior and ritual correctness: it is the ability to make use of ritual forms to give full outward expression to the love and obligation by which one is bound to others. *Li* is the acting out of veneration and love, not only for parents, for one's sovereign, for one's people, but also for "Heaven-and-earth." It is a liturgical contemplation of the religious and metaphysical structure of the person, the family, society, and the cosmos itself. The ancient Chinese liturgists "made observations of all the movements under the sky, directing their attention to the interpenetrations which take place in them, this with a view to putting into effect right rituals."

One's individual self should be lost in the "ritual disposition" in which one emerges as a higher "liturgical self," animated by the compassion and respect which have traditionally informed the deepest responses of one's family and people in the presence of "Heaven," *Tien.* One learns by *Li* to take one's place gratefully in the cosmos and in history. Finally there is "wisdom," *Chih,* that embraces all the other virtues in a mature and religious understanding which orients them to their living fulfillment. This perfect understanding of the "way of Heaven" finally enables a man of maturity and long experience to follow all the inmost desires of his heart without disobeying Heaven. It is St. Augustine's "Love and do what you will!" But Confucius did not claim to have reached this point until he was seventy. In any case, the man who has attained Chih, or wisdom, has learned spontaneous inner obedience to Heaven, and is no longer governed merely by external standards. But a long and arduous discipline by external standards remains absolutely necessary.

These sound and humane ideals, admirable in themselves, were socially implemented by a structure of duties, rites, and observances that would seem to us extraordinarily complex and artificial. And when we find Chuang Tzu making fun of the Confucian practice of Li (for example the rites of mourning), we must not interpret him in the light of our own extremely casual mores, empty of symbolic feeling and insensitive to the persuasion of ceremony.

We must remember that we ourselves are living in a society which is almost unimaginably different from the Middle Kingdom in 300 B.C. We might perhaps find analogies for our own way of life in Imperial Rome, if not Carthage, Nineveh, or Babylon. Though the China of the fourth century was not without its barbarities, it was probably more refined, more complex, and more humane than these cities that the Apocalypse of John portrayed as typical of worldly brutality, greed, and power. The climate of Chinese thought was certainly affected by the fact that the Ju ideal was taken seriously and was already to some extent built in, by education and liturgy, to the structure of Chinese society. (We must not however imagine, anachronistically, that in the time of Chuang Tzu the Chinese governing class was systematically educated en masse according to Confucian principles, as happened later.)

If Chuang Tzu reacted against the Ju doctrine, it was not in the name of something lower—the animal spontaneity of the individual who does not want to be bothered with a lot of tiresome duties—but in the name of something altogether higher. This is the most important fact to remember when we westerners confront the seeming antinomianism of Chuang Tzu or of the Zen Masters.

Chuang Tzu was not demanding less than Jen and Yi, but more. His chief complaint of Ju was that it did not go far enough. It produced well-behaved and virtuous officials, indeed cultured men. But it nevertheless limited and imprisoned them within fixed external norms and consequently made it impossible for them to act really freely and creatively in response to the ever new demands of unforeseen situations.

Ju philosophy also appealed to Tao, as did Chuang Tzu. In fact all Chinese philosophy and culture tend to be "Taoist" in a broad sense, since the idea of Tao is, in one form or other, central to traditional Chinese thinking. Confucius could speak of "my Tao." He could demand that the disciple "set his heart on the Tao." He could declare that "If a man hears the Tao in the morning and dies in the evening, his life has not been wasted." And he could add that if a man reaches the age of forty or fifty without ever "hearing the Tao," there is "nothing worthy of respect in him." Yet Chuang Tzu believed that the Tao on which Confucius set his heart was not the "great Tao" that is invisible and incomprehensible. It was a lesser reflection of Tao as it manifests itself in human life. It was the traditional wisdom handed down by the ancients, the guide to practical life, the way of virtue.

In the first chapter of the Tao Teh Ching, Lao Tzu distinguished between the Eternal Tao "that can not be named," which is the nameless and unknowable source of all being, and the Tao "that can be named," which is the "Mother of all things." Confucius may have had access to the manifest aspects of the Tao "that can be named," but the basis of all Chuang Tzu's critique of Ju philosophy is that it never comes near to the Tao "that can not be named," and indeed takes no account of it. Until relatively late works like the Doctrine of the Mean which are influenced by Taoism, Confucius refused to concern himself with a Tao higher than that of man precisely because it was "unknowable" and beyond the reach of rational discourse. Chuang Tzu held that only when one was in contact with the mysterious Tao which is beyond all existent things, which cannot be conveyed either by words or by silence, and which is apprehended only in a state which is neither speech nor silence could one really understand how to live. To live merely according to the "Tao of man" was to go astray. The Tao of Ju philosophy is, in the words of Confucius, "threading together into one the desires of the self and the desires of the other." This can therefore be called an "ethical Tao" or the "Tao of man," the manifestation in act of a principle of love and justice. It is identifiable with the Golden Rule—treating others as one would wish to be treated oneself. But it is not the "Tao of Heaven." In fact, as Confucianism developed, it continued to divide and subdivide the idea of Tao until it became simply a term indicating an abstract universal principle in the realm of ethics. Thus we hear of the "tao of fatherhood," the "tao of sonship," the "tao of wifeliness" and the "tao of ministership." Nevertheless, when Confucian thought was deeply influenced by Taoism, these various human taos could and did become fingers pointing to the invisible and divine Tao. This is clear for instance in the *Tao of Painting:* "Throughout the course of Chinese painting the common purpose has been to reaffirm the traditional (human) *tao* and to transmit the ideas, principles and methods that have been tested and developed by the masters of each period as the means of expressing the harmony of the *Tao.*"

Chuang Tzu drily observed that the pursuit of the ethical Tao became illusory if one sought for others what was good for oneself without really knowing what was good for oneself. He takes up this question of the good in the meditation that I have called "Perfect Joy." First of all he denies that happiness can be found by hedonism or utilitarianism (the "profit motive" of Mo Ti). The life of riches, ambition, pleasure, is in reality an intolerable servitude in which one "lives for what is always out of reach," thirsting "for survival in the future" and "incapable of living in the present." The Ju philosopher would have no difficulty in agreeing that the motive of profit or pleasure is unworthy of a true man. But then Chuang Tzu immediately turns against Ju, and criticizes the heroic and self-sacrificing public servant, the "Superior Man" of virtue formed in the school of Confucius. His analysis of the ambiguities of such a life may perhaps seem subtle to us, living as we do in such a different moral climate. Chuang Tzu's concern with the problem that the very goodness of the good and the nobility of the great may contain the hidden seed of ruin is analogous to the concern that Sophocles or Aeschylus felt a little earlier, in the west. Chuang Tzu comes up with a different answer in which there is less of religious mystery. To put it simply, the hero of virtue and duty ultimately lands himself in the same ambiguities as the hedonist and the utilitarian. Why? Because he aims at achieving "the good" as object. He engages in a self-conscious and deliberate campaign to "do his duty" in the belief that this is right and therefore productive of happiness. He sees "happiness" and "the good" as "something to be attained," and thus he places them outside himself in the world of objects. In so doing, he becomes involved in a division from which there is no escape: between the present, in which he is not yet in possession of what he seeks, and the future in which he thinks he will have what he desires: between the wrong and the evil, the absence of what he seeks, and the good that he hopes to make present by his efforts to eliminate the evils; between his own idea of right and wrong, and the contrary idea of right and wrong held by some other philosophical school. And so on.

Chuang Tzu does not allow himself to get engaged in this division by "taking sides." On the contrary, he feels that the trouble is not merely with the *means* the Ju philosopher chooses to attain his ends, but with the ends themselves. He believes that the whole concept of "happiness" and "unhappiness" is ambiguous from the start, since it is situated in the world of objects. This is no less true of more refined concepts like virtue, justice, and so on. In fact, it is especially true of "good and evil," or "right and wrong." From the moment they are treated as "objects to be attained," these values lead to delusion and alienation. Therefore Chuang Tzu agrees with the paradox of Lao Tzu, "When all the world recognizes good as good, it becomes evil,'' because it becomes something that one does not have and which one must constantly be pursuing until, in effect, it becomes unattainable.

The more one seeks ''the good'' outside oneself as something to be acquired, the more one is faced with the necessity of discussing, studying, understanding, analyzing the nature of the good. The more, therefore, one becomes involved in abstractions and in the confusion of divergent opinions. The more ''the good'' is objectively analyzed, the more it is treated as something to be attained by special virtuous techniques, the less real it becomes. As it becomes less real, it recedes further into the distance of abstraction, futurity, unattainability. The more, therefore, one concentrates on the means to be used to attain it. And as the end becomes more remote and more difficult, the means become more elaborate and complex, until finally the mere study of the means becomes so demanding that all one's effort must be concentrated on this, and the end is forgotten. Hence the nobility of the Ju scholar becomes, in reality, a devotion to the systematic uselessness of practicing means which lead nowhere. This is, in fact, nothing but organized despair: ''the good'' that is preached and exacted by the moralist thus finally becomes an evil, and all the more so since the hopeless pursuit of it distracts one from the real good which one already possesses and which one now despises or ignores.

The way of Tao is to begin with the simple good with which one is endowed by the very fact of existence. Instead of self-conscious cultivation of this good (which vanishes when we look at it and becomes intangible when we try to grasp it), we grow quietly in the humility of a simple, ordinary life, and this way is analogous (at least psychologically) to the Christian ''life of faith.'' It is more a matter of *believing* the good than of seeing it as the fruit of one's effort.

The secret of the way proposed by Chuang Tzu is therefore not the accumulation of virtue and merit taught by Ju, but *wu wei*, the non-doing, or non-action, which is not intent upon results and is not concerned with consciously laid plans or deliberately organized endeavors: ''My greatest happiness consists precisely in doing nothing whatever that is calculated to obtain happiness . . . Perfect joy is to be without joy . . . if you ask 'what ought to be done' and 'what ought not to be done' on earth to produce happiness, I answer that these questions do not have [a fixed and predetermined] answer'' to suit every case. If one is in harmony with Tao—the cosmic Tao, "Great Tao"—the answer will make itself clear when the time comes to act, for then one will act not according to the human and self-conscious mode of deliberation, but according to the divine and spontaneous mode of wu wei, which is the mode of action of Tao itself, and is therefore the source of all good.

The other way, the way of conscious striving, even though it may claim to be a way of virtue, is fundamentally a way of self-aggrandizement, and it is consequently bound to come into conflict with Tao. Hence it is self-destructive, for "what is against Tao will cease to be." This explains why the Tao Teh Ching, criticizing Ju philosophy, says that the highest virtue is non-virtuous and "therefore it has virtue." But "low virtue never frees itself from virtuousness, therefore it has no virtue." Chuang Tzu is not against virtue (why should he be?), but he sees that mere virtuousness is without meaning and without deep effect either in the life of the individual or in society.

Once this is clear, we see that Chuang Tzu's ironic statements about "righteousness" and "ceremonies" are made not in the name of lawless hedonism and antinomianism, but in the name of that genuine virtue which is "beyond virtuousness."

Once this is clear, one can reasonably see a certain analogy between Chuang Tzu and St. Paul. The analogy must certainly not be pushed too far. Chuang Tzu lacks the profoundly theological mysticism of St. Paul. But his teaching about the spiritual liberty of wu wei and the relation of virtue to the indwelling Tao is analogous to Paul's teaching on faith and grace, contrasted with the "works of the Old Law." The relation of the Chuang Tzu book to the Analects of Confucius is not unlike that of the Epistles to the Galatians and Romans to the Torah.

For Chuang Tzu, the truly great man is therefore not the man who has, by a lifetime of study and practice, accumulated a great fund of virtue and merit, but the man in whom "Tao acts without impediment," the "man of Tao." Several of the texts in this present book describe the "man of Tao." Others tell us what he is not. One of the most instructive, in this respect, is the long and delightful story of the anxiety-ridden, perfectionistic disciple of Keng Sang Chu, who is sent to Lao Tzu to learn the "elements." He is told that "if you persist in trying to attain what is never attained . . . in reasoning about what cannot be understood, you will be destroyed." On the other hand, if he can only "know when to stop," be content to wait, listen, and give up his own useless strivings, "this melts the ice." Then he will begin to grow without watching himself grow, and without any appetite for self-improvement.

Chuang Tzu, surrounded by ambitious and supposedly "practical men," reflected that these "operators" knew the value of the "useful," but not the greater value of the "useless." As John Wu has put it:

> To Chuang Tzu the world must have looked like a terrible tragedy written by a great comedian. He saw scheming politicians falling into pits they had dug for others. He saw predatory states swallowing weaker states, only to be swallowed in their turn by stronger ones. Thus the much vaunted utility of the useful talents proved not only useless but self-destructive.

The "man of Tao" will prefer obscurity and solitude. He will not seek public office, even though he may recognize that the Tao which "inwardly forms the sage, outwardly forms the King." In "The Turtle," Chuang Tzu delivers a curt and definite refusal to those who come to tempt him away from his fishing on the river bank in order to give him a job in the capital. He has an even more blunt response when his friend Hui Tzu suspects him of plotting to supplant him in his official job (cf. "Owl and Phoenix").

On the other hand, Chuang Tzu is not merely a professional recluse. The "man of Tao" does not make the mistake of giving up self-conscious virtuousness in order to immerse himself in an even more self-conscious contemplative recollection. One cannot call Chuang Tzu a "contemplative" in the sense of one who adopts a systematic program of spiritual self-purification in order to attain to certain definite interior experiences, or even merely to "cultivate the interior life." Chuang Tzu would condemn this just as roundly as the "cultivation" of anything else on an artificial basis. All deliberate, systematic, and reflexive "self-cultivation," whether active or contemplative, personalistic or politically committed, cuts one off from the mysterious but indispensable contact with Tao, the hidden "Mother" of all life and truth. One of the things that causes the young disciple of Keng Sang Chu to be so utterly frustrated is precisely that he shuts himself up in a cell and tries to cultivate qualities which he thinks desirable and get rid of others which he dislikes.

A contemplative and interior life which would simply make the subject more aware of himself and permit him to become obsessed with his own interior progress would, for Chuang Tzu, be no less an illusion than the active life of the "benevolent" man who would try by his own efforts to impose his idea of the good on those who might oppose this idea—and thus in his eyes, become "enemies of the good." The true tranquillity sought by the "man of Tao" is *Ying ning,* tranquillity in the action of non-action, in other words, a tranquillity which transcends the division between activity and contemplation by entering into union with the nameless and invisible Tao.

Chuang Tzu insists everywhere that this means abandoning the "need to win" (see "The Fighting Cock"). In "Monkey Mountain," he shows the peril of cleverness and virtuosity, and repeats one of his familiar themes that we might summarize as: No one is so wrong as the man who knows all the answers. Like Lao Tzu, Master Chuang preaches an essential humility: not the humility of virtuousness and conscious self-abasement, which in the end is never entirely free from the unconsciousness of Uriah Heep, but the basic, one might say, "ontological," or "cosmic" humility of the man who fully realizes his own nothingness and becomes totally forgetful of himself, "like a dry tree stump . . . like dead ashes."

One may call this humility "cosmic," not only because it is rooted in the true nature of things, but also because it is full of life and awareness, responding with boundless vitality and joy to all living beings. It manifests itself everywhere by a Franciscan simplicity and connaturality with all living creatures. Half the "characters" who are brought before us to speak the mind of Chuang Tzu are animals—birds, fishes, frogs, and so on. Chuang Tzu's Taoism is nostalgic for the primordial climate of paradise in which there was no differentiation, in which man was utterly simple, unaware of himself, living at peace with himself, with Tao, and with all other creatures. But for Chuang this paradise is not something that has been irrevocably lost by sin and cannot be regained except by redemption. It is still ours, but we do not know it, since the effect of life in society is to complicate and confuse our existence, making us forget who we really are by causing us to become obsessed with what we are not.

It is this self-awareness, which we try to increase and perfect by all sorts of methods and practices, that is really a forgetfulness of our true roots in the "unknown Tao" and our solidarity in the "uncarved block" in which there are as yet no distinctions.

Chuang Tzu's paradoxical teaching that "you never find happiness until you stop looking for it" must not, therefore, be negatively interpreted. He is not preaching a retreat from a full, active, human existence into inertia and quietism. He is, in fact, saying that happiness can be found, but only by non-seeking and non-action. It can be found, but not as the result of a program or of a system. A program or a system has this disadvantage: it tends to situate happiness in one kind of action only and to seek it only there. But the happiness and freedom which Chuang Tzu saw in Tao is to be found *everywhere* (since Tao is everywhere), and until one can learn to act with such freedom from care that all action is "perfect joy because without joy," one cannot really be happy in anything. As Fung Yu Lan sums it up in his *Spirit of Chinese Philosophy* (p. 77), the sage will "accompany everything and welcome everything, everything being in the course of being constructed and in the course of being destroyed. Hence he cannot but obtain joy in freedom, and his joy is unconditional."

The true character of wu wei is not mere inactivity but *perfect action*—because it is act without activity. In other words, it is action not carried out independently of Heaven and earth and in conflict with the dynamism of the whole, but in perfect harmony with the whole. It is not mere passivity, but it is action that seems both effortless and spontaneous because performed "rightly," in perfect accordance with our nature and with our place in the scheme of things. It is completely free because there is in it no force and no violence. It is not "conditioned" or "limited" by our own individual needs and desires, or even by our own theories and ideas.

It is precisely this *unconditional* character of wu wei that differentiates Chuang Tzu from other great philosophers who constructed systems by which their activity was necessarily conditioned. The abstract theory of "universal love" preached by Mo Ti was shrewdly seen by Chuang Tzu to be false precisely because of the inhumanity of its consequences. In theory, Mo Ti held that all men should be loved with an equal love, that the individual should find his own greatest good in loving the common good of all, that universal love was rewarded by the tranquillity, peace, and good order of all, and the happiness of the individual. But this "universal love" will be found upon examination (like most other utopian projects) to make such severe demands upon human nature that it cannot be realized, and indeed, even if it could be realized it would in fact cramp and distort man, eventually ruining both him and his society. Not because love is not good and natural to man, but because a system constructed on a theoretical and abstract principle of love ignores certain fundamental and mysterious realities, of which we cannot be fully conscious, and the price we pay for this inattention is that our "love" in fact becomes hate.

Hence, the society of "universal love" planned by Mo Ti was drab, joyless, and grim since all spontaneity was regarded with suspicion. The humane and ordered satisfactions of the Confucian life of friendship, ritual, music, and so on, were all banned by Mo Ti. It is important to remember that in this case, Chuang Tzu defends "music" and "rites" though in other places he laughs at exaggerated love of them. "Mo Ti," he said, "would have no singing in life, no mourning in death . . . Notwithstanding men will sing, he condemns singing. Men will mourn, and still he condemns mourning, men will express joy, and still he condemns it—is this truly in accord with man's nature? In life toil, in death stinginess: his way is one of hard heartedness!"

From such a passage as this we can see that Chuang Tzu's own irony about elaborate funerals is to be seen in the right light. The amusing and of course entirely fictitious description of "Lao Tzu's Wake" gives Chuang an opportunity to criticize not mourning as such, or even piety toward one's master, but the artificial attachments formed by a cult of the master as Master. The "tao of discipleship" is for Chuang Tzu a figment of the imagination, and it can in no way substitute for the "Great Tao," in which all relationships find their proper order and expression.

That Chuang Tzu should be able to take one side of a question in one place, and the other side in another context, warns us that in reality he is beyond mere partisan dispute. Though he is a social critic, his criticism is never bitter or harsh. Irony and parable are his chief instruments, and the whole climate of his work is one of tolerant impartiality which avoids preaching and recognizes the uselessness of dogmatizing about obscure ideas that even the

philosophers were not prepared to understand. Though he did not
follow other men in their follies, he did not judge them severely—
he knew that he had follies of his own, and had the good sense to
accept the fact and enjoy it. In fact he saw that one basic characteristic of the sage is that he recognizes himself to be *as other men are.*
He does not set himself apart from others and above them. And yet
there is a difference; he differs "*in his heart*" from other men, since
he is centered on Tao and not on himself. But "he does not know in
what way he is different." He is also aware of his relatedness to others, his union with them, but he does not "understand" this either.
He merely lives it.

The key to Chuang Tzu's thought is the complementarity of
opposites, and this can be seen only when one grasps the central
"pivot" of Tao which passes squarely through both "Yes" and
"No," "I" and "Not-I." Life is a continual development. All
beings are in a state of flux. Chuang Tzu would have agreed with
Herakleitos. What is impossible today may suddenly become possible tomorrow. What is good and pleasant today may, tomorrow,
become evil and odious. What seems right from one point of view
may, when seen from a different aspect, manifest itself as completely wrong.

What, then, should the wise man do? Should he simply remain
indifferent and treat right and wrong, good and bad, as if they were
all the same? Chuang Tzu would be the first to deny that they were
the same. But in so doing, he would refuse to grasp one or the other
and cling to it as to an absolute. When a limited and conditioned view
of "good" is erected to the level of an absolute, it immediately becomes an evil, because it excludes certain complementary elements
which are required if it is to be fully good. To cling to one partial
view, one limited and conditioned opinion, and to treat this as the
ultimate answer to all questions is simply to "obscure the Tao" and
make oneself obdurate in error.

He who grasps the central pivot of Tao, is able to watch "Yes"
and "No" pursue their alternating course around the circumference.
He retains his perspective and clarity of judgment, so that he knows
that "Yes" is "Yes" in the light of the "No" which stands over
against it. He understands that happiness, when pushed to an extreme, becomes calamity. That beauty, when overdone, becomes ug-
liness. Clouds become rain and vapor ascends again to become

clouds. To insist that the cloud should never turn to rain is to resist the dynamism of Tao.

These ideas are applied by Chuang Tzu to the work of the artist and craftsman as well as to the teacher of philosophy. In "The Woodcarver," we see that the accomplished craftsman does not simply proceed according to certain fixed rules and external standards. To do so is, of course, perfectly all right for the mediocre artisan. But the superior work of art proceeds from a hidden and spiritual principle which, in fasting, detachment, forgetfulness of results, and abandonment of all hope of profit, discovers precisely the tree that is waiting to have this particular work carved from it. In such a case, the artist works as though passively, and it is Tao that works in and through him. This is a favorite theme of Chuang Tzu, and we find it often repeated. The "right way" of making things is beyond self-conscious reflection, for "when the shoe fits, the foot is forgotten."

In the teaching of philosophy, Chuang Tzu is not in favor of putting on tight shoes that make the disciple intensely conscious of the fact that he has feet—because they torment him! For that very reason Chuang is critical not only of Confucians who are too attached to method and system, but also of Taoists who try to impart knowledge of the unnameable Tao when it cannot be imparted, and when the hearer is not even ready to receive the first elements of instruction about it. "Symphony for a Sea Bird" is to be read in this light. It does not apply merely to the deadening of spontaneity by an artificial insistence on Ju philosophy, but also to a wrong-headed and badly timed zeal in the communication of Tao. In fact, Tao cannot be communicated. Yet it communicates itself in its own way. When the right moment arrives, even one who seems incapable of any instruction whatever will become mysteriously aware of Tao.

Meanwhile, though he consistently disagreed with his friend the dialectician, Hui Tzu, and though his disciples, who were not without "the need to win" always represented Chuang as beating Hui in debate, Chuang Tzu actually used many of Hui Tzu's metaphysical ideas. He realized that, by the principle of complementarity, his own thought was not complete merely in itself, without the "opposition" of Hui Tzu.

One of the most famous of all Chuang Tzu's "principles" is that called "three in the morning," from the story of the monkeys whose keeper planned to give them three measures of chestnuts in the morning and four in the evening but, when they complained, changed his plan and gave them four in the morning and three in the evening. What does this story mean? Simply that the monkeys were foolish and that the keeper cynically outsmarted them? Quite the contrary. The point is rather that the keeper had enough sense to recognize that the monkeys had irrational reasons of their own for wanting four measures of chestnuts in the morning, and did not stubbornly insist on his original arrangement. He was not totally indifferent, and yet he saw that an accidental difference did not affect the substance of his arrangement. Nor did he waste time demanding that the monkeys try to be "more reasonable" about it when monkeys are not expected to be reasonable in the first place. It is when we insist most firmly on everyone else being "reasonable" that we become, ourselves, unreasonable. Chuang Tzu, firmly centered on Tao, could see these things in perspective. His teaching follows the principle of "three in the morning," and it is at home on two levels: that of the divine and invisible Tao that has no name, and that of ordinary, simple, everyday existence.

V

THEOSOPHY

We have already, in the introductory chapter of this book, glanced at the founding and basic outlook of the Theosophical Society. The role of this extraordinary movement in disseminating Eastern ideas in America should not be underestimated. Its lectures, periodicals, and gifts of books to public libraries have reached not only major cities, but numerous American small towns as well, to leave behind a general awareness of such concepts as karma and the spiritual evolution of the universe. Sometimes an ongoing group was the reward of Theosophical promotional efforts as well. For example, according to the *Theosophic Messenger* of January 1900, there were some seventy-one branches of the society in America. They were not restricted to such expected haunts of the occult as Boston, New York, and Los Angeles, but were also found in such places as Council Bluffs (Iowa), Honolulu, Sheridan (Wyoming), and Pierre (South Dakota). The White Lotus Lodge in Pierre reported "very interesting and instructive meetings every Saturday." The group had gone through seven theosophical manuals and was engaged in discussion of karma as the century turned.

So it was that, through Theosophy, Eastern ideas trickled down into the American heartland. For part of the legacy of Theosophy was a sense that the spiritual East was important. It was not necessarily more important than Western religion, rightly understood in light of its esoteric symbolism. But the East was equally significant, for both East and West were veils under which ancient wisdom was concealed, yet through which the wise could nonetheless discern its true contours.

Bibliography

Campbell, Bruce, *Ancient Wisdom Revived: A History of the Theo-sophical Movement*. Berkeley and Los Angeles: University of California Press, 1980.

Ellwood, Robert, "The American Theosophical Synthesis," in *The Occult in America: New Historical Perspective,* ed. Howard Kerr and Charles L. Crow. Urbana and Chicago: University of Illinois Press, 1983, pp. 111–34.

Neff, Mary K. *Personal Memoirs of H. P. Blavatsky*. New York: Dutton, 1937.

Olcott, Henry S. *Old Diary Leaves: The History of the Theosophical Society*. 6 vols. Adyar: Theosophical Publishing House, 1895–1935. See especially volume 1 for the writing of *Isis Unveiled*.

Theosophy Selection

The penetrating of those veils is the task of *Isis Unveiled*, the first major book of Theosophy's premier modern interpreter, H. P. Blavatsky, and the only important work she penned on American soil. Scattered throughout it are Eastern examples of the ancient wisdom. To be sure, the cofounder and chief intellectual mentor of Theosophy does not here develop Eastern-inspired teaching as systematically as in her later work, *The Secret Doctrine*. But it does appear as one legitimation of her basic theme.

At first opening, the sprawling two volumes called *Isis Unveiled* may seem little more than a farrago of stories about magic and wonders around the world, especially as associated with shamans and witch doctors in obscure places, together with frequently acerbic comments on conventional science and religion. Gradually, however, a position emerges behind all the rambling material. In the universe there is not only matter, but also an invisible energy, rather like the Taoist *ch'i*, which can be wielded by those who know its science, which is what is ordinarily called magic.

The universe and the individual are permeated by the two principles: this energy, called spirit, and matter. Both stem from the ultimate, God, the Universal Soul. Consciousness derives from the union of spirit and matter, and so reflects God, the unity from which both derive.

This wisdom, Blavatsky believed, was better understood in antiquity than today, when it has been so much obscured by dogmatic religion and shallow but no less arrogant science. It is still, however, preserved in some fullness by adepts in isolated places and semi-secret lodges. The passage following offers a typical account of hidden learning, of the working of so-called magic, which involves knowledge of the invisible energy on both popular and higher levels, together with some puncturing of the pretensions of Christians and other "civilized" Westerners, who really understand little of the mysterious world they presume to convert and rule.

Isis Unveiled*

Both in Western and Eastern Thibet, as in every other place where Buddhism predominates, there are two distinct religions, the

---

*From H. P. Blavatsky, *Isis Unveiled* (New York: J. W. Bouton, 1877, pp. 607–20).

same as it is in Brahmanism—the secret philosophy and the popular religion. The former is that of the followers of the doctrine of the sect of the Sutrântika.* They closely adhere to the spirit of Buddha's original teachings which show the necessity of *intuitional* perception, and all deductions therefrom. These do not proclaim their views, nor allow them to be made public.

"All *compounds* are perishable," were the last words uttered by the lips of the dying Gautama, when preparing under the Sâl-tree to enter into Nirvana. "Spirit is the sole, elementary, and primordial unity, and each of its rays is immortal, infinite, and indestructible. Beware of the illusions of matter." Buddhism was spread far and wide over Asia, and even farther, by Dharm-Asôka. He was the grandson of the miracle-worker Chandragupta, the illustrious king who rescued the Punjâb from the Macedonians—if they ever were at Punjâb at all—and received Megasthenes at his court in Pataliputra. Dharm-Asôka was the greatest King of the Maûrya dynasty. From a reckless profligate and atheist, he had become Pryâdasi, the "beloved of the gods," and never was the purity of his philanthropic views surpassed by any earthly ruler. His memory has lived for ages in the hearts of the Buddhists, and has been perpetuated in the humane edicts engraved in several popular dialects on the columns and rocks of Allahabad, Delhi, Guzerat, Peshawur, Orissa, and other places.† His famous grandfather had united all India under his powerful sceptre. When the Nâgas, or serpent-worshippers of Kashmere had been converted through the efforts of the apostles sent out by the Sthaviras of the third councils, the religion of Gautama spread like wild-fire. Gândhara, Cabul, and even many of the Satrapies of Alexander the Great, accepted the new philosophy. The Buddhism of Nepâl being the one which may be said to have diverged less than any other from the primeval ancient faith, the Lamaism of Tartary, Mongolia, and Thibet, which is a direct offshoot of this country, may be thus shown to be the purest Buddhism; for we say it again, Lamaism properly is but an external form of rites.

---

*From the compound word sûtra, maxim or precept, and antika, close or near.

†It sounds like injustice to Asôka to compare him with Constantine, as is done by several Orientalists. If, in the religious and political sense, Asôka did for India what Constantine is alleged to have achieved for the Western World, all similarity stops there.

The Upâsakas and Upâsakis, or male and female semi-monastics and semi-laymen, have equally with the lama-monks themselves, to strictly abstain from violating any of Buddha's rules, and must study *Meipo* and every psychological phenomenon as much. Those who become guilty of any of the "five sins" lose all right to congregate with the pious community. The most important of these is *not to curse upon any consideration, for the curse returns upon the one that utters it, and often upon his innocent relatives who breathe the same atmosphere with him.* To love each other, and even our bitterest enemies; to offer our lives even for animals, to the extent of abstaining from defensive arms; to gain the greatest of victories by conquering one's self; to avoid all vices; to practice all virtues, especially humility and mildness; to be obedient to superiors, to cherish and respect parents, old age, learning, virtuous and holy men; to provide food, shelter, and comfort for men and animals; to plant trees on the roads and dig wells for the comfort of travellers; such are the moral duties of Buddhists. Every Ani or Bikshuni (nun) is subjected to these laws.

Numerous are the Buddhist and Lamaic saints who have been renowned for the unsurpassed sanctity of their lives and their "miracles." So Tissu, the Emperor's spiritual teacher, who consecrated Kublaï-Khan, the Nadir Shah, was known far and wide as much for the extreme holiness of his life as for the many wonders he wrought. But he did not stop at fruitless miracles, but did better than that. Tissu purified completely his religion; and from one single province of Southern Mongolia is said to have forced Kublai to expel from convents 500,000 monkish impostors, who made a pretext of their profession, to live in vice and idleness. Then the Lamaists had their great reformer, the Shaberon Son-Ka-po, who is claimed to have been immaculately conceived by his mother, a virgin from Koko-nor (fourteenth century), who is another wonder-worker. The sacred tree of Kounboum, the tree of the 10,000 images, which, in consequence of the degeneration of the true faith had ceased budding for several centuries, now shot forth new sprouts and bloomed more vigorously than ever from the hair of this avatar of Buddha, says the legend. The same tradition makes him (Son-Ka-po) ascend to heaven in 1419. Contrary to the prevailing idea, few of these saints are *Khubilhans,* or Shaberons—reïncarnations.

Many of the lamaseries contain schools of magic, but the most celebrated is the collegiate monastery of the Shu-tukt, where there are over 30,000 monks attached to it, the lamasery forming quite a little city. Some of the female nuns possess marvellous psychological powers. We have met some of these women on their way from Lha-Ssa to Candi, the Rome of Buddhism, with its miraculous shrines and Gautama's relics. To avoid encounters with Mussulmans and other sects they travel by night alone, unarmed, and without the least fear of wild animals, *for these will not touch them.* At the first glimpses of dawn, they take refuge in caves and viharas prepared for them by their co-religionists at calculated distances; for notwithstanding the fact that Buddhism has taken refuge in Ceylon, and nominally there are but few of the denomination in British India, yet the secret Byauds (Brotherhoods) and Buddhist viharas are numerous, and every Jain feels himself obliged to help, indiscriminately, Buddhist or Lamaist.

Ever on the lookout for occult phenomena, hungering after sights, one of the most interesting that we have seen was produced by one of these poor travelling Bikshu. It was years ago, and at a time when all such manifestations were new to the writer. We were taken to visit the pilgrims by a Buddhist friend, a mystical gentleman born at Kashmir, of Katchi parents, but a Buddha-Lamaist by conversion, and who generally resides at Lha-Ssa.

"Why carry about this bunch of dead plants?" inquired one of the Bikshuni, an emaciated, tall and elderly woman, pointing to a large nosegay of beautiful, fresh, and fragrant flowers in the writer's hands.

"Dead?" we asked, inquiringly. "Why they just have been gathered in the garden?"

"And yet, they are dead," she gravely answered. "To be born in this world, is this not death? See, how these herbs look when alive in the world of eternal light, in the gardens of our blessed Foh?"

Without moving from the place where she was sitting on the ground, the Ani took a flower from the bunch, laid it in her lap, and began to draw together, by large handfuls as it were, invisible material from the surrounding atmosphere. Presently a very, very faint nodule of vapor was seen, and this slowly took shape and color, until, poised in mid-air, appeared a copy of the bloom we had given her. Faithful to the last tint and the last petal it was, and lying on its side like the original, but a thousand-fold more gorgeous in hue and exquisite in beauty, as the glorified human spirit is more beauteous than its physical capsule. Flower after flower to the minutest herb was thus reproduced and made to vanish, reappearing at our desire, nay, at our simple thought. Having selected a full-blown rose we held it at arm's length, and in a few minutes our arm, hand, and the flower, perfect in every detail, appeared reflected in the vacant space, about two yards from where we sat. But while the flower seemed immeasurably beautified and as ethereal as the other spirit flowers, the arm and hand appeared like a mere reflection in a looking-glass, even to a large spot on the fore arm, left on it by a piece of damp earth which had stuck to one of the roots. Later we learned the reason why.

A great truth was uttered some fifty years ago by Dr. Francis Victor Broussais, when he said: "If magnetism were true, medicine would be an absurdity." Magnetism *is* true, and so we shall not contradict the learned Frenchman as to the rest. Magnetism, as we have shown, is the alphabet of magic. It is idle for any one to attempt to understand either the theory or the practice of the latter until the fundamental principle of magnetic attractions and repulsions throughout nature is recognized.

Many so-called popular superstitions are but evidences of an instinctive perception of this law. An untutored people are taught by the experience of many generations that certain phenomena occur under fixed conditions; they give these conditions and obtain the expected results. Ignorant of the laws, they explain the fact by supernaturalism, for experience has been their sole teacher.

In India, as well as in Russia and some other countries, there is an instinctive repugnance to stepping across a man's shadow, especially if he have red hair; and in the former country, natives are extremely reluctant to shake hands with persons of another race. These are not idle fancies. Every person emits a magnetic exhalation or aura, and a man may be in perfect physical health, but at the same time his exhalation may have a morbific character for others, sensitive to such subtle influences. Dr. Esdaile and other mesmerists long since taught us that Oriental people, especially Hindus, are more susceptible than the white-skinned races. Baron Reichenbach's experiments—and, in fact, the world's entire experience—prove that these magnetic exhalations are most intense from the extremities. Therapeutic manipulations show this; hand-shaking is, therefore, most calculated to communicate antipathetic magnetic conditions, and the Hindus do wisely in keeping their ancient "superstition"— derived from Manu—constantly in mind.

The magnetism of a red-haired man, we have found, in almost every nation, is instinctively dreaded. We might quote proverbs from the Russian, Persian, Georgian, Hindustani, French, Turkish, and even German, to show that treachery and other vices are popularly supposed to accompany the rufous complexion. When a man stands exposed to the sun, the magnetism of that luminary causes his emanations to be projected toward the shadow, and the increased molecular action develops more electricity. Hence, an individual to whom he is antipathetic—though neither might be sensible of the fact—would act prudently in not passing through the shadow. Careful physicians wash their hands upon leaving each patient; why, then, should they not be charged with superstition, as well as the Hindus? The sporules of disease are invisible, but no less real, as European experience demonstrates. Well, *Oriental experience for a hundred centuries has shown that the germs of moral contagion linger about localities, and impure magnetism can be communicated by the touch.*

Another prevalent belief in some parts of Russia, particularly Georgia (Caucasus), and in India, is that in case the body of a drowned person cannot be otherwise found, if a garment of his be thrown into the water it will float until directly over the spot, and then sink. We have even seen the experiment successfully tried with the sacred cord of a Brahman. It floated hither and thither, circling about as though in search of something, until suddenly darting in a straight line for about fifty yards, it sank, and at that exact spot the divers brought up the body. We find this "superstition" even in America. A Pittsburgh paper, of very recent date, describes the finding of the body of a young boy, named Reed, in the Monongahela, by a like method. All other means having failed, it says, "a curious superstition was employed. One of the boy's shirts was thrown into the river where he had gone down, and, it is said, floated on the surface for a time, and finally settled to the bottom at a certain place, which proved to be the resting-place of the body, and which was then drawn out. The belief that the shirt of a drowned person when thrown into the water will follow the body is well-spread, absurd as it appears."

This phenomenon is explained by the law of the powerful attraction existing between the human body and objects that have been long worn upon it. The oldest garment is most effective for the experiment; a new one is useless.

From time immemorial, in Russia, in the month of May, on Trinity Day, maidens from city and village have been in the habit of casting upon the river wreaths of green leaves—which each girl has to form for herself—and consulting their oracles. If the wreath sinks, it is a sign that the girl will die unmarried within a short time; if it floats, she will be married, the time depending upon the number of verses she can repeat during the experiment. We positively affirm that we have personal knowledge of several cases, two of them our intimate friends, where the augury of death proved true, and the girls *died* within twelve months. Tried on any other day than Trinity, the result would doubtless be the same. The sinking of the wreath is attributable to its being impregnated with the unhealthy magnetism of a system which contains the germs of early death; such magnetisms having an attraction for the earth at the bottom of the stream. As for the rest, we are willing to abandon it to the friends of coincidence.

The same general remark as to superstition having a scientific basis applies to the phenomena produced by fakirs and jugglers, which skeptics heap into the common category of trickery. And yet, to a close observer, even to the uninitiated, an enormous difference is presented between the *kîmiya* (phenomenon) of a fakir, and the *batte-bâzi* (jugglery) of a trickster, and the necromancy of a *jâdûgar,* or *sâhir,* so dreaded and despised by the natives. This difference, imperceptible—nay incomprehensible—to the skeptical European, is instinctively appreciated by every Hindu, whether of high or low caste, educated or ignorant. The *kangâlin,* or witch, who uses her terrible *abhi-châr* (mesmeric powers) with intent to injure, may expect death at any moment, for every Hindu finds it lawful to kill her; a *bukka-baz,* or juggler, serves to amuse. A serpent-charmer, with his *bâ-îni* full of venomous snakes, is less dreaded, for his powers of fascination extend but to animals and reptiles; he is unable to charm human beings, to perform that which is called by the natives *mantar phûnknâ,* to throw spells on men by magic. But with the yogi, the sannyâsi, the holy men who acquire enormous psychological powers by mental and physical training, the question is totally different. Some of these men are regarded by the Hindus as demigods. Europeans cannot judge of these powers but in rare and exceptional cases.

The British resident who has encountered in the *maidans* and public places what he regards as frightful and loathsome human beings, sitting motionless in the self-inflicted torture of the *ûrddwa bahu,* with arms raised above the head for months, and even years, need not suppose they are the wonder-working fakirs. The phenomenon of the latter are visible only through the friendly protection of a Brahman, or under peculiarly fortuitous circumstances. Such men are as little accessible as the real Nautch girls, of whom every traveller talks, but very few have actually seen, since they belong exclusively to the pagodas.

It is surpassingly strange, that with the thousands of travellers and the millions of European residents who have been in India, and have traversed it in every direction, so little is yet known of that country and the lands which surround it. It may be that some readers will feel inclined not merely to doubt the correctness but even openly contradict our statement? Doubtless, we will be answered that all that it is desirable to know about India is already known? In fact this very reply was once made to us personally. That resident Anglo-Indians should not busy themselves with inquiries is not strange; for, as a British officer remarked to us upon one occasion, ''society does not consider it well-bred to care about Hindus or their affairs, or even show astonishment or desire information upon anything they may see extraordinary in that country.'' But it really surprises us that at least travellers should not have explored more than they have this interesting realm. Hardly fifty years ago, in penetrating the jungles of the Blue or Neilgherry Hills in Southern Hindustan, a strange race, perfectly distinct in appearance and language from any other Hindu people, was discovered by two courageous British officers who were tiger-hunting. Many surmises, more or less absurd, were set on foot, and the missionaries, always on the watch to connect every mortal thing with the *Bible,* even went so far as to suggest that this people was one of the lost tribes of Israel, supporting their ridiculous hypothesis upon their very fair complexions and ''strongly-marked Jewish features.'' The latter is perfectly erroneous, the Todas, as they are called, not bearing the remotest likeness to the Jewish type; either in feature, form, action, or language. They closely resemble each other, and, as a friend of ours expresses himself, the handsomest of the Todas resemble the statue of the Grecian Zeus in majesty and beauty of form more than anything he had yet seen among men.

Fifty years have passed since the discovery; but though since that time towns have been built on these hills, and the country has been invaded by Europeans, no more has been learned of the Todas than at the first. Among the foolish rumors current about this people, the most erroneous are those in relation to their numbers and to their practicing polyandry. The general opinion about them is that on account of the latter custom their number has dwindled to a few hundred families, and the race is fast dying out. We had the best means of learning much about them, and therefore state most positively that the Todas neither practice polyandry nor are they as few in number as supposed. We are ready to show that no one has ever seen children belonging to them. Those that may have been seen in their company have belonged to the Badagas, a Hindu tribe totally distinct from the Todas, in race, color, and language, and which includes the most direct "worshippers" of this extraordinary people. We say *worshippers,* for the Badagas clothe, feed, serve, and positively look upon every Toda as a divinity. They are giants in stature, white as Europeans, with tremendously long and generally brown, wavy hair and beard, which no razor ever touched from birth. Handsome as a statue of Pheidias or Praxiteles, the Toda sits the whole day inactive, as some travellers who have had a glance at them affirm. From the many conflicting opinions and statements we have heard from the very residents of Ootakamund and other little new places of civilization scattered about the Neilgherry Hills, we cull the following:

"They never use water; they are wonderfully handsome and noble looking, but extremely unclean; unlike all other natives they despise jewelry, and never wear anything but a large black drapery or blanket of some woollen stuff, with a colored stripe at the bottom; they never drink anything but pure milk; they have herds of cattle but neither eat their flesh, nor do they make their beasts of labor plough or work; they neither sell nor buy; the Badagas feed and clothe them; they never use nor carry weapons, not even a simple stick; the Todas can't read and won't learn. They are the despair of the missionaries and apparently have no sort of religion, beyond the worship of themselves as the Lords of Creation."*

---

*See "Indian Sketches;" Appleton's "New Cyclopedia," etc.

We will try to correct a few of these opinions, as far as we have learned from a very holy personage, a Brahmanam-guru, who has our great respect.

Nobody has ever seen more than five or six of them at one time; they will not talk with foreigners, nor was any traveller ever inside their peculiar long and flat huts, which apparently are without either windows or chimney and have but one door; nobody ever saw the funeral of a Toda, nor very old men among them; nor are they taken sick with cholera, while thousands die around them during such periodical epidemics; finally, though the country all around swarms with tigers and other wild beasts, neither tiger, serpent, nor any other animal so ferocious in those parts, was ever known to touch either a Toda or one of their cattle, though, as said above, they never use even a stick.

Furthermore the Todas do not marry at all. They seem few in number, for no one has or ever will have a chance of numbering them; as soon as their solitude was profaned by the avalanche of civilization—which was, perchance, due to their own carelessness—the Todas began moving away to other parts as unknown and more inaccessible than the Neilgherry hills had formerly been; they are not born of Toda mothers, nor of Toda parentage; they are the children of a certain very select sect, and are set apart from their infancy for special religious purposes. Recognized by a peculiarity of complexion, and certain other signs, such a child is known as what is vulgarly termed a Toda, from birth. Every third year, each of them must repair to a certain place for a certain period of time, where each of them must meet; their "dirt" is but a mask, such as a sannyâsi puts on in public in obedience to his vow; their cattle are, for the most part, devoted to sacred uses; and, though their places of worship have never been trodden by a profane foot, they nevertheless exist, and perhaps rival the most splendid pagodas—*goparams*—known to Europeans. The Badagas are their special vassals, and—as has been truly remarked—worship them as half-deities; for their birth and mysterious powers entitle them to such a distinction.

The reader may rest assured that any statements concerning them, that clash with the little that is above given, are false. No missionary will ever catch one with his bait, nor any Badaga betray them, though he were cut to pieces. They are a people who fulfill a certain high purpose, and whose secrets are inviolable.

Furthermore, the Todas are not the only such mysterious tribe in India. We have named several in a preceding chapter, but how many are there besides these, that will remain unnamed, unrecognized, and yet ever present!

What is now generally known of Shamanism is very little; and that has been perverted, like the rest of the non-Christian religions. It is called the "heathenism" of Mongolia, and wholly without reason, for it is one of the oldest religions of India. It is spirit-worship, or belief in the immortality of the souls, and that the latter are still the same men they were on earth, though their bodies have lost their objective form, and man has exchanged his physical for a spiritual nature. In its present shape, it is an offshoot of primitive theurgy, and a practical blending of the visible with the invisible world. Whenever a denizen of earth desires to enter into communication with his invisible brethren, he has to assimilate himself to their nature, *i.e.*, he meets these beings half-way, and, furnished by them with a supply of spiritual essence, endows them, in his turn, with a portion of his physical nature, thus enabling them sometimes to appear in a semi-objective form. It is a temporary exchange of natures, called theurgy. Shamans are called sorcerers, because they are said to evoke the "spirits" of the dead for purposes of necromancy. The true Shamanism—striking features of which prevailed in India in the days of Megasthenes (300 B.C.)—can no more be judged by its degenerated scions among the Shamans of Siberia, than the religion of Gautama-Buddha can be interpreted by the fetishism of some of his followers in Siam and Burmah. It is in the chief lamaseries of Mongolia and Thibet that it has taken refuge; and there Shamanism, if so we must call it, is practiced to the utmost limits of intercourse allowed between man and "spirit." The religion of the lamas has faithfully preserved the primitive science of *magic,* and produces as great feats now as it did in the days of Kublaï-Khan and his barons. The ancient mystic formula of the King Srong-ch-Tsans-Gampo, the "Aum mani padmé houm,"* effects its wonders now as well as in

---

Aum (mystic Sanscrit term of the Trinity), *mani* (holy jewel), *padmé* (in the lotus, padma being the name for lotus), *houm* (be it so). The six syllables in the sentence correspond to the six chief powers of nature emanating from Buddha (the abstract deity, not Gautama), who is the *seventh,* and the Alpha and Omega of being.

the seventh century. Avalokitesvara, highest of the three Boddhis-attvas, and patron saint of Thibet, projects his shadow, full in the view of the faithful, at the lamasery of Dga-G'Dan, founded by him; and the luminous form of Son-Ka-pa, under the shape of a fiery cloudlet, that separates itself from the dancing beams of the sunlight, holds converse with a great congregation of lamas, numbering thousands; the voice descending from above, like the whisper of the breeze through foliage. Anon, say the Thibetans, the beautiful appearance vanishes in the shadows of the sacred trees in the park of the lamasery.

At Garma-Khian (the mother-cloister) it is rumored that bad and unprogressed spirits are made to appear on certain days, and *forced* to give an account of their evil deeds; they are compelled by the lamaic adepts to redress the wrongs done by them to mortals. This is what Huc naïvely terms "personating evil spirits," *i.e.*, devils. Were the skeptics of various European countries permitted to consult the accounts printed daily* at Moru, and in the "City of Spirits," of the business-like intercourse which takes place between the lamas and the invisible world, they would certainly feel more interest in the phenomena described so triumphantly in the spiritualistic journals. At Buddha-lla, or rather Foht-lla (Buddha's Mount), in the most important of the many thousand lamaseries of that country, the sceptre of the Boddhisgat is seen floating, unsupported, in the air, and its motions regulate the actions of the community. Whenever a lama is called to account in the presence of the Superior of the monastery, he knows beforehand it is useless for him to tell an untruth; the "regulator of justice" (the sceptre) is there, and its waving motion, either approbatory or otherwise, decides instantaneously and unerringly the question of his guilt. We do not pretend to have witnessed all this personally—we wish to make no pretensions of any kind. Suffice it, with respect to any of these phenomena, that what we have not seen with our own eyes has been so substantiated to us that we indorse its genuineness.

---

*Moru (the pure) is one of the most famous lamaseries of Lha-Ssa, directly in the centre of the city. There the Shaberon, the Taley Lama, resides the greater portion of the winter months; during two or three months of the warm season his abode is at Foht-lla. At Moru is the largest typographical establishment of the country.

A number of lamas in Sikkin produce *meipo*—"miracle"—by magical powers. The late Patriarch of Mongolia, Gegen Chutuktu, who resided at Urga, a veritable paradise, was the sixteenth incarnation of Gautama, therefore a Boddhisattva. He had the reputation of possessing powers that were phenomenal, even among the thaumaturgists of the land of miracles *par excellence.* Let no one suppose that these powers are developed without cost. The lives of most of these holy men, miscalled idle vagrants, cheating beggars, who are supposed to pass their existence in preying upon the easy credulity of their victims, are miracles in themselves. Miracles, because they show what a determined will and perfect purity of life and purpose are able to accomplish, and to what degree of preternatural asceticism a human body can be subjected and yet live and reach a ripe old age. No Christian hermit has ever dreamed of such refinement of monastic discipline; and the aërial habitation of a Simon Stylite would appear child's play before the fakir's and the Buddhist's inventions of will-tests. But the theoretical study of magic is one thing; the possibility of practicing it quite another. At *Brâs-ss-Pungs,* the Mongolian college where over three hundred magicians (*sorciers,* as the French missionaries call them) teach about twice as many pupils from twelve to twenty, the latter have many years to wait for their final initiation. Not one in a hundred reaches the highest goal; and out of the many thousand lamas occupying nearly an entire city of detached buildings clustering around it, not more than two per cent become wonder-workers. One may learn by heart every line of the 108 volumes of *Kadjur,** and still make but a poor practical magician. There is but one thing which leads surely to it, and this particular study is hinted at by more than one Hermetic writer. One, the Arabian alchemist Abipili, speaks thus: "I admonish thee, whosoever thou art that desirest to dive into the inmost parts of nature; if that thou seekest thou findest not *within thee,* thou wilt *never find it without thee.* If thou knowest not the excellency of thine own house, why dost thou seek after the excellency of other things? . . . O Man, Know Thyself! in thee is hid the treasure of treasures."

---

*The Buddhist great canon, containing 1,083 works in several hundred volumes, many of which treat of magic.

In another alchemic tract, *De manna Benedicto,* the author expresses his ideas of the philosopher's stone, in the following terms: "My intent is for certain reasons not to prate too much of the matter, which yet is but one only thing, already too plainly described; for it shows and sets down such magical and natural uses of it [the stone] as many that have had it never knew nor heard of; and such as, when I beheld them, *made my knees to tremble and my heart to shake, and I to stand amazed at the sight of them!*"

Every neophyte has experienced more or less such a feeling; but once that it is overcome, the man is an ADEPT.

Within the cloisters of Dshashi-Lumbo and Si-Dzang, these powers, inherent in every man, called out by so few, are cultivated to their utmost perfection. Who, in India, has not heard of the Banda-Chan Rambouchi, the *Houtouktou* of the capital of Higher Thibet? His brotherhood of Khe-lan was famous throughout the land; and one of the most famous "brothers" was a *Peh-ling* (an Englishman) who had arrived one day during the early part of this century, from the West, a thorough Buddhist, and after a month's preparation was admitted among the Khe-lans. He spoke every language, including the Thibetan, and knew every art and science, says the tradition. His sanctity and the phenomena produced by him caused him to be proclaimed a shaberon after a residence of but a few years. His memory lives to the present day among the Thibetans, but his real name is a secret with the shaberons alone.

The greatest of the *meipo*—said to be the object of the ambition of every Buddhist devotee—was, and yet is, the faculty of walking in the air. The famous King of Siam, Pia Metak, the Chinese, was noted for his devotion and learning. But he attained this "supernatural gift" only after having placed himself under the direct tuition of a priest of Gautama-Buddha. Crawfurd and Finlayson, during their residence at Siam, followed with great interest the endeavors of some Siamese nobles to acquire this faculty.*

Numerous and varied are the sects in China, Siam, Tartary, Thibet, Kashmir, and British India, which devote their lives to the cultivation of "supernatural powers," so called. Discussing one of such sects, the *Taossé,* Semedo says: "They pretend that by means of cer-

---

*"Crawfurd's Mission to Siam," p. 182.

tain exercises and meditations one shall regain his youth, and others will attain to be *Shien-sien, i.e.,* 'Terrestrial Beati,' in whose state every desire is gratified, whilst they have the power to transport themselves from one place to another, *however distant,* with speed and facility.''* This faculty relates but to the *projection* of the *astral entity,* in a more or less corporealized form, and certainly not to bodily transportation. This phenomenon is no more a miracle than one's reflection in a looking-glass. No one can detect in such an image a particle of matter, and still there stands our double, faithfully representing, even to each single hair on our heads. If, by this simple law of reflection, our double can be seen in a mirror, how much more striking a proof of its existence is afforded in the art of photography! *It is no reason, because our physicists have not yet found the means of taking photographs, except at a short distance, that the acquirement should be impossible to those who have found these means in the power of the human will itself, freed from terrestrial concern.*** Our thoughts are *matter,* says science; every energy produces more or less of a disturbance in the atmospheric waves. Therefore, as every man—in common with every other living, and even inert object—has an *aura* of his own emanations surrounding him; and, moreover, is enabled, by a trifling effort, to transport himself in

---

*''Semedo,'' vol. iii., p.114.

**There was an anecdote current among Daguerre's friends between 1838 and 1840. At an evening party, Madame Daguerre, some two months previous to the introduction of the celebrated Daguerrean process to the *Académie des Sciences,* by Arago (January, 1839), had an earnest consultation with one of the medical celebrities of the day about her husband's mental condition. After explaining to the physician the numerous symptoms of what she believed to be her husband's mental aberration, she added, with tears in her eyes, that the greatest proof to her of Daguerre's insanity was his firm conviction that he would succeed in nailing his own shadow to the wall, or fixing it on *magical* metallic plates. The physician listened to the intelligence very attentively, and answered that he had himself observed in Daguerre lately the strongest symptoms of what, to his mind, was an undeniable proof of madness. He closed the conversation by firmly advising her to send her husband quietly and without delay to Bicêtre, the well-known lunatic asylum. Two months later a profound interest was created in the world of art and science by the exhibition of a number of pictures taken by the new process. The *shadows* were fixed, after all, upon metallic plates, and the ''lunatic'' proclaimed the father of photography.

imagination wherever he likes, why is it scientifically impossible that his thought, regulated, intensified, and guided by that powerful magician, the educated WILL, may become corporealized for the time being, and appear to whom it likes, a faithful double of the original? Is the proposition, in the present state of science, any more unthinkable than the photograph or telegraph were less than forty years ago, or the telephone less than fourteen months ago?

If the sensitized plate can so accurately seize upon the *shadow* of our faces, then this shadow or reflection, although we are unable to perceive it, must be something substantial. And, if we can, with the help of optical instruments, project our *semblances* upon a white wall, at several hundred feet distance, sometimes, then there is no reason why the adepts, the alchemists, the savants of the secret art, should not have already found out that which scientists deny to-day, but may discover true tomorrow, *i.e.,* how to project electrically their astral bodies, in an instant, through thousands of miles of space, leaving their material shells with a certain amount of animal vital principle to keep the physical life going, and acting within their spiritual, ethereal bodies as safely and intelligently as when clothed with the covering of flesh? There is a higher form of electricity than the physical one known to experimenters; a thousand correlations of the latter are as yet veiled to the eye of the modern physicist, and none can tell where end its possibilities.

BIBLIOGRAPHY OF
GENERAL WORKS ON
EASTERN SPIRITUALITY IN AMERICA

*For further bibliography, see lists at the ends of
introductory sections above.*

Ellwood, Robert S. *Alternative Altars: Unconventional and Eastern Spirituality in America*. Chicago: University of Chicago Press, 1979. Emphasis on Theosophy and Zen in America.

Fields, Rick. *How the Swans Came to the Lake: A Narrative History of Buddhism in America*. Boulder, Colo.: Shambhalla, 1981. Informal but highly informative.

Harper, Marvin Henry, *Gurus, Swamis, and Avataras: Spiritual Masters and Their American Disciples*. Philadelphia: Westminster, 1972. Interesting insights into Americans involved in Indian spirituality through the 1960s era.

Jackson, Carl T. *The Oriental Religions and American Thought: Nineteenth-Century Explorations*. Westport, Conn.: Greenwood, 1981. A superb overview of the topic up to the World's Parliament of Religions.

Layman, Emma. *Buddhism in America*. Chicago: Nelson-Hall, 1976. A useful survey, covering both ethnic and occidental Buddhism.

Melton, J. Gordon. *The Encyclopedia of American Religions*. 2 vols. Wilmington, N.C.: McGrath, 1978. Valuable information on a large number of particular Eastern groups.

Needleman, Jacob. *The New Religions*. Garden City, N.Y.: Doubleday, 1970. Well-written survey, largely of Eastern groups; reflects the 1960s era.

Prebish, Charles S. *American Buddhism*. North Scituate, Mass.: Duxbury, 1979. Good historical and interpretive survey.

Richardson, E. Allen. *East Comes West*. Boston: Pilgrim Press, 1985.

INDEX TO INTRODUCTION

Adams, Hannah, 8
American religion (*See also*
    Eastern religious groups,
    American): and Buddhism, 19–
    22; currents of Eastern religion
    in, 6–7; focuses of, 5–6;
    Hinduism in, 42; history of
    Eastern religion in, 32–34;
    intellectual influence of Eastern
    religion on, 7–11; and
    Mesmerism, 13–15; and
    occultism, 11–12; preparation
    of, for East, 11–16; and
    romanticism, 11; and science,
    15–16; and Swedenborgianism,
    13–14; and theosophy, 16–19
Arnold, Sir Edwin, 19
Asian religion, ethnic, 42

Beat movement, 40
Bhajan, Yogi, 39
Bhaktivedanta, Swami, 33, 38
Blavatsky, Helena P. (*See also Isis
    Unveiled*): character of, 25–26;
    and founding of theosophy, 16–
    19; and Mesmerism, 14
Block, Marguerite, 13
Brooks, Phillips, 19
Buddhism: in America, 19–22;
    Nichiren, 40; Theravada, 41;
    Tibetan, 40–41
Buddhist groups, 39–41

Confucian Enlightenment, 7–8
Cross, Whitney, 15

Davis, Andrew Jackson, 14
Dayal, Shiv, 38
Divine Light Mission, 37

Eastern religion (*See also* Eastern
    religious groups, American): and
    Buddhism, in America, 19–22;
    currents of, in America, 6–7;
    focus on, in America, 5–6;
    history of, in America, 32–34;
    intellectual influences of, on
    America, 7–11; preparation for,
    in America, 11–16; and
    theosophy, 16–19
Eastern religious groups,
    American: appeal of, 22; Asian
    religion, ethnic, 42–43;
    Buddhist, 39–41; and charisma,
    22-23; desire of, for new
    religion, 34; experience of,
    intensity of, 27-28; Hindu-
    derived, 36-38; intellectual
    expression of, 23–27; overview
    of, 34–35; Sikhism-related, 38–
    39; sociology in, 28-32; Taoism,
    41–42; theosophical, 35–36;
    worship in, 28-32
Eckanka, 39
Emerson, Ralph Waldo, 8–9, 19

Fox sisters, 14–15
Franklin, Benjamin, 7–8

Gakkai, Soka, 40
Goldstein, Joseph, 41
Gustaitis, Rasa, 29

Hare Krishna movement, 30–31
Hindu-derived groups, 36–38
Hinduism, 8, 42

In My Own Way (Watts), 26
Intellectual Orientalism, 6
International Society for Krishna
    Consciousness, 38
Isherwood, Christopher, 24
Isis Unveiled (Blavatsky), 18, 35
Islam, 7

Ji, Maharaj, 37
Johnson, Gregory, 31
Jones, Sir William, 8
Judah, J. Stillson, 30–31

Kennett, Jiyu, 33
Kornfield, Jack, 41

Lao Tzu, 41
"Light of Asia, The" (Arnold), 19

Magic, 18
Mesmer, Franz, 14
Mesmerism, 13–15
My Guru and His Disciple
    (Isherwood), 24

Nanak, Guru, 38
"New religions," 6
Nichiren Buddhism, 40
Nichiren Shoshu of American
    (NSA), 40

Occultism, 11–12, 17
Olcott, Henry Steel: and character

of Blavatsky, 25-26; and
    founding of theosophy, 16–19
Old Diary Leaves (Olcott), 25–26

"Passage to India" (Whitman), 10
Prabhavananda, Swami, 25, 36
*Principles of Nature, Her Divine
    Revelation and a Voice to
    Mankind* (Davis), 14

Radhasoami Satsang, 38–39
Rajneesh, 38
Rajneesh Movement, 38
Ramakrishna Mission, 21, 36
Religion (*See* American religion;
    Eastern religion)
Ricci, Matteo, 7
Romanticism, 11
Roshi, Sokei-an Sasaki, 39
Roy, Ram Mohan, 8–9
Ruhani Satsang, 39

Satya Sai Baba, 38
Satya Sai Baba Movement, 38
Science, 15–16, 18
Secret Doctrine, The (Blavatsky),
    26, 35
Self-Realization Fellowship, 6, 33,
    36–37
Senzaki, Nyogen, 39–40
Shaku, Soyen, 21, 39
Shigemitus, Sasaki, 21–22
Sikh Dharma, 39
Sikhism-related groups, 38–39
Singh, Gobind, 38
Singh, Kirpal, 39
Sivananda, 37
Soami, Radha, 39
Suzuki, D. T., 21
Swedenborg, Emmanuel, 13–14
Swedenborgianism, 13–14

Taoism, 41–42

Tao te ching (Tzu), 41

Theosophical groups, 35–36

Theosophical Society: branches of, 35-36; and Eastern religion in America, 32; founding of, 16–19

Theosophy: in American religion, 16–19; in twenties and thirties, in America, 33

Theravada Buddhism, 41

Thoreau, Henry David, 8–9

Tibetan Buddhism, 40–41

Transcendentalism, 6, 11

Transcendental Meditation (TM), 37

Turner, Victor, 5

Turning On (Gustaitis), 29

Twitchell, Paul, 39

Upanishads, 8

Vedanta Society, 6, 32, 36

View of Religion, The (Adams), 8

Vivekananda, Swami, 21, 36

Walden (Thoreau), 9

Watts, Alan, 26–27

Weber, Max, 22–23

Whitman, Walt, 10

World's Parliament of Religions, 20–22

Yoga groups, 37

Yogananda, Parmahansa, 36

Yogi, Maharishi Mahesh, 37

Zazen, 30

Zen, American, 33

Zen centers: description of, 39–40; and Eastern religion in America, 6; worship in, 28–29

Zen Mountain Center, 29

INDEX TO TEXTS

Adbhutananda, Swami, 64
After-death state, 189–190
Aggregate of Matter, 186
Ahaṅkara, 102–103
Akhilananda, 47
Antinomianism, 127
Aquinas, St. Thomas, 85
Arya Samaj, 45
Augustine, St., 70–71
Avatar, 66–72

Bardo Thödol (See also Wisdom
  Teachings): and after-death
  state, 189–190; aim of, 194;
  First, 189; Second, 189–190;
  Third, 189; visions of, 190–194
Beat movement, 116
Beat Zen, 168–171, 175, 179
Beat Zen, Square Zen, and Zen
  (Watts): and beat Zen, 168–171,
  175, 179; and creation of Zen,
  163; and Dharma Bums, The,
  173–175; and li, 171–172; and
  samurai, 164; and square zen,
  175–179; and Tao, 163–164;
  and te, 172; and Western interest
  in Zen, 164–169; and yang, 173;
  and yin, 172–173
Benedict, Ruth, 164
Bhagavad-Gita: and bhakti-yoga,
  107–108; and Perennial
  Philosophy, 87; and perfection,

99; position of, 80; and Song of
  God, 87
Bhakti, 97
Bhaktivedanta, Swami (See also
  Krishna Consciousness):
  background of, 98; and bhakti-
  yoga, 107–113; and Hare Kṛṣṇa
  mantra, 104–107
Bhakti-yoga: and conquering God,
  110; and illusion, 111–112; and
  process to understanding God,
  110–111; and reading of
  Bhagavad-Gita, 107–108; and
  understanding of God, 108–109
Bible, The, 194
Blavatsky, Helena P., 219 (See
  also Isis Unveiled)
"Blessed are the meek," 63
Bliss, 55, 88–91 (See also
  Happiness)
Bliss-consciousness, 92–94
Body, 52–53
Brahmananda, Swami, 46
Brahmo Samaj, 45
Broussais, Francis Victor, 223
Buddha, 158
Buddha's Mind, 152–153
Buddha's Words, 152–153
Buddhism (See also Zen): and
  American life, 156–161; and
  cause and effect, 121–124;
  distinct religions of, 219–220;

and enlightenment, 129–136; fundamental idea of, 125, 127; Hinayana, 152–153; and ignorance, 125–128; and Lamaism, 220–222; Mahayana, 152–153; parts of, 152; spreading of, 220; Tibetan, 180; and universe, reason of, 134; Zen school of, 114–116, 163

Buddhist selections (*See Beat Zen, Square zen, and Zen; Bardo Thödol; Senzaki; Shaku; Wisdom Teachings*)

Cage, John, 170
Calligraphy, 172
Cause and effect, 121–124
Chanting, 100–101
Chapman, Abbot John, 84–85
Chih, 202
Chuang Tzu (*See Way of Chuang Tzu, The*)
Clelland-Holmes, John, 174–175
Confucius: and Ju philosophy, 201, 203–204; and realization, 139–140; and righteousness, 163; and Zen, 158
Consciousness, 53, 57
Contemplation, 135
Continence, 76–77
Coomaraswamy, Ananda K., 80

Dayananda, 45
Devotionalism, 97
Dharma Bums, The (Kerouac), 173–175
Dharma-Dhātu, 186
Dharmakaya, 137–139
Dharma-Kāya, 183–184
Divine Body-Aggregate, 187–188
Divine Ground, 81–83

Earth-Element, 187
Education, 111–112
Ego, 102
Element Air, 187
Emptiness, 135
Enlightenment, spiritual: and contemplation, 135–136; definition of, 129; and emptiness, 135–136; and faith, 131–132; and intellect, 129–130; and knowledge, 131–132; and natural course of human activity, 133–134; and Prajñâ, 131–132, 136; and religion, 129–130, 134; and religious sense, 130–134; and trance, 132–133; and tranquillity, 135–136
Etheral things, 101–102
Evans-Wentz, W. Y., 181–182; and *Bardo Thödol*, 189–194; and Wisdom Teachings, 182–189

Faith, 131–132
False ego, 103
Fire-Element, 187
Five Wisdoms, 186–189
Freedom, 56
Fruit, ripe/unripe, 153–156

Genro, 145
God: as absolute good, 71–72; conception of, 94–95; conquering, 110; existence of, 91–92, 131; laughter of, 78; loving, 55–56, 72; power of, 78; reaching, 56–57; realization of, 65–66; understanding, 108–111
God-consciousness, 92–94
Good: 71–72, 204–206
Grace, 63
Gross things, 101

Happiness, 210 (*See also* Bliss)
Harā, 106
Hare Kṛṣṇa mantra, 104–107
Hinduism: and bhakti, 97; and
   bliss, immortal, 55;
   contradictions to, 51–52, 60;
   and doctrines of Perennial
   Philosophy, 80–83; and love,
   55–56; Neo-Vedanta, 45–47;
   and perfection, 56–57; purpose
   of, 60–61; and realization, 59;
   as religion, 51–61; and Rishis,
   52; and science, 57–58; and
   soul, 56; and spirit, 54; and
   Vedas, 52
Hindu selections (*See Krishna
   Consciousness*; "Salt of the
   Earth"; *Science of Religion,
   The*; *Song of God, The*;
   Vivekananda's address at
   World's Parliament of
   Religions)
Hsin-hsin Ming, 169
Humility, 209–210
Huxley, Aldous, 79 (*See also Song
   of God, The*)

Idolatry, 58, 60
Ignorance, 125–128
Incarnation, divine, 66–72
Incarnation, human, 83–85
Individualism, 57, 201
Intelligence, 102
Isis Unveiled (Blavatsky): and
   Bikshu, 222–223; and distinct
   religions of Buddhism, 219–220;
   and Lamaism, 220–222; and
   magic, 230–233; and miracles,
   231–232; and spreading of
   Buddhism, 220; and
   supernatural powers, 232–234;

and superstitions, 223–226; and
   Todas, 226–230

Jakushitsu, 140, 146–147, 160
Jen, 201
Jnana yoga, 83
Ju Philosophy, 201–204

Karma, 69, 190–191
Karma-relation, 151
Kerouac, Jack, 173–175
Knowledge, 64–65, 130–132
Koans, 115, 149–150
Koran, The, 194
Krishna: and incarnation, 67; as
   mouthpiece of Hinduism, 85;
   power of, 68–69; relationship
   with, 112–113; worship of, 70
Krishna Consciousness
   (Bhaktivedanta): and ahaṅkara,
   102–103; and chanting, 100–
   101; and ego, 102; and etheral
   things, 101–102; and false ego,
   103; and Hare Kṛṣṇa mantra,
   105; and intelligence, 102; and
   reasoning power, 99–100; and
   soul, 102
Kriya Yoga, 47
Kṛṣṇa, 106
Kṛṣṇa consciousness, 105, 112–
   113

Lamaism, 220–222
Lan, Fung Yu, 210
Lao Tzu, 203–204
Li, 171–172, 202
Libertinism, 127–128
Lin-chi, 164
Logos, 66–69
Love, 55, 72–73, 211

Magic, 230–233
Mahāmantra, 106

Māya, 106
Meditation, 73
Meipo, 231–232
Memory, 53
Merton, Thomas, 199–200 (*See also Way of Chuang Tzu*)
Miracles, 231–232
Mohammed, 82
Monologism, 147
Moonlight Party, 145–149
Morning Talk, 143–145
Mo Ti, 210–211

Neo-Vedanta, 45–47
Nikhilananda, 47
Nirvâna, 114, 127–128
"Noble-Minded Man," 201

Ox, straying, 149–151

Paramparā, 107
Passions, 74–75
Perennial Philosophy: corollaries of, 85–86; doctrines of, 79–83
Perfection, 56–57, 99
Personalism, 201
Philo, 66
Philosophy: and religion, 129–131, 134; teaching of, by Cuang Tzu, 213
Plato, 66
Play of world, 96–97
Pleasure, 89–90
Polytheism, 58
Prabhavananda, Swami, 61–62 (*See also* "Salt of the earth")
Pragmatism, 159–161
Prajñâ, 131–132, 136
Prakriti, 69
Prayer, 73–74

Rāma, 106
Ramakrishna, 45–46, 63, 65, 67
Ramakrishna Order of Monks, 46–47
Realization, 139–141
Reasoning power, 99–100
Religion (*See also* Buddhism; Hinduism; Taoism; Theosophy): and causal law, 123; and facts, 131; and philosophy, 129–131, 134; self-alienation in, 130; and spiritual enlightenment, 129–130; Universal, 91
Religious sense, 130–131
Rishis, 52
Roy, Ram Mohan, 45
Rumi, Jalaluddin, 85
Ryder, Japhy, 173

"Salt of the earth" (Prabhavanada): and avatar, 66–71; and continence, 76–77; and good, absolute, 71–72; and grace, 63; and knowledge, 64–65; and Logos, 66–69; and love, 72; and meekness, 63; passage of, 62; and passions, control of, 74–77; and power of God, 78; and prayer, 73–74; and realization of God, 65–66; and strength, 74; and teachers, 62–64
Samurai, 164
Satori, 175–176, 178
Science: and ether, 102; and knowledge, 130; and perfect unity, 57–58; self-alienation in, 130
Science of Religion, The (Yogananda): and bliss, 88–91; and Bliss-consciousness, 92–94;

and conception of God, 94–95; and play of world, 95–96; and pleasure, 89–90
Self-abnegation, 85–86
Self-alienation, 130
Self-assertion, 125–127
Self-formation, 123–124
Self-realization, 151
Self-Realization Fellowship, 47
Semedo, 232–233
Senzaki, Nyogen: background of, 136–137; and Buddha's mind, 152–153; and Buddha's words, 152–153; and Dharmakaya, 137–139; and fruit, ripe/unripe, 153–156; and moonlight party, 145–149; and morning talk, 143–145; and realization, 139–141; and this lifetime, 141–143; and three pictured fans, 149–151; and Zen in American life, 156–161
Shaku, Soyen: background of, 121, 125; and cause and effect, 121–124; and enlightenment, 129–136; and ignorance, 125–128; and religion, 144; sermons by, 125–128
Shaku's address at World's Parliament of Religions: and cause and effect, 121–124; and enlightenment, 129–136; and ignorance, 125–128
Shankara, 85
Snyder, Gary, 173–174
Song of God, The (Huxley): and *Bhagavad-Gita*, 87; and corollaries of Perennial Philosophy, 85–86; and doctrines of Perennial Philosophy, 79–83; and Incarnation, human, 83–85

Soul, 53–54, 56, 102
Spirit, 54
Square Zen, 175–179
"Superior Man," 201, 205
Supernatural powers, 232–234
Superstitions, 223–226
Suzuki, D. T., 144

Tagore, Rabindranath, 150–151
Taoism: in China, 195–196; description of, 195; ethical, 204–206; and Ju philosophy, 203; and view of world, 168; and Zen, 163–164, 179
Taoist selection (*See Way of Chuang Tzu, The*)
Te, 172
Theosophy, 215
Theosophy selection (*See Isis Unveiled*)
This lifetime, 141–143
Three Bodies, 183–186
Three in the morning, 213–214
Three Pictured Fans, 149–151
Three Treasures, 138
Tibetan Book of the Dead, The (Evans-Wentz) (*See Bardo Thödol*; Wisdom Teachings)
Tibetan Buddhism, 180
Tobey, Mark, 172
Todas, 226–230
Torei, 137
Trance, 132–133
Tranquillity, 135
Tri-Kāya, 185

Unconditioned Reality, 114
Universal mysticism, 79 (*See also* Perennial Philosophy)

Vedas, 52, 66
Visions, *Bardo*, 190–194

Vivekananda, Swami, 46–47, 51 (*See also* Vivekandanda's address at World's Parliament of Religions)

Vivekananda's address at World's Parliament of Religions: and bliss, immortal, 55; and body, 52–53; and consciousness, 53, 57; contradictions to Hinduism, 51–52, 60; and Hindu religion's purpose, 60–61; and idolatry, 58–60; and individuality, 57; and love, 55–56; and memory, 53; and perfection, 56–57; and polytheism, 58; and realization, 59; and religions in world, 51; and Rishis, 52; and science, 57–58; and soul, 53–54, 56; and spirit, 54; and Vedas, 52

Voidness, 183

Water-Element, 186–187

Watts, Alan, 162–163 (*See also Beat Zen, Square Zen, and Zen*)

Way of Chuang Tzu, The (Merton): and contempt of politics, 200–201; and ethical Tao, 204–205; and happiness, 210; and humility, 209–210; and individualism, 201; and Ju philosophy, 201–204; and love, 210–211; and man of Tao, 207–209; and opposites, 212–213; and personalism, 201; and philosophy of Chuang Tzu, 213; and principles of Chuang Tzu, 213–214; and thought of Chuang Tzu, 212; and three in the morning, 213–214; and way of Tao, 206–207; and work of Chuang Tzu, 211–212; and wu wei, 210

Wisdom Teachings (*See also Bardo Thödol*): and Five Wisdoms, 186–189; and Three Bodies, 183–186; and voidness, 183

Woolman, John, 86

World's Parliament of Religions (*See* Shaku's address at; Vivekandanda's at)

Wu wei, 210

Yamaoka, Tessu, 139

Yang, 173

Yang Chu, 200

Yi, 201

Yin, 172–173

Yogananda, Paramahansa, 47, 87 (*See also Science of Religion, The*)

Yun-men, 169

Zen: and American life, 156–161; background of, 114–116; beat, 168–171, 175, 179; creation of, 163; experiencing, 147; and li, 171–172; and Pragmatism, 159–161; and realization, 140–141; and samurai, 164; square, 175–179; and Tao, 163–164, 179; and te, 172; and this lifetime, 141–143; and view of world, 168; Western interest in, 164–169; and yang, 173; and yin, 172–173

Zen riddles, 115, 149–150

Other Volumes in This Series

Walter Rauschenbusch: Selected Writings
William Ellery Channing: Selected Writings
Devotion to the Holy Spirit in American Catholicism
Horace Bushnell: Sermons
Alaskan Missionary Spirituality
Elizabeth Seton: Selected Writings
Charles Hodge: The Way of Life
Henry Alline: Selected Writings

75226